CISTERCIAN STUDIES SERIES: NUMBER FIVE / TWO

COMMUNITY AND ABBOT IN THE RULE OF ST BENEDICT

EDITOR'S NOTE

According to the Translator's Note in Volume I, p. 11, and contrary to what has been erroneously printed in volume I, p. 253, the RB and RM references throughout the work are *not* to the editions of Butler and Vanderhoven-Masai (chapter and line), but to the following editions by Adalbert de Vogüé (chapter and verse): *La Règle de saint Benoît, Sources Chrétiennes 181–182, Paris, 1972. La Règle du Maître, Sources Chrétiennes 105–106, Paris, 1964.*

CISTERCIAN STUDIES SERIES: NUMBER FIVE / TWO

COMMUNITY AND ABBOT IN THE RULE OF ST BENEDICT

by

Adalbert de Vogüé
Monk of La Pierre-que-Vire

translated by
Charles Philippi and Ethel Rae Perkins

Cistercian Publications
Kalamazoo, Michigan
1988

Translated from the French *La Communauté et l'Abbé dans la Règle de saint Benoît* (Paris-Brussels: Desclée-de-Brouwer, 1961).

The editors of Cistercian Publications express their appreciation to Dr Joan M. Petersen for editing this English translation.

Cistercian Publications Inc.
WMU Station
Kalamazoo, Michigan 49008

Available in Great Britain and Europe from
A.R. Mowbray & Co Ltd Saint Thomas House
Becket Street Oxford OX1 1SJ

The work of Cistercian Publications is made possible in part by support from Western Michigan University for the Institute of Cistercian Studies.

Library of Congress Cataloging in Publication Data
Vogüé, Adalbert de.
Community and abbot in the rule of Saint Benedict
(Cistercian studies series: no. 5/2)
Translation of La communauté et l'abbé dans la règle de saint Benoît.
Bibliography: p 491
1. Benedictus, Saint, Abbot of Monte Cassino. Regula.
I. Title. II. Series.
BX3004.Z5V613
ISBN 0-87907-905-3

TABLE OF CONTENTS

Volume Two

Chapter 5

THE ABBOT'S COLLABORATORS (RB 21 and 31)

IN STUDYING THE CHAPTERS devoted to the deans and the cellarer, we propose to bring into focus certain characteristics of the abbot, which stand out with particular clarity when he is set alongside his collaborators. The monastic hierarchy is an example of these characteristics. Its various degrees express, each in its own manner, a single idea. In this very coherent system, certain aspects of the function of the leader appear more clearly when we examine the subordinate ranks.

THE DEANS (RM 11 and RB 21)

Those men whom RB will call 'deans' (*decani*) are still styled 'provosts' (*praepositi*) in RM. This linguistic peculiarity of the Master is of an archaic character. The Master is adhering in this to the terminology of Cassian, who, while using the term *decania* to designate a group of ten monks (*Inst* 4.10 and 17), ignores the title *decanus*, which Jerome and Augustine had given to the head of this group,[1] and entitles this officer the *praepositus* (*Inst* 4.10; Petschenig, p. 53, 25 and 54, 13. *Inst* 4.27; Petschenig, p. 66, 4), sometimes also *senior.*[2] The archaic character of *praepositus* as the head of a group of ten is well testified by certain variants in the manuscript, Paris Latin 12634, which substitutes *decanus* (singular) for *praepositi* (plural)[3] several times; elsewhere any mention of provost or provosts is omitted.[4] That we are dealing with emendations and not the primitive text is demonstrated in turn by the incoherent and obviously glossed E reading of RM 73:3, and by the numerous passages in which the E redactor let *praepositus* stand, either in the singular[5] or in the plural.[6] Thus at the time and place in which MS E was transcribed, we were simultaneously embarrassed by the use of *praepositus* in the sense of dean, and by the presence of *two* officers at the head of each decade.[7]

Furthermore, the Master had a particular fondness for the function of 'provost'. Nothing shows this better than the numerous close parallels which emerge between the directory for the abbot (RM 2) and which come to light as soon as the place, structure, and content of RM 11. The place of honor this chapter holds is quite well indicated by the two transitions of RM 10:123–11, T and 11:1–3. Just as the treatise *qualis debeat esse abbas* headed the section *actus militiae cordis* (or *actus iustitiae*), so the chapter on provosts begins the *ordo monasterii*. The spiritual doctrine of the first chapters of the rule was wholly dominated by the figure of the abbot as teacher and architect of the *ars sancta*. When we pass to the practical ordering of the life of the brethren, new subordinate teachers who will be present at every moment and will exercise a continual supervision over every detail emerge; these are the provosts.

A long prologue (RM 11:1–14) explains the meaning of the institution, exactly as RM 1:76–92 served as a prologue to the treatise on the abbot by explaining the meaning of the abbatial function. In both, the author resumes his tone of exhortation in the first person plural. In both, he shows the need for the office, for which he is about to set out a directory. The function of the provosts is presented, furthermore, as the indispensable complement to that of the abbot. It is not enough, in fact, for the abbot to instruct his disciples in the acts of justice, which were described in chapters 3 through 10 of the rule. It is also necessary to fend off the machinations of the devil, who is intent on preventing the brethren from accomplishing these good works. Hence the need of associating with the abbot two provosts in each group of ten brethren, in order that the 'teacher' may be constantly represented before his disciples by trustworthy men, who are capable of putting his teaching into practice. The provosts are therefore in the Master's eyes, rather like assistant masters in a school, who always and everywhere extend the educational work of the abbot.

Likewise, the prologue to the directory for provosts is comparable to the prologue to the directory for the abbot in the loftiness of its viewpoint, breadth of perspective, and solemnity of tone. The same doctrine is developed in both. Like the abbot, the provosts are in some sense, a divine institution. Lk 10:16, 'Anyone who listens to you, listens to me', applies to them, too. This solemn investiture, like that of the abbot, gives rise to a parallel between churches and monasteries,[8] and between the ecclesiastical hierarchy and the monastic hierarchy. This important text requires no further comment, after what we have said about it in studying RB 2. We need only remark that if the abbot is there likened to a bishop, the provosts in their turn see themselves placed on the same level as priests, deacons and clerics.

When he comes to regulate the order of readings during the office, the Master will delineate a new parallel between the two hierarchies, ecclesiastical and monastic. Just as in churches the Letters of the apostles are read by clerics and the Gospel by a deacon, so in monasteries the provosts read the Lesson from the Apostle in turn, but the Gospel is reserved for the abbot when he is present (RM 46:3–7). This time the abbot is likened not to the bishop but to the deacon, and the provosts similarly descend from the status of priests to that of minor clerics. With this exception, the idea is the same. The abbot and the provosts constitute a genuine hierarchy comparable to that of the Church, and like her, are surrounded with liturgical honors.

The importance which the Master attaches to the provosts, moreover, results from the fact that these officers are solemnly 'ordained' in the chapel (RM 11:15–19). The ceremony consists only of their being given the rod, symbol of their authority,[9] but in its simplicity, it recalls the ordination of the abbot, which is described at the end of the rule. No other officer, according to the Master, is 'ordained' in this fashion. Such a rite is the privilege of the abbot and provosts.[10]

Yet a difference does exist between the abbot and the provosts. Whereas the supreme 'teacher' is unique, there are two provosts for each group of ten brethren (RM 11:20–26, 35–36).[11] The Master took pains to explain to us the meaning of this number: it is a question of ensuring the continual presence of a provost with the members of a *decania*, if work requirements oblige the *decania* to split into two groups. The two provosts thus amount to colleagues on an equal footing. The Master never indicates a relationship of subordination between them. Possibly the Master is here recollecting the system of Pachomius, whereby each 'house provost' was backed up by a 'Second'; in any case, he employs a different terminology—the two officers are called praepositi indisciminately —and he gives the institution a precise and original significance, which refers only to his concerns as a teacher.

The same must be said of the number ten, chosen as the unit entrusted to the provosts. This number surely cannot go back to Pachomian origins, where a 'house' had a far higher membership,[12] but it was traditional in Egypt, according to the testimony of Jerome, Augustine and Cassian. As we shall see shortly, in commenting on RB, such a decimal organization was inspired by biblical precedent. Surprisingly, the Master makes no allusion to it, absorbed as he is with his educational activities. If ten brethren and no more (*non amplius*, vs 22) are to be entrusted to the guardianship of two provosts, this is only to render their supervision more effective. The number ten does not recall Israel in the desert; it is merely regarded as the ideal small number for letting nothing escape the guardians' attention.

A directory for provosts, rightly so-called, clearly expounds this educational method (RM 11:27–43, 40–90). the provosts' first duty is always to be present with their men. This recommendation recurs like a *leitmotiv* throughout the chapter; this is what ensures a certain continuity between its various parts.[13] Next, the provosts must be constantly alert to the faults of their subordinates, reprimanding the slightest manifestations of sin with appropriate admonitions. The Master gives us no less than ten examples of such little warnings. There we see a considerable part of the chapters on silence and humility gone over once again, no longer in the form of doctrinal expositions, but, as it were, struck like coins, as brief recalls to order. The provosts repeat what the abbot has taught and cause his doctrine to pass into the lives of the brethren. Thus the 'teacher' can extend his protective influence over every moment of each disciple's day.[14] A suit of armor without chinks thus guarantees the monastery against every attack by the devil.

The directory for provosts concludes like that for the abbot. The Master had assured the abbot that his task as 'teacher' would oblige him to correct himself (RM 2:39–40). He hopes for the same progress in respect of the provosts (RM 11:91–93).

What follows next (RM 11:94–123) may be considered as a lengthy appendix not unlike that of the abbatial directory (RM 2:41–52). After dealing with the duties of the office, it consists of a series of more practical instructions: reduction of manual labor for the benefit of the provosts' spiritual mission (94–106); their exercise of supervision over clothing (107); the brethren's sleep (108–121); the table (122); and a final recommendation that they never allow a brother to slip away from the *decania* (123).

The directory for provosts, therefore, offers more than one analogy with that for the abbot. Their charge is truly complementary to his. The provosts are an extension of the abbot; they are his teaching, which permeates every detail of the lives of the brethren. It was necessary for us to look at what the Master tells us about them, in order to realize the extent to which the monastery really is a school in his eyes. The modern reader is stunned at seeing imposed on adults a system of supervision which in our day is not conceivable even for children. Let us not be too quick to impute this naïve theory to the educational zeal of our author. The picture of cenobitic life which he gives us here does, in fact, correspond exactly with Jerome's description of the egyptian cenobites (Lr 22.35). There too the monk is taken in charge day and night by superiors, whose solicitude and competence he praises to us: the 'father' who is an incomparable orator, the provosts, whose vigilance is incessant, marvelously charitable and resourceful, the steward, who keeps his eye on everyone and makes sure that no one ever lacks anything, the aged infirmarians, who look after you like mothers. . . . Activity of the superiors and passivity of the subjects: the monk abandons himself like a child into the hands of his teachers.

Cassian also insists on the role of the provost in the education of the young monk,[15] but, unlike what we have observed in RM, the abbot seems to fade completely into the background. Once he has "entrusted" the new cenobite to the provost (*Inst* 4.7), he is never again seen to intervene. Apparently it is the provost who took over the formation of the young monk. It is specifically he who teaches obedience, mortifies self-will, and hears confessions. The role, which RM attributes to the provosts, seems much more modest. To judge from the ten examples of warnings given in this chapter, the provosts are satisfied with being vigilant regarding the rules of silence, of speaking, and of exterior behavior. In addition, they are entrusted in Chapter 15 with the task of questioning the brethren about their evil thoughts, and of bringing these to the attention of the abbot. Even in that case, however, they play only the role of intermediaries between the brethren and the abbot, who alone is qualified to attend to evil through prayer and exhortation. In the small community for which he is legislating, the Master intends the educational work to be entirely in the abbot's hands. In this we perceive a tangible difference from the responsibility left to the provost in the more numerous communities which Cassian had in mind.

Passing from RM to RB (chapter 21), we are struck first by the change of terminology. The *praepositi* of the Master are now called *decani*, while *praepositus* henceforth designates the 'prior', the abbot's lieutenant. This evolution of *praepositus* entailed the substitution of *decani* for *praepositi* to designate the heads of the groups of ten which, we might add, constitutes not an innovation but a return to the vocabularly previously used by Jerome and Augustine in their descriptions of the egyptian monks.

The term *decanus*, moreover, is used sparingly in RB. Apart from this chapter, where it figures four times, the term reappears only in Chapters 62 and 65: *regulam decanis vel praepositis constitutam* (62:7), *per decanos ordinetur, ut ante disposuimus, omnis utilitas monasterii* (65:12). Both of these texts hark back to Chapter 21. Thus the term appears only in three chapters of the Rule, closely linked to one another. Nowhere else is there any mention of *decani*. Nevertheless, the redactor did have them in mind, beyond any possible doubt, when he spoke of the *seniores*, who supervise the dormitory (22:3, Cf. RM 11:108, 121), give commands (23:1, Cf. RM 12:1), and issue warnings (23:2, Cf. RM 12:2). These instances, where the *seniores* are certainly equivalent to *decani*, lead us to identify the deans in a good number of other passages referring to *seniores*.[16] This word is therefore a true equivalent to *decanus*, or to put it better, with the exception of the three chapters mentioned above, it is the usual term for designating the heads of the groups of ten throughout the Rule.

As for the term *praepositi*, it never designates deans in RB, despite the interpretation of RB 62:7 and 71:3 that Kassius Hallinger believed it possible to give (*abbatis aut praepositorum qui ab eo constituuntur imperio*). The plural in these two passages seems to me to apply to the successive incumbents of the single office of prior or lieutenant of the abbot.[17] It is not a relic of the provosts.

Thus *seniores* is preferred to *decani* to designate the deans in RB. This partially revives the terminology of Cassian, who as we saw, ignores *decanus* and employs *senior* concurrently with *praepositus*. But in realizing that *seniores* and *decani* are synonymous, we come to the question of the number of such officers for each group of ten.[18] Is there just one dean per decury, as is generally supposed,[19] or are there really two, as in RM?

The question cannot be resolved by the fact that *decani* always occurs in the plural, since this plural can in every case be explained by the plural number *decaniae*. But an indication can be gleaned from certain uses of *seniores*. When RB 23:1 says of a recalcitrant monk, *contrarius existens*. . . *praeceptis seniorum suorum*, this does seem to assume that there are several deans for each religious. No doubt this plural, *seniorum suorum*, might be explained as a simple transposition of *praepositis suis*, which the RB redactor read in RM 12:4. But if the RB redactor had intended to reduce the number of leaders for each *decania* from two to one, nothing would have prevented him from writing *senioris sui* in the singular. Since the term for deans was changed (*seniores* instead of *praepositi*), there would have been no problem in altering the number (singular instead of plural). So this passage furnishes serious evidence for the survival in RB of the RM system of 'two provosts per decade'. The rest of the text confirms this hypothesis: a disobedient brother (singular) shall be twice admonished in private by his elders (plural).

On the other hand there exists, to our knowledge, no positive indication of a reduction to a single dean per *decania*. The case of RB 58:6 (*senior eis talis deputetur*. . .) is not conclusive, for we are dealing here with a function unknown to RM (that of master of novices), and one which does not fall within the ordinary framework of the decanal system. The novices, being of a variable and unpredictable number, do not form a true *decania*. One might also refer to RB 4:50 (*et seniori spiritali patefacere*), but it would be necessary to take account as well of RB 46:5 (*aut spiritalibus senioribus patefaciat*), where we find the plural.

Moreover, we must admit that RB, here as in the chapter on the weekly kitchen helpers, shows itself surprisingly imprecise about the number of holders of this job. The point is left unclear. RB 48:17 shows well the writer's indifference for the arithmetical precisions fixed so seriously by the Master: as roundsmen, 'one or two elders' shall be deputed.[20] So it is probable, judging from RB 23, that the number of deans remains, as with the Master, two for each *decania*, but that RB has not taken the trouble of saying so clearly, or of justifying this duplication by educational considerations such as those proffered by RM.

Furthermore, this entire little chapter on deans is concise to the point of dryness. The very full directory of the Master has been reduced to a few lines on the election of deans, which is apparently the only subject of interest to our redactor. After dealing with it, in his opening words, he comes back to it a second and a third time:

vs 1: *si maior fuerit congregatio, elegantur de ipsis . . .*
vs 3: *qui decani tales elegantur . . .*
vs 4: *et non elegantur per ordinem . . .*

In each instance there is a new description of the requisite qualities:

vs 1: *fratres boni testimonii et sanctae conuersationis.*
vs 3: *in quibus securus abbas partiat onera sua.*
vs 4: *sed secundum uitae meritum et sapientiae doctrinam.*

This insistence on the choice of holders of this office and on the criteria for their election is all the more striking because RM mentioned the question only briefly (RM 11:4).[21] The high point of the text is to be sought without a doubt in the third formula (*non per ordinem sed secundum uitae meritum et sapientiae doctrinam*), which will recur in the chapter on the ordination of the abbot. Let us note in passing these parallels between the criteria for the choice of an abbot and those for the choice of deans. The exclusion of any *ordo* or rank on a bais of seniority is patently a peculiar characteristic of RB, which alone regulates that order, in Chapter 63. But this peculiar characteristic gives an opportunity for the redactor to stress the analogy between the two offices, a principle whose importance we saw in RM 11.

The question of the election of deans therefore captures all our attention in RB. Three lines only are given to the brief description of the function which, moreover, exactly summarizes the long directory of the Master. The deans must exercise total supervision over their *decaniae*, according to the commandments of God and the precepts of their abbot (vs 2).[22] One may also see in the words *in quibus securus abbas partiat onera sua* an allusion to the theme developed at length in the RM prologue,[23] but if RB thus summarizes the Master's theory on the relationships between the abbot and his collaborators, it is to emphasize the qualities that they ought to display: *tales elegantur in quibus*. This reminiscence of RM therefore only aims at organizing the single theme of interest to our author: the deans must be well chosen and perfectly fitted for their function.

We meet this theme again, in a special form, in the last lines of the chapter (5–7), in which we are told about the correction of a dean 'puffed up with pride', his disposition, and his replacement by 'another man who is worthy'. This passage, which will be repeated almost in its entirety in the chapter on the provost,[24] stands in complete continuity with what has preceded it: after dealing with the election of the deans, the writer seeks to provide a remedy, in case all his efforts to guarantee a good choice in the end prove futile. His sole preoccupation—*that the incumbent of the office be 'worthy'*![25]—continues to haunt him.

This entire conclusion, which almost equals the body of the chapter in length, constitutes an addition in relation to RM, where the case under consideration here is not even envisaged. The Master has no more imagined that provosts may act reprehensibly than he has foreseen failings on the part of the abbot. In his mind the dignitaries of the cenobitic hierarchy are safe from such suspicions. How could he, given his educational perspective, make an issue of the educators' possible faults, and in a document meant for daily public reading at that? Only once does the Master provide for a sanction affecting the provosts, but it is for the situation where one of their men might arrive late for the office.[26] Then the provosts bear responsibility for their subordinates according to a principle which the Master takes very seriously,[27] but their own guilt is not directly involved. Only in RB do we come across warnings addressed to the abbot,[28] and coercive measures against officers guilty of insubordination.[29] The prestige of the educators is no longer strong enough to ensure silence about human weaknesses, which experience has revealed. In RM, the peril of pride threatened only the 'under-abbot' (RM 93) but now it is foreseen that even deans will be open to it.[30]

Since RB lays particular emphasis on the qualities required for a good choice, we must devote special attention to the three formulas, referred to above, which set forth these criteria for election. It will be seen that the redactor has given them a very meaningful content.

Brothers chosen as deans must be *boni testimonii*. This expression is taken from Acts 6:3, where it characterizes the candidates for the diaconate.[31] By *sanctae conuersationis* one is immediately reminded of Deut 1:13, that is, one of the texts which narrate the establishment of the hierarchy of Israel by Moses in the desert.[32] This allusion is fully confirmed by the propinquity of the words *constituantur decani*: the Deuteronomic text, of course, goes on to relate how Moses has taken wise and noble men from the tribes of Israel and made them leaders: captains of thousands, of hundreds, of fifties, and of tens.[33]

The same expression (*constituantur decani*) recurs in the parallel pericope of Ex 18:21–22. Now Cassian explicitly refers to this text of Exodus when he introduces the decanal system to his readers (*Inst.* 4.7), the young monk is given into the keeping of an elder, *qui decem iunioribus praeest, quos sibi creditos ab abbate instituit pariter et gubernat, secundum illud scilicet quod ordinatum in Exodo legimus per Moysen.* There can be no doubt that RB is here harking back to that passage of the Pentateuch. This is again perceptible when the redactor prescribes that deans *tales elegantur in quibus securus abbas partiat onera sua*. The idea, as we have seen, comes from RM 11, but its expression is certainly inspired by Ex 18:21–22 (*leuiusque sit tibi, partito in alios onere*), a text about which we have no indication on the Master's thought.[34] Thus it is obvious that St Benedict, following Cassian, looks upon the captains of the monastic as the successors of the captains of ten in Exodus. In both cases the meaning of the institution is the same: Moses on one hand, the abbot on the other, have to judge a numerous people; since this responsibility exceeds their strength, they must employ the help of subordinate officers, under whose orders the people will be divided up into groups of ten.

The third expression employed by RB (*secundum uitae meritum et sapientiae doctrinam*) does not include any characteristic allusion to the Pentateuch texts relating to the establishment of captains of ten. But this expression nevertheless remains in keeping with the tone of these texts and the qualities that they attribute to the men selected by Moses: *uiros sapientes et gnaros et quorum conuersatio sit probata* (Deut 1:13), *uiros potentes et timentes Deum, in quibus sit ueritas, et qui oderint auaritiam* (Ex 18:21). The two elements of the expression (conduct and wisdom) are precisely those which recur, though in different words and in inverse order, in the Deut 1:13 definition. The same text notes a little further on that the *decani* have a 'doctrinal' mission (*decanos, qui docerent uos singula*; Deut 1:15).

The word *decanus*, along with the idea of the function it designates, is therefore certainly of biblical origin. Cassian and St Benedict, each in his respective fashion, affirm this beyond any shadow of doubt. On the other hand, they make no mention of another reference, for which an important case has been made out in recent times: that the *decani* were allegedly the subordinate officers of the roman army, and that once again RB is betraying a dependence on secular institutions.[35] We do not deny that the roman *decurio* could have served as a model for the organizers of cenobitism. But if it did, it did so in a secondary manner; the decisive influence, attested by the texts, was that of biblical precedent. It was not the roman army, which the Fathers wished to reproduce, but Israel, the people of God in the Old Testament and the type of Christian Church in the New Testament. The jewish monasticism of Qumran had already taken the organization of Israel in the desert as a pattern.[36] This idea from scripture again imposed itself quite naturally on Christian monasticism.[37]

Thus, the monastic community again begins the story of Israel in the desert. The Moses of this new exodus is the abbot. In revealing this to us, the chapter on deans projects a new and living light on the abbatial function. We knew already that the abbot, like the bishop, is the representative of Christ in the community entrusted to him. Even here, reference to the *fratres boni testimonii*, that is, the deacons of early times, tends to emphasize this close relationship to the ecclesiastical hierarchy. In calling upon the assistance of the deans, the abbot resembles the apostles when they 'constituted' the deacons.[38] But here, in addition, we are referred to Moses as a type. Such typology is all the more expressive as the monks are close to the desert life of Israel after the exodus from Egypt. The abbot really is for them what Moses was for Israel: the man of God who makes known the divine will, the reliable guide on the long journey leading from the land of sin to the Promised Land.

This exodus theme often prompted descriptions of the *coenobium* and its head. The coptic lives of St Pachomius delight in comparing the assistants of Pachomius—Theodorus and Horsiesios—to 'Jesus son of Nun', that is, to Joshua, which is tantamount to likening Pachomius himself to Moses.[39] Consequently, Msgr Lefort seems quite right in affirming that the pachomian 'house' is also a reminiscence of the patriarchical organization of Israel.[40] The word 'tribe', itself, which according to Jerome, designated a cluster of three or four 'houses', tends in the same direction.[41] Pachomius does not seem to have been thinking precisely of the decimal system described in the books of Exodus and Deuteronomy, but by referring to the Israelites dividing themselves by 'tribes' and 'houses', he linked his congregation to the same basic type, that of the people of God under Moses and Joshua.

In his turn, Faustus of Riez recalls Moses and Joshua, when he writes to depict Honoratus transferring his powers to Maximus.[42] This episode gives rise to a long comparison of the new abbot with the two great leaders of the people of God in the desert.

Again, we could cite RM 11, which as we have seen, makes the delivery of the *virga* the ordination rite of the provosts and refers back to the rods of the Messiah (Ps 2:9), the Apostle (1 Cor 4:21), and Moses. This slightly veiled allusion, however, should not make us forget what we recognized above: all in all, RM shows scarcely any interest in Old Testament typology. The merit of the Master lies in having thrown into relief, with incomparable clarity, the analogy between abbot and bishop, and between the hierarchy of the cloister and the ecclesiastical hierarchy. This essential point occupies his full attention and relegates the parallel with the Ancient Law to the background.

Nevertheless we should be wrong if we were to set the Old and New Testaments in opposition, as if it were a question of two distinctive typologies to which the writers on cenobitism might have appealed. In fact, to lay claim to one is implicitly to appeal to the other. The Church gives proof of this when it has recourse to Moses' institution of the seventy 'elders' (Num 11:16–17) to elucidate the ordination of its priests (or 'elders') by the bishop. This typology forms a part of the most primitive stratum of the prayers for presbyteral ordination: it is already found in Hippolytus' *Apostolic Tradition*,[43]and in the consecratory prayer of the roman pontifical attested by the Leonine Sacramentary. It completes the network of analogies which we have already brought forward. If the Master is right in comparing provosts to priests, this is because both are successors of the subordinate captains of Israel mentioned in the Pentateuch. The church hierarchy, like that of the *coenobium*, refers back to the type of Moses-and-collaborators, and this common point of reference quite naturally invites us to liken one to the other.[44]

We must point out, nevertheless, that ecclesiastical and monastic literature have spontaneously divided between themselves the Pentateuch texts, which do in fact fall into two series, one narrating the institution of the captains of thousands, of hundreds, and of tens (Ex 18:21–22 and Deut 1:13), and the other telling of the seventy elders receiving a share in the spirit of Moses (Num 11:16–17). The monastic *decania* appeals to the first series of texts, while the ecclesiastical order of priests (or 'elders') attributes its origins to the second. Such a division ought not to be exaggerated, since the *decani* of cenobitism are also called *seniores* by a good number of texts, by Cassian and RB in particular, which thus likens them to the second series. It remains nevertheless true that the ecclesiastical hierarchy and the cenobitic hierarchy are joined to the same Old Testament type by different paths. Just as Moses serves as the type of both abbot and bishop, the 'deans' are in line with the *decani* of Exodus-Deuteronomy, and the 'priests' with the 'elders' of the book of Numbers.[45]

To conclude: the decanal system which RB inherits from the Master plainly situates both rules in the great tradition of egyptian cenobitism as Jerome and Cassian had made it known to the latin west. This affiliation is all the more remarkable in that another tradition, that of Basil and Caesarius of Arles, says not a word about the decanal system.[46]

RB has scarcely modified the indications which it found in the Master on the subject of deans. It has merely summarized them, to the point of reducing the highly expressive and pictorial directory of the master to a somewhat colorless schema. On the other hand, it has laid an energetic emphasis on the selection of deans, on the qualities they ought to possess, and on their eventual replacement by subjects truly 'worthy' of this charge. We note lastly the suppression of the 'appendix' (RM 11:107–123) which in RB becomes a separate chapter (22) dealing with the sleep of the monks.[47] This amputation performed on the directory for deans does not lack an analogy with the fate of the appendix to the abbatial directory (RM 2:41–52), which became the treatise on the counsel of the brethren in RB. In the present case, it tends to tone down still more the role of the deans.

The parallel between abbots and deans, so strongly emphasized by the Master, loses much of its distinctness in the remnant preserved by our rule. Even the place of RB 21 separated from the 'spiritual' chapters by the liturgical section, keeps the deans at some kind of distance from the abbot. A serious effort of concentration is necessary, in order to rediscover the meaning of the decanal function in RB, in relation either to the initial treatise on spirituality or to the *ordo monasterii* which follows, something which stood out so clearly at a first reading of RM 11.

We may regret this loss of doctrinal substance. We may also deplore the disappearance of the Master's interesting prologue, which deprives us of very stimulating insight into the cenobitic hierarchy as compared to that of the Church. But it is our good fortune that RB, in abridging the text has spontaneous recourse to expressions redolent with biblical vigor. They constitute a return to a thoroughly traditional Old Testament typology which the Master had neglected. More than in RM, the abbot emerges in RB as a new Moses 'unburdening' himself on carefully selected 'captains of ten'. This typology in its turn tends towards the ecclesial parallel developed by the Master, that of the bishop encircled by priests, deacons, and clerics.

THE CELLARER (*RM 16 and RB 31*)

The two directories—RM 16 and RB 31—form an arresting contrast. After a lengthy prologue in the first person plural (RM 16:1–26) reminiscent of those of the directories for the abbot and the provosts, the Master finally arrives[48] at the conclusion which deals with the cellarer. If it is true that he 'is none other than a dispenser of *divine* things' (vs 11)—for it is from God himself that the brethren receive their food, clothing, and footwear—a heavy responsibility weighs upon him. Like the abbot (RM 2 and 11), the cellarer will have to give an account before God's tribunal (vss 27–30). After these preliminaries, the Master passes immediately to the regulation of the life of the cellarer which will occupy almost the whole chapter (vss 32–61). The holder of this position is given precise and practical instructions. First to be outlined are his duties, carried out in complete dependence on the abbot, in particular, those concerning distributions to sick brethren and alms for the poor. Only in the absence of the abbot may he take the initiative in such matters (vss 32–37).

These recommendations still bear a close relation to the principles laid down in the prologue. But what comes next is no more than a chain ofdetailed directions regulating the conduct of the cellarer throughout the day and the week: exact directions are given as to the moment when he is to go to communion, his relations with the weekly kitchen helpers as regards the kitchen utensils,[49] his behavior and that of his companions at table during meals, his occupations during those hours when his employment leaves him free, and what he should do to link himself with the office when his work prevents him from going to it (vss 38–52).

Next, the Master specifies the situation of the cellarer, who is outside all the *decaniae* and under the immediate supervision of the abbot, and attributes as the motive for this state of affairs some not very complimentary considerations: were the cellarer to belong to a *decania* he would be able to try to bribe his provosts by offering them additional payments (vss 53–56). Here one again finds one of the preoccupations of the prologue.[50] Finally, the Master notes the role that the cellarer plays in maintaining the law of renunciation of property. It is he who receives and distributes all the implements of the monastery, which plainly means that no one apart from the abbot possesses the least object (vss 57–61).

The RM directory closes with a note on the qualities demanded of the cellarer (vss 62–66). The Master wants the abbot to recognize him as 'faithful and abstinent, never overcome by desires from the direction of his *gula*, nor overfond of eating and drinking', for he will surely not lack temptations of this sort.

Thus the directory for the cellarer in RM is of a decidedly practical nature. Apart from the prologue, which is inflated by digressions on Providence, and the final notice indicating the qualities required of him, the Master here gives the cellarer a real rule of life. Brief and precise notations succeed one another like articles of a code, whereas spiritual considerations all but cease after the end of the prologue.[51] Compared to the directory for the abbot or even to the provosts', the chapter on the cellarer impresses us by its down-to-earth aspect. This is not surprising, since with the present chapter, we move from the spiritual domain, where the abbot and his provosts exercise their educational function in the material organization of the monastery.

Moreover, if the prologue lays so much stress on Providence, it is to remind us that material things belong all the same to the divine sphere and that the cellarer *himself* has a spiritual responsibility. But such insistence is only meant to put the holder of this office on his guard against bad administration, not to attach importance to the dignity of his functions. Plainly, the Master does not have any very lofty view of this responsibility, attaching no importance to it from the standpoint of the spiritual formation of the brethren.

Not only does the cellarer play no educational role in the community, but he is himself classed among the subjects to be educated. He too needs to be 'watched'[52]—nothing of the sort had been noted concerning the provosts—and if he is not placed under a provost, this is precisely because he is mistrusted. Even though 'faithful and abstinent'—the minimum required to avoid the worst—the cellarer belongs to the category of *minores*,[53] those who are supervised and instructed. The directory composed for him does not exude the confidence which RM furnishes for provosts, as for the abbot, who are in principle considered irreproachable religious, impeccable educators and men accomplished in spirituality.

Moving to RB, we find ourselves faced with a passage with quite a different aspect. There are of course a certain number of identical directions: the cellarer ought not to be a 'big eater'; he must obey the abbot in everything; the sick and the poor are entrusted to his care; the monastic patrimony should be 'divine' and 'sacred' to him; he will have to render an account to the Lord, so he must not be guilty of wasting the goods of the monastery. These points of contact, however, give way to some quite perceptible differences, which we shall point out in the course of this study. They are less remarkable as they are to be found here and there in the directories for the cellarer in other rules, notably in the remarkable Chapter 25 of R Or.[54] What is striking, on the contrary, is the large number of original remarks found in RB 31, and especially the interest that the redactor seems to have towards this office. Let us look more closely into this.

The initial words *eligatur de congregatione sapiens* betray that overriding preoccupation for the 'right choice' affirmed so forcefully, as we saw, in the chapter on the deans. Whereas RM 16 treats the requisite qualities only in a sort of postscript,[55] RB broaches the question from the outset. The list of qualities is considerably developed and includes no fewer than ten terms—three positive, six negative, and another positive—most of which lack a parallel in the Master. The Master spoke neither of wisdom nor of maturity; he did not think of excluding pride, rowdiness, a tendency to be abusive, slowness, or extravagance, nor to commend the fear of God.[56]

Almost all these qualities and defects will reappear in the course of the development; in enumerating them, the redactor indicates at the outset the principal themes and the general meaning of his directory. Instead of providing a rule of life, he sketches a portrait of a good cellarer. Practical dispositions are almost entirely missing, but the virtues that the cellarer ought to practice in his relations with persons and things are set out in detail.

This list of qualities, moreover, displays the analogous enumeration found in the second directory for the abbot, a passage peculiar to RB chapter 64. There, as we shall see, the redactor repeats certain recommendations made previously to the cellarer: like him, the abbot shall be 'sober' and '*non turbulentus*'. The lists of qualities drawn up in the Pastoral Letters, and the portrait of the Servant of Yahweh in Is 42, inspire both these exhortations in RB.

Without at present delving into the details of these scriptural references, we must nevertheless emphasize the link made between the cellarer and the deacon, which is similar to that between abbot and bishop, through recourse to the literary device of enumerating virtues and vices which, in the pastoral epistles, serves to describe the ecclesiastical hierarchy. Let us also note the first two qualities in the list: *sapiens, maturus moribus*. They will recur in the description of the porter (RB 66). In that instance, as in the present one, RB transforms the rule of life furnished by RM into a piece of spirituality, in which practical preoccupations give way to psychological and moral interest.[57]

The cellarer, then, ought to be picked carefully, in accordance with a series of criteria enumerated in the 'list of qualities'. The directory next insists on the universal scope of his responsibility: 'the whole community', that is to say, all the persons who make it up or who become attached to it in some capacity (such as the guests and the poor), and perhaps also the things which are in the monastery.[58] This universal solicitude is compared to that of a father, a comparison which places the cellarer very close to the abbot, who is rightly called the true father of the community.[59] So honorable a proximity contrasts somewhat with the more reserved appreciation of the Master. Nor had the Master any thought of commending to the cellarer to care for people. This preoccupation for the common good is indeed indicated in passing by RM,[60] in the same way as the alms that are to be given the poor and the appropriate distribution made to the sick,[61] but all that seems to go of its own accord, without saying and is not made the object of any positive recommendation.[62]

The next two recommendations (*sine iussione abbatis nihil faciat, quae iubentur custodiat*) do no more than proclaim in more general fashion the specific directions of RM 16:32–34. From some of the Master's specific observations RB derives a principle valid in all circumstances. Note the sequence of short phrases stating as many distinct precepts, in the style of a list of good works. The RB 64 abbatial directory presents the same stylistic feature, which one seeks in vain in RM 2–RB 2.

The list ends, as will also be the case with RB 64:10, with a singularly important feature, which produces the following development: *fratres non contristet*, referring to unreasonable demands addressed to the cellarer by the brethren. We shall see shortly how much this theme of avoiding 'sadness' engrosses our redactor. Here we would only observe that it is absent from the RM directory. The Master, moreover, paid no attention at all to the relationships of the cellarer with the brethren, that is, to the *manner* in which he ought to deal with them. He is told what to do, but not *how* to do it.

This commentary on the *non contristet* phrase shows us, on the other hand, the significance of two of the qualities enumerated at the beginning of the chapter. If the cellarer must not be *elatus* nor *iniuriosus*, it is because—as we are now learning—his office exposes him to temptations to pride, contempt, and giving disobliging answers. 'Humility' is particularly necessary, when one's job provides opportunities for discovering the unreasonable characters of certain brothers! In such circumstances, the cellarer will thus have to answer 'reasonably', opposing good to evil and the contrary to its contrary, like a good schoolmaster. In this, the educational role already attributed to him will be brought into broad daylight in the second part of the text. *Rationabiliter* is, moreover, a word of which RB is very fond.[63]

There is perhaps an echo of RM in the words, *animam suam custodiat*. The Master does indeed prescribe that the abbot be 'on guard' against the cellarer's faults (RM 16:53), but the allusion, if there is one, does not pass without a total alteration of the idea: it is not the abbot but the cellarer himself who is urged to 'guard his soul'. Once again we see the difference between the two rules in respect of the cellarer. He is held in higher esteem in RB and greater confidence is shown in him. He passes from the category of subjects to be educated, where the Master kept him, to that of the educators or at least of mature spiritual men responsible for themselves.

RB supports this recommendation with a scriptural *testimonium* of great importance for the ecclesial typology of the cellarer's function. The cellarer ought constantly to bear in mind the apostolic dictum, 'Those who carry out their duties well will earn a high standing' (1 Tim 3:13). Whatever be the authentic meaning of this Pauline text, the fact that it concerns deacons is enough to suggest a parallel between them and the cellarer. We shall see that this Pauline parallel is well attested in cenobitic tradition. RM, on the other hand, does not seem to have given it a thought. The mild interest that it displays in the cellarer has apparently prevented it from noticing a parallel, which had nonetheless been in the line traced by the RM 11 prologue: abbot = bishop, provosts = priests, deacons and clerics. . . This silence well indicates, that in the eyes of the Master, the cellarer does not belong to the cenobitic hierarchy, properly so-called.

The exhortation to care for people is then continued in the form of a list of categories, which names in detail those for whom the cellarer is responsible: the sick, the children, the guests and the poor. The first and last were named by the Master, but without this appeal to watch over them with all possible care; the second and third are not even mentioned in the RM directory. 'For all these categories' shall the cellarer have accounts to render on the Day of Judgement. We shall come back especially to his duties towards the sick in RB 36:10. Let us observe that the theme of accountability to the Lord has already been indicated by RM (16:27–31), but there it is a question of the victuals, the *annona*, whereas in RB the accountability relates to the care of people.

The next phrase, moreover, connects precisely with the idea developed in the RM prologue: 'The cellarer is the dispenser of *divine* things', said the Master; 'He ought to look upon all vessels as if they were consecrated vessels,' rejoins RB. The thought is very similar. However, the Master has in mind only the *annona*, that is, food and perhaps also clothing and footwear;[64] it is the divine origin of these material goods, the fact that they have been dispensed by Providence, in conformity with Mt 6: 25–33, which renders them worthy to be looked upon as divine. In speaking of 'all the *vasa monasterii* and of all the *substantia*,' RB has in view a more vast assemblage of objects. There again, it does not refer to the Sermon on the Mount or to the providential origin of these objects, as RM does, but rather to the concept of consecration that is dear to Basil[65] and attested by Cassian.[66] Since the monastery is a church and a house of God, everything that is found there acquires a sacred character. Basil was addressing himself especially to craftsmen; Cassian had the weekly kitchen helpers in mind; here it is question of the cellarer, and the goods of the monastery in general. Within the same general context, R 4 Pat prescribes that the brothers consider everything as sanctified, and adds a reference to the sacrilege of King Belshazzar.[67] In transferring to the cellarer what Basil, Cassian, and R 4 Pat said of the brethren, RB remains consistent with its very lofty conception of this responsibility. In RB the cellarer is the officer responsible for the economic life of the community. The sacred character of things handled by the cellarer might also be related to his quality of 'deacon'. In both instances, it is the same ecclesial theme which is affirmed.

In the prolongation of this exhortation to deal with the case of objects RB puts the cellarer on his guard against every sort of negligence. The word appears in RM 16:30. Like the Master, the RB redactor condemns all wastefulness.[68] However, he introduces here a counterpart unknown to the Master: *neque auaritiae studeat*. One extreme is as much to be avoided as the other. This theme of the middle way is emphasized in the conclusion of the passage: *omnia mensurate faciate*, which clearly paves the way for chapter 64. The *ne quid nimis* is a concept dear to the redactor. He will develop with insistence in the second directory for the abbot, even referring back to it in different words in his praise of 'discretion', which brings that directory to a close. Here, he makes only a rapid allusion to it in relation to the cellarer, but this allusion is like a signature.[69]

All in all, the caution against 'avarice' serves hardly any other purpose than to furnish the indispensable counterpart to the admonition against 'prodigality,' in order that the theme of the just mean may come to be understood. The important element is the *non prodigus*, as is indicated at the same time by the context (*nihil ducat negligendum*), by the redundant expression (*et stirpator substantiae monasterii*), and by the reference to the list of qualities at the beginning, where *non prodigus* was already read, minus any allusion to 'avarice'.

The exhortation to show care for objects concludes with a reminder of the abbot's supervision (*et iussione abbatis*). This note which repeats the *sine iussione abbatis nihil faciat* of vs 4, is completely alien to the context. Hitched on to the end of a development, which deals with an entirely different matter, it does indeed look like a later addition. However, nothing prevents it from having been added by the redactor himself, betraying as it does one of his main interests, or dare it be said, one of his obsessions.

At the point that we have reached, it is indispensable to take an overall look at this chapter. The end of the text (vss 13–19) is really no more than a repetition of what comes before. This can be easily verified by examining the following list of doublets:

vss 3–5: *curam gerat de omnibus; sine iussione abbatis nihil faciat; quae iubentur custodiat;*	vs 15: *omnia quae ei iniunxerit abbas ipsa habeat sub cura sua; a quibus eum prohibuerit non praesumat.*
vss 6–7a: *fratres non contristet. Si quis frater ab eo forte aliqua inrationabiliter postulat, non spernendo eum contristet . . .*	vs 16: *fratribus constitutam annonam sine aliquo typho uel mora offerat, ut non scandalizentur . . .*
vs 7b: *sed rationabiliter cum humilitat male petenti deneget.*	vs 13: *humilitatem ante omnia habeat, et cui substantia non est quod tribuatur, sermo responsionis porrigatur bonus.*

We are not, of course, dealing with pure and simple repetitions, but the themes are the same: submission to the abbot under two aspects: positive (all that he commands or entrusts) and negative (*only* what he commands or entrusts); good relationships with the brethren, neither saddening them nor scandalizing them by a proud attitude, humility, especially in refusals; reasonable or kind words. . . .

This bipartite structure has already been encountered in the abbatial directory and in the RM 2 treatise on the council of the brethren. We shall find it again in the second directory for the abbot, peculiar to RB (Chapter 64). Thus it is a habitual stylistic practice of our authors to juxtapose two parallel developments, the second taking up with some variations the themes proposed in the first.

This method provides us, in the present case, with some interesting, precise examples. It is obvious that the cellarer has a role to play in the spiritual growth of his brethren. He can, and even should give them the 'good word' that is of greater worth than the best of gifts (Si 18:17).

Giving the word in RM is the monopoly of the abbot and his deputies, the provosts. By extending this privilege to the cellarer, RB whether consciously or not, is advancing this personage into the category of educators and members of the hierarchy. Likewise, as we shall see, it will finally credit all the brethren with a share in the abbot's educational mission.[70]

No less significant is the caution against scandalizing the little ones (Mt 18:6). If the cellarer can and ought to contribute to the spiritual edification of the brethren, he is also in a position to 'scandalize' them. The word may not perhaps have the wide meaning given it by the Evangelist. In the language of St Benedict as well as that of the Master, 'to scandalize' means 'to anger', and 'scandal' means 'dispute'.[71] Such a limited sense well suits the present context. The 'scandal' which one dreads for the brethren is not just any 'stumbling-block', but precisely the sin of wrath and of resentment which the arrogance or the dawdling of the cellarer might occasion.[72] The idea, as one can see, closely approaches the *non contristet* of the first part.

The cellarer ought therefore to guard himself against causing the brethren to fall into anger. Such a recommendation prepares the way for the developments on fraternal charity which we shall meet when commenting on RB 63 through 72. As we have seen, the cellarer in RB resembles the abbot and his deans more closely; like them, he bears the responsibility of an educator. But he is at the same time one of the brethren, frail and sinful as they are, and liable to be an occasion of sin for them. He is therefore requested here to watch his relationships with his brethren. Just as RB 63 will prescribe that the elders (and the abbot himself) call the younger men 'brothers', so the cellarer is urged to show humility towards those whom he serves, in order to avoid affronts. This concern for 'horizontal relations' is missing in the Master, both in his directory for the cellarer and in the whole of his rule.

The finale (vss 17–19) prolongs these considerations on fraternal charity. The rule provides for the possibility of assistants to relieve the cellarer, when the community is too numerous.[73] *Si congregatio maior fuerit.* This was already the reason given for creating the deans. The cellarer, like the abbot, ought to be relieved of an excessive burden. But we should be ungracious if we stressed this comparison, for RB provides also for helpers in different categories of employment: weekly kitchen-helpers, guests' cooks, the porter. The cellarer therefore, is just one particular instance of a general rule, which will be formulated explicitly in RB 53:19– 20.[74]

No less remarkable is the fact that RB here manifests a concern foreign to the Master, who makes no provision for relieving the cellarer. On the contrary, he foresees the necessity of giving him extra work to keep him occupied (RM 16:45–46). This contrast between the two rules signifies that the community has increased, and the work of the cellarer become more absorbing. Only once does RM envisage a situation when work is excessive, owing to the large number of brethren and when it would be necessary to assigning helpers for the service; it is then a question of the weekly kitchen-helpers.[75] RB has renewed this devotion concerning the weekly helpers (RB 35:3–4), but has extended it to other cases as well: guests, cooks and the porter,[76] and here even to the cellarer. In the same way, we must call attention to the change from singular to plural in the chapter on the custodian of the tools. RM 17 provides for only one holder of this office, RB 32 for several. All this indicates a numerical increase of the community and a corresponding burden on the services.

We would be mistaken, however, if we were to see in this direction, dealing with the assistance to be provided for the cellarer, only a consequence of the development of the *congregatio*. In the eyes of the redactor the spiritual interests of the cellarer are at stake: *a quibus adiutus et ipse aequo animo impleat officium sibi commissum*. It is not therefore the smooth running of the service which is the object of attention here, but the moral well-being of the person who fulfills it.

The same thought will be expressed in different words in the chapter on the weekly kitchen-helpers: *ut non cum tristitia hoc faciant* (RB 35:3). This case of the weekly kitchen-helpers is particularly interesting, for it allows us to compare the Master's and the RB redactor's concern with the same direction. For the Master, the motive given is the punctuality of the service,[77] while in RB, it is the spiritual consolation of the servants. The Master's only concern is the peace of the abbot and community, which would be upset by lateness. RB is only interested in the state of soul of those who minister.[78]

Here, likewise, it watches over the spiritual well-being of the cellarer, after attending to that of the brethren. The link between the two series of directions is explicit: the cellarer, too (*et ipse*), ought to keep his soul in peace.[79] Neither of these directions figures in RM, which is content to indicate the mutual duties of cellarer and brethren at the time of prayer: while one alone is working outside the chapel, for the good of all, it is only fair that these last make a special remembrance of him in their prayers (RM 16:51–52). This charitable consideration has its cost, but it does not equal RB's recommendations. One could say that RB is entirely original in its concern for the moral equilibrium of the cellarer as much as the brethren's. In describing the cellarer's task it introduces an interest in person-to-person relations, a solicitude for the spiritual well-being of both parties conditioned by these relations, and finally a concern for the individual, beyond the letter of the regulations, all of which give this directory significantly higher value and weight than it had in the Master.

The last sentence manifests the same fundamental concern for the peace of souls. Cellarer and brethren have an equal interest in doing everything at the appointed time: 'giving' is the cellarer's business, 'asking' that of the brethren. Here therefore we see a resumption of the alternation which governs the two preceding formulas.[80] The redactor's thought embraces with the same solicitude both the parties involved; 'no one'—the cellarer no more than the monks—'should feel troubled or sadness in the house of God'. An admirable and justly famous conclusion to a chapter devoted to the most material of tasks![81]

This question of 'suitable times' had previously been the object of a reference in R Aug 13.162–165, immediately after a sentence relating to the cellarer. The reference deserves the more attention, in that it brings to notice other connections between this directory for the cellarer and the Augustinian texts. Butler rightly points out a reminiscence of *Enarr. in Ps 103* (1.19) and a trace of Lr 22.6. These two references furnished by Butler, like the one which we have just indicated, cannot be paid too much attention. On considering them carefully, one is inclined to seek in St Augustine the source of what had seemed to us the particular merit of this directory in comparison with the Master's: care to bring about good fraternal relations between cellarer and brethren and concern for the peace of their hearts.

Furthermore, these Augustinian references emphasize the relationship between RB 31 and RB 64. The second directory for the abbot, as we shall see, bears the undeniable imprint of Augustine's influence, and this influence makes itself very much felt in the direction that we have just indicated, even more precisely, in that of the theme of charity.

Indeed, it is by insisting upon the relation between the directories for the cellarer and for the abbot, that we should bring this commentary to a close. From the stylistic point of view as well as from that of fundamental concern, the two texts bear the impress of a single personality. In both, lists of qualities are followed by developments abounding in short aphorisms; in both, there are reminiscences of Augustine and of the Pastoral Letters, and in both, above all, the same search for a just mean, the same concern for peace of souls (*non turbulentus*!), and the same appeal to humility and love.

When this fundamental harmony between the two directories has been perceived, one cannot fail to be struck through such a parallel by the importance given to the cellarer. Both offices are obviously of almost equal standing in the estimation and concern of the redactor. He has devoted directories of them of almost equal length (that for the cellarer even surpasses the exhortation for the abbot by several lines), orchestrating largely the same themes and drafted with the same love. These two passages, which are so much alike, are also the only ones of their kind in RB, once the first abbatial directory transmitted by RB 2 has been restored to the Master.

The predilection thus shown for the cellarer forms a lively contrast with the much less favorable appreciation of the Master. It contrasts equally with the dryness of the RB chapter on the deans. In short, our Rule has exactly reversed the scale of values that it found in RM, by reducing the notice devoted to the deans to a few points, and by showing an extraordinary interest in the office of cellarer.

With this shift of accent, it may perhaps be that a different conception of cenobitic education is dawning. In the Master, such educational work was conceived according to a very simple, purely vertical plan, in which the action of the abbot and his provosts, the school-master and his assistants, counted for everything. This elementary plan remains in RB, but loses something of its clear-cut simplicity through its inclusion in a broader and more subtle concept, in which personal relations hold an important place, and in which a new sense of the value of the individual is affirmed. The directory for the cellarer has been for the redactor a privileged opportunity to give expression for the first time to this relatively new vision. It reappears with many a detail in the course of the rule before revealing itself with complete clarity in the additional chapters of the appendix.

Several times, while commenting on RB, we have noted indications, which compare the cellarer to the deacon. It will be useful to retrace briefly the history of this theme, for the purpose of bringing its traditional character into relief.

Sulpicius Severus already points out a 'deacon' alongside St Martin at Marmoutiers,[82] but the hybrid nature of Martin's foundation, half-monastic and half-clerical, makes one hesitate over the meaning of this *datum*. We are indeed told how this man Cato had the administration of the monastery in his hands—something which corresponds to the office of cellarer—but would it not be a question of a 'deacon' properly so-called, invested with the holy order, to whom Martin had confided the temporalities of the community? At all events, this text clearly indicates the affinity between the two offices.

Gregory of Nyssa's mention of a *diakonos*, moreover, at the monastery of his sister Macrina[83] reveals that the name 'deacon' had been given to simple cellarers, not invested with the ecclesiastical diaconate. Cassian in turn attests the existence of a 'deaconry' affiliated to each of the four churches of Scete.[84] Of course, he never calls the holder of this office *diaconus*, but rather 'president of the *diaconia*' or 'steward', the title of deacon being reserved for the altar minister.[85] Nevertheless, the particular structure of the community, to which this steward is attached, strongly suggests, no less than the very name of the office and a comparison with the diaconate: the hermits of Scete were in fact grouped round a church, in which they assembled once a week; their head is the priest of this church. What could be more natural than to see in the steward a deacon?[86]

The same comparison asserts itself when we turn to the verbs expressing the ministry (in Greek *diakonein*), which ordinarily comprises the activity of the steward. Thus Palladius, speaking of a distribution made to the members of a group of anchorites by their confrère Diocles, calls it *diakonesai tois adelphois*.[87]

Finally, the citation which R 4 Pat 123 makes of the Pauline text on deacons, when applying it to the cellarer (1 Tim 3:13) must be taken into account. RB probably lifted this citation from R 4 Pat, likewise phrasing it in the singular rather than in the plural of St Paul. In R 4 Pat the example of Judas is added to this scriptural reference, which quite capable of arousing a salutary fear in the cellarer since the betrayer had also been in some sense steward of the group of Twelve. Whether the ecclesiastical diaconate or the college of the apostles is cited when talking of the cellarer, it is always the same ecclesial type, which is set before our eyes. The monastic community is a quasi-church and its cellarer the analogue of the deacon.

Thus, in this directory for the cellarer, RB has preserved a valuable im pression of the traditional idea of the 'cellarer-deacon', inadequately indicated by RM.[88] It deserves to be pointed out along with the indications furnished by our two rules on the subject of deans. In both instances, a new light is thrown upon the significance of the abbacy as an ecclesial function analogous to the episcopate. The meaning given to the subordinate offices of the *coenobium* shows in its turn the meaning of the abbot's function.

And since, in consequence, we converge upon the figure of the abbot-head of a church, that is, the abbot-bishop, may we point out the connection between this authentically traditional concept and the question —rather a subject of discussion today—of the abbot-pontiff?[89] It might seem as though the pontificals of modern abbots result quite naturally from the ancient theme, whose history we have traced. If the abbot really is, in the eyes of monastic tradition, a sort of bishop, why should the liturgical marks of the episcopate not befit him?

The question is in fact much more complex. On the one hand we must note that the pontifical insignia are rather a tribute of honor than a specific sign of the episcopal charge,[90] while on the other hand we must take account of the historical circumstances in which abbots were, little by little, vested with such insignia. It seems that the external prestige of medieval abbeys has contributed more to this evolution than did a deep consciousness of the role of the abbacy *intra muros*. We should also take account of the weighing-down of the monastic liturgy, which resulted from this; the liturgy was required to be a pompous display, in imitation of cathedral pageantry. Lastly, let us not forget that the ancient tradition is as firm in maintaining the nonclerical character of the monastic hierarchy as in indicating its relationship with the hierarchy of the Church.[91]

This obviously does not prejudice the legitimacy of a more recent evolution, but it ought to forewarn us against any exploitation of the ancient texts in terms of the modern perspective of abbot-priest and abbot-pontiff. For the ancient writers, the abbot is indeed analogous to the bishop, but he is so in his own way and in his particular line, which is that of a complete monk become spiritual father. This is to say that he is, in principle, only a layman. It also bespeaks the simplicity of manner which should be his.

We should not on that account neglect the traditional comparison between abbot and bishop, and set the two types of authority that they represent in an exaggerated opposition. Such a tendency makes its appearance in certain pages of Olivier Rousseau.[92]

In the conception of cenobitism, which is that of our two Rules, the abbot is in all respects analogous to the bishop. His election by the brethren signifies nothing other than that of a bishop by the faithful. It is only a matter of acknowledging the charisma given by God, of discovering the man gifted with the grace of the necessary spiritual worth and teaching gifts required for a pastor of souls in truth.[93] Such a charisma ranks the abbot in the category of 'doctors' who rule over the people of God in the footsteps of the prophets and apostles.[94] It sets him alongside the bishop in this category, while his collaborators, the deans and the cellarer, are in similar fashion ranked alongside the priests, deacons, and clerics. His teaching will be traditional like that of the head of a church, for he is bound to a rule which actualizes the exigencies of the Gospel and epitomizes the experience of the perfect disciples of Christ, that is, those who have embraced the apostolic life. In brief, though he is no bishop, he is in every respect similar to a bishop.

NOTES TO CHAPTER FIVE

1. Jerome, Lr 22.35; Augustine, *De moribus ecclesiae* 1.36.7. These two authors also employ *praepositus* as a synonym for *decanus* in the same passage.

2. *Inst* 4.7; 4.9; 4.10 (Petschenig, p 54, 4). In *Inst* 4.17, Cassian paraphrases: *eum qui suae decaniae praeest.*

3. RM 73:3: *cum praepositis* (PA), *cum decano suo* (E). RM 73:7: *cum suis . . . praepositis* (PA), *cum suis . . . praeposito hoc est decano* (E).

4. RM 12:1: *praepositis suis*; 13.55: *a praeposito suo*; 30:30: *a praepositis*, according to P and A. In RM 13:5, 67, omission of this term by E is not typical, for the whole passage has disappeared in E.

5. RM 12:3; 13:1, 5.

6. RM 13:44, 51.

7. The word itself (*decada*) is not attested in E, but the only reason for its absence is that this term did not occur in the passages recopied by this manuscript. *Decada* furthermore stands isolated, as far as I know, in tradition. Jerome says *decuria*, Cassian *decania*.

8. Monasteries are mentioned by name in RM 11:8, 11, whereas RM 1:83 spoke only of *scolae* (cf. The 45). The two texts have the expression *gradus doctrinae* (1:82; 11:13), but by that the first means the three *successive* authorities of the people of God (prophets, apostles, teachers), while the second has in view the various hierarchical echelons which simultaneously govern this people at the present time, either in churches or in monasteries.

9. The symbolism of the *uirga* is explained with the help of two texts (Ps 2:9; 1 Cor 4:21) already noticed in RM Pr 23–27. This little series of *testimonia* seems better placed here than in the Prologue, where it is somewhat foreign to the context. The Prologue adds two further texts on the *uirga* (Ps 45:7–8; Ps 89:3) which might have been rather expected here, while RM 11 proceeds in evoking the rod of Moses.

10. No such provision is made for the cellarer, the guardian of the tools, or the porters. The cases of the weekly kitchen-helpers and of the reader, who receives a blessing, is different, since it is a matter of a simple weekly rotation.

11. RM 1:87

12. Jerome says: *quadraginta plus minusue fratres* (R Pac *Praef* 2).

13. RM 11:22, 28 (cf. 38), 40, 108, 121, 122.

14. *Custodire*, which recurs so often in this directory, means both 'to guard someone [from sin]' (RM 11:40, 44, 46, 49, 91, 92) and 'to mount guard against [sin]' (RM 11:22, 37, 94), depending upon whether the direct object is 'the brethren' or 'the faults.' In 11:14 the text carries *custodiendis ratiociniis*, an expression difficult to translate. In 11:23 there is no direct object.

15. *Inst* 4.8ff.

16. In particular RB 46:5; 56:3; 58:6. Cf. also 3:12; 4:50; 27:2; 48:17.

17. See below, Chapter 8, p 347–348.

18. Styled *decania* as in Cassian. Cf. above, n.7.

19. Kassius Hallinger, *Gorze-Kluny: Studien zu den Monastischen Lebensformen und Gegensätzen im Hochmittelalter*, 2 vols (Rome, Studia Anselmiania, 1950), vol 2, p 784; G. Penco, *Regula*, p lv. The latter, however, suspects RB 48:17 (*unus aut duo seniores*) of harboring an allusion to the *two* provosts of RM. Cf. RB 56:3: *seniorem . . . unum aut duo*, corresponding to *praepositos . . . ambos* (RM 84:3–4).

20. The same as in RB 22:3: *deni aut uiceni*; 56:3: *unum aut duo*. There is the same flexibility of numerical determination among the Pachomians, if one is to believe Jerome (R Pac *Praef* 2: *quadraginta plus minusue fratres . . . triginta uel quadraginta domus . . . ternae uel quaternae domus*). On the number of weekly helpers in the kitchen, according to RB, see below, Chapter 8 n.6; on that of porters, see Chapter 9, n.35.

21. With an allusion further on (RM 11:21), to this designation according to 'merit', *eligere* figures but once, as a passive participle, in RM 11 (*duo electi fratres*, vs 4), whereas *ordinari* is not uncommon there. (vss 4, 5, 8, 14, 15, 35).

22. CF. RM 11:27: *in eis . . . sollicitudinem exercere*; 11:32: *circa os omnium auribus sollicita*. In RB, *sollicitudinem gerere* is used with regard to the abbatial charge: 2:33; 27:5 (cf. 27:1). See also 31:3: *curam gerat de omnibus* (the cellarer); 22:3: *super eos solliciti sint* (the deans); 58:6–7: *super eos omnio curiose intendat. Et sollicitudo sit. . . .* (the novice master).

23. Cf. *securus* in RM 11:6, 14, and in RB 32:1. *Onera* also recalls RB 64:7: *quale onus suscepit* (*abbas*).

24. Cf. RB 65:18–21; even here (vss 6–7) the redactor refers us expressly to that text. Deans and provosts are again associated in RB 62:7.

25. This preoccupation with 'worthiness' reappears in RB 62:1 (*de suis elegat qui dignus sit sacerdotio fungi*); 63:14 (*ut dignus sit tali bonore*); 64:5 (*domus Dei dignum constituant dispensatorum*). CF. RB 2:1 = RM 2:1 (*abbas qui praeesse dignus est monasterio*). This incidental clause in RM becomes an express and often reiterated recommendation in RB. There is the same preoccupation concerning the cellarer (RB 31): the qualities required for this employment are more thoroughly developed in RM 16:62–66. On the porter, see below, Chapter 9; aptitudes and virtues not mentioned in RM 95 are demanded of him. Note also what is said about the guest master (RB 53:22), the guests' cook (53:17), the infirmarian (36:7), the reader (38:12; cf. 47:3–4); all these remarks on the competence demanded of the officers of the monastery lack parallels in RM.

26. RM 73:3–7 (cf. 32:9). Add the suspicions of 16:53–56.

27. Cf. RM 2:7–10 (2:35–36; 7:55–56).

28. Cf. below, Chapter Nine, pp 396–397.

29. See, besides this chapter, the case of the monk ordained priest (RB 62, something for which RM does not provide. The sanctions against the provost (RB 65) reproduce the procedure already described in RM 93, though giving it a juridical precision unknown to the Master (the four warnings) and adding, like RB 62, the threat of expulsion.

30. Despite the hope expressed by RB 65:13 (*ut dum pluribus committitur unus non superbiat*).

31. Acts 6:3: *uiros ex uobis boni testimonii . . . quos constituamus super hoc opus*. Cf. Cassian, Conf 21:1 (appointment to the deaconry of Scete).

32. Deut 1:13: *date ex uobis uiros sapientes et gnaros quorum conuersatio sit probata*.

33. Deut 1:15: *constitui eos decanos*. This text, like Acts 6:3 (see n. 31 above), could have suggested to RB the use of *constituere*, whereas the Master, referring to the provosts, says *ordinari* and *praeponi*. Note also the *ex uobis* in the text of Acts, the *ex uobis . . . de tribubus uestris* of Deueronomy, and the *de omni plebe . . . ex eis* of Ex 18:21–22; similarly, RB 21:1 says *elegantur de ipsis* (cf 62:1: *de suis elegat*; 31:1: *eligatur de congregatione*).

34. On *onus*, see above, n.23.

35. Herwegen, *Sinn und Geist* p 191, citing Vegetius, *Epit. de re militari* 2.13 and 2.8.

36. See 'Le monastère, Eglise du Christ,' *Studia Anselmiana* 42, (1957), pp 40–41 and n. 65.

37. In translating 'captains of thousands, of hundreds, and of tens' by *tribuni, centuriones, decani*, the Vulgate itself uses the Roman military vocabulary. In fact, the same decimal system governed both the Roman legion and the Israelite army, such as the Pentateuch describes it. It is probably to the Latin version of the Bible that the monastic decury owes its resemblance to the Roman institution of the same name, on which it depends perhaps only indirectly, through the intermediary of the biblical text.

38. Note in this respect another implicit comparison between abbots and apostles in RB Pr 50 (=RM Ths 46): *in eius doctrina . . . perseuerantes*, a reminiscence of Acts 2:42.

39. *Vies Coptes*, 139, 19 (Bo 78: Theodore), and 274, 3 (S 5 126: Horsiesios); cf. 338, 4 (S 3b, p 156).

40. *Vies Coptes*, p 97, n. 1, citing Joshua 7:16–18.

41. Cf. Jerome, R Pac *Praef* 2 (Boon, p 5, 1. 17).

42. *Hom. de S. Maximo* in *Bibl. Vet. Pat.* (Lyons, 1677), vol 6, p 655ab.

43. Hippolytus, *Apostolic Tradition* 8 (Botte, p 38).

44. Is this why, in the Roman Missal, the Mass for the common of abbots has for the first reading the eulogy of Moses (Eccles 45:1–6)?

45. A distinction that we did not make in 'Le monastère, Eglise du Christ,' p 41.

46. On these two traditions, see Kassius Hallinger, 'Papst Gregor der Grosse undder Hl. Benedikt,' *Studia Anselmiana* 42 (1957), pp 305–306.

47. RM itself subscribed to this interpretation in its digressions on the brethren's sleep. Yet this question was not the only one with which the appendix dealt. It begins with a direction about clothing (RM 11:107), which has purely and simply disappeared in RB, and ends with a direction relating to the table (RM 11:122), which is found in RB 56:3 (a passage immediately dependent on RM 84:2–4). The general recommendation which follows (RM 11:123) has left no trace in RB. The RB redactor has therefore reduced the RM 11 appendix to a treatise 'on the brethren's sleep' (a treatise inflated by elements drawn from RM 29), leaving aside the characteristics contained in the directions on the dormitory.

48. This prologue, the principal theme of which is announced in a few words in vs 11, is overloaded with digressions on confidence and indifference to things here below (RM 16:1–26; cf. 82:1–15; 86:1–13; 89:21–23; 91:8–34).

49. At this point comes a note on penances for objects broken (vss 41–42).

50. Cf. RM 16:48: *fraudulenter*.

51. Note, however, (vss 51–52) the solidarity established between cellarer and brethren, who pray while the former is working.

52. RM 16:53. There we recognize the key word of RM 11. Cf. above, p . The two uses of *custodire* found here belong to the second series: 'to mount guard *against* sin.' Likewise RM 18:5.

53. Cf. RM 11:8.

54. Cf. also R 4 Pat 138–144; R Aug 160–165. The R Or calls the cellarer *cellarius*. If the text of Holste is accurate, one could see in this fact an indication of the antiquity of R Or (cf. R Aug 13, 160 and *Vita Caesarii* 1, 6). According to Philip Corbett, *The Latin of the Regula Magistri. A Guide to the Establishment of the Text* (Louvain, 1958), pp 214–215, *cellarius* instead of *cellararius* in RM 16:1 and 16:11 would, on the contrary, be simply a scribe's error.

55. Same position for the corresponding note on the subject of the custodian of tools (RM 17:21–22), but the Master had already said at the beginning of the chapter: *uni fratri cuius diligentiam abbas agnoverit* (17:1), just as he had spoken of the qualities of the provosts right from the prologue of their directory (RM 11:4).

56. This last quality will still be demanded of the custodian of the tools (RM 17:22).

57. See below, Chapter 9.

58. *Curam gerat de omnibus* (vs 3). Penco translates: *di tutto e di tutti*. But really, in RB 27:1, 6, *curam gerere* regards only care for persons. Similarly, *sollcitudinem gerere* (RB 21:2).

59. Cf RB 33:5: *a patre monasterii*.

60. *Omnium sollicitudine* (RM 16:51); *communis utilitas* (16:52).

61. RM 16:32–36.

62. The point of the text concerning the sick and the poor, is not to incite the cellarer to be concerned for others, but to lay down precise rulings as to his obligations when the abbot is present and when he is absent.

63. Cf. RB 61:4 (*rationabiliter et cum humilitate caritatis*); 65:14 (*rationabiliter cum humilitate*). In RB 7:60, *rationabilia* is substituted for *sancta* (cf. RM 10.80). *Rationabilis* in RB 2:18 makes up part of an RB addition.

64. Cf. RM 16:12: *quid induamini*; 16:19: *uestiarii, calciarii*.

65. R Bas 103–104. See also '*Le monastère, Eglise du Christ*,' p 37, nn 53–55.

66. *Inst* 4.20.

67. R 4 Pat 144–150 (cf. Dan 5:3). The passage follows on some directives for the cellarer (1.138–144) where the 1 Tim 3:13 citation appears, as in RB.

68. *Neque stirpator substantiae monasterii* (RB 31:12) recalls RM 16:30–31: *per negligentiam . . . stricari . . . ab euersoribus stricari*. In this passage, E exchanges *stricari* first for *exterminari*, which renders the sense satisfactorily, but secondly for *custodiri*, which changes the meaning. This last fact escaped Corbett (*The Latin*, pp 215 and 280).

69. Cf. RB 48:9: *Omnia mensurate fiant*, and the *uestimenta mensurata* of RB 55:8. In these two passages, the idea of 'measure' is opposed not to two contrary extremes, between which one would try to find a just mean, but to a single excess (too much work, thereby disheartening the weak; clothing too short). Here likewise, as we have noted, the burden of the text is especially directed against all prodigality. Again, similarly, in RB 64, the theme of discretion is in fact developed uniquely against the 'too much,' while leaving the 'too little' out of the picture (cf. below, Chapter 7, p 327–28).

70. Cf. below, Chapter 9.

71. Cf. RB 13:12; 65:1, 2; 69:3.—RM 83:19; 94:5. The case of RM 13:13, 23 should be set apart. In 13:23 the Master is citing Ps 50:20, where *scandalum* seems to signify detraction, dishonor, injury to one's reputation. 13:13 has a similar sense, probably 'grave injustice, wrong'.

72. Note *sine mora* (vs 16), echoing *non tardus* of vs 1, just as *sine aliquo typho* recalls *non elatus* (vs 1). So the redactor is continuing a commentary on the virtues and vices enumerated in the initial list.

73. *Solatia*. CF. RB 35:3–4; 53:18, 20; 66:5. The word is already employed in the same context by RM 13:45, 49; 18:4–5, 12; 19:18, 20; 23:52; 53:44; 95:11. However, it does not signify in the Master the *personnel* given as reinforcements, as is the case in all the passages peculiar to RB, but rather the *help* and the *companionship* which these additional personnel offer (cf. RM 15:49; 91:53). It will be observed that this is also the meaning of RM 1:4 (= RB 1:4): *multorum solatio iam docti* (the help brought by the brothers, not *the brothers* themselves in so far as they constitute help). Here we have quite a remarkable case in which MB, as regards the meaning of a word, is found to be in agreement with M and not with B. *Solacium* occurs only exceptionally in RM with the meaning of a helper (☐ a person). Cf. RM 56:15: *solacio laico* designates a lay travelling companion (the same personage is designated otherwise in RM 62:5: *illis uiae collegis*). Possibly this meaning of 'companion' is already that of RM 13:49 (*sit ei sola culpa solacium*). The same meaning is possible, but more dubious still, in RM 79:14 (*caritatem solacii adinplere*). In these two cases, the meaning 'companionship' remains probable.

74. This RB passage combines, moreover, an article from the RM directory for the cellarer (RM 16:45–46) with an article on the government of the weekly kitchen helpers (RM 19:18; 23:51–52). The whole is erected into a general law for all occupations.

75. RM 23:51–52 (*one* brother of the same *decania* is added to them for serving at table; RM 19:18 (*several* brothers are added to them for kitchen work, and they begin after prime).

76. RB 66:5. It is true that conceding an assistant to the porter does no more than reconstitute the *two-man* crew prescribed by RM 95.

77. Cf. n. 75. The Master lays a good deal of insistence on this point, which affects the peace of the community (see RM 21:4–6, 13–14). Certain sanctions are prescribed in the event of lateness (19:13–17). In line with the same preoccupations, cf. 23:53–56: the serving must be performed well.

78. Same viewpoint in RB 36:4. There once again, the redactor successively envisages the good of the sick and that of those who serve them.

79. Here we perhaps have a doublet with *animam suam custodiat* (vs 8). This new doublet would have to be added to the list given above. By understanding *animam suam custodiat* in

this sense, the citation which follows (1 Tim 3:13) can be explained rather well as an encouragement in the difficulties of an important office.

80. *Horis competentibus* (vs 18) alludes to *sine mora* (vs 16), itself announced by *non tardus* (vs 1; cf. above, n. 72).

81. Note, however, that this finale recalls very much that of RM 21:14: *ut cum omnia exiens abbas inuenerit praeparata non sit locus irae uel occasio coleris uel clamoris sed sit monasterium taciturnitatis et pacis*. Here as well, the issue is one of exactitude in serving, but relevant to those who wait at table (cf. above, n. 77). Condemnation of sadness is found again in RB 27:3 (cf. 2 Cor 2:7); 34:3, 35:3; 36:4; 48:7; 54:4. The Master had already warned against the harm that such sadness might cause (RM 55:13; 56:14–15; 61:23). The monastery is called *domus Dei* in RB 55:22 and 64:5, which are moreover two very similar passages. The Master speaks of *domus diuina* in RM 11:8, 13, meaning thereby churches and monasteries, that is to say, the *familia*, the community of the servants of God, a meaning which fits RB 64:5 and the present citation well enough, but is less suitable perhaps for RB 53:22, where the context suggests a local sense (the house, the building and its furnishings). Cf. also RM 94:5: *domus pacis*, recalling 21:14: *monasterium . . . pacis*.

82. *Dial* 3.10: *Cato diaconus ad quem monasterii administratio pertinebat*.

83. *Vita Macrinae*, Jaeger, 406, 11; cf. 402, 5: the same Lampadion is *en tô tès diaconias bathmô*.

84. *Conf* 21. 1–9. The qualities required of the administrator recall the selection of the deacons in Acts 6:3 (cf. above, n. 31). It is probably the same *abba* John who appears in *Inst* 5.40 as 'steward' of Scete. As Maïeul Cappuyns well appreciated, (art. '*Cassien*' in *Dictionnaire d'Histoire et de Géographie Ecclésiastiques*, Paris: Letouzey et Ané, 1949, vol 11, col 1323) ths deaconry described in *Conference* 21 is probably located in Scete, and not in Diolcos, as is generally supposed. In this respect, the article '*Diaconia*' in the *Enciclopedia Cattolica* requires emendation. Otherwise this article gives a good survey of the moastic ecclesiastic deaconries of antiquity.

85. Cf. *Conf* 4.1: Daniel, a future priest, exercises the liturgical functions of deacon together with the priest Paphnutius. Note that it is also to the same church of the priest Paphnutius that John the steward, his contemporary, is attached. Thus one clearly grasps the duality of functions: the deacon ministers at the altar, the steward administers the deaconry, the deacon being selected by the priest and the steward by the elders.

86. Cf. *dispensationem ecclesiae* (*Inst* 5.40).

87. LH 58.2. The issue is moreover only that of an *ad hoc* steward, chosen expressly for the occasion by the priest Dorotheus, head of the group. Dorotheus declares that Diocles surpasses himself (Dorotheus) for wisdom. Palladius, in his turn, qualifies Diocles as *gnôstikôtatos*. We shall observe the lofty conception formed in their milieux of the qualities required for such down-to-earth functions. Palladius (LH 10) also points out a 'priest and steward', one Origen, in company of the hermit Pambo.

88. Steidle does not take up this point, but Herwegen notes it (p 250).

89. Steidle, p 315–316: 'Der äbtliche Pontifex'; Louis Bouyer, in *Le message des moines à notre temps* (Paris 1958), p 171; B. Beseret, *ibid.* pp 246–47.

90. See the study by Pierre Salmon in *L'Ami du clergé* (1954), pp 651–54; 674–81; 753–60, published also under the title *Etude sur les insignes de Pontife dans le Rite romain* (Rome, Officium Libri Catholici, 1955).

91. Cf. below, Chapter Six.

92. Oliver Rousseau, 'Communauté ecclésiale et communauté monastique,' *Maison-Dieu* 51 (1957), pp 10–30, especially pp 26–27. 'The abbot is by no means the successor of an apostle', he writes in commenting on RB 2. Instead of deriving his authority from the apostolic succession like the bishop, the abbot would owe it to the choice of his brethren,

that is, to say in the ultimate analysis, to the 'desire' they have 'to be under an abbot' (RB 5:12), in order that Christ may be visibly represented as 'present in their midst', according to the promise of Mt 18:20.

Rousseau is logically led to these views by the contrast which he makes between the ecclesial and the monastic community. The monastic community was born of eremitism, that is to say, of a repudiation of the ecclesial community, but, in cenobitism, the eremitical tendency would combine with an 'apostolic' tendency, to follow Christ not only into the desert but also on his mission of accomplishing good among men. In other words, Rousseau represents the *coenobium* as the result of a reorganization of hermits on the 'horizontal' level of fraternal charity. The abbot would emanate from the community thus constituted, and his authority would arise from their desire for a common life as an affirmation of the presence of Christ among the brethren.

Here, as also in his essay *Monasticism and Religious Life*, (*Monachisme et vie religieuse d'après l'ancienne tradition de l'Eglise*, Chevetogne: Collection Irénikon, 1957). Rousseau seems to be unaware of RM. Had he known it, he would have found it hard to set the two types of community and authority in such radical opposition. In this respect RM does no more than explain, as we have shown, the constant data of the cenobitic tradition. In the eyes of that tradition, the abbot does not emanate from the community, but rather the community is engendered by the abbot. The role of the abbot is before all else that of teacher. The gathering of the brethren results from their joint dependence upon this father in God, with whom they have come to serve an apprenticeship in the perfect life. The role of spiritual direction is therefore decisive in the genesis of cenobitism. It is organized round a principal axis which is the master-disciple relationship, at least in the great tradition which stretches from Pachomius to Benedict, and including Cassian and the Master (for Basil certainly does have a conception of the community of the same kind as that analysed by Rousseau).

93. Finally, we would mention that election by the brethren is not an essential characteristic of the abbacy. As we shall see, other methods of appointment often competed with it, in particular appointment by the predecessor. If, moreover, election by the community seems the normal mode, it is precisely by analogy with the election of a bishop by the people.

94. This role of the charisma is moreover very well noted by Rousseau in *Monachisme et vie religieuse*, pp 78–79.

Chapter 6

PRIESTS AT THE MONASTERY (RB 60 and 62)

THE FIRST OF THESE CHAPTERS clearly belongs to the section on recruitment, beginning with Chapter 58. The second, on the contrary, is not part of this section because of the subject with which it deals; it concerns not the recruitment of monks, but the promotion of monks to the priesthood. Nevertheless it is obvious that Chapter 62 is connected with Chapter 60 not only because it deals with the priesthood, but also by reason of the directions regarding the rank to be given to priests and clerics. This theme of rank is indeed already well-placed in Chapters 60 and 61; Chapter 63 soon comes to deal with it *ex professo*. Chapter 62 is thus immediately connected with both what preceded it and with what follows. It stands as an appendix to the section on recruitment, while at the same time it heralds the Chapter *De ordine congregationis*, which goes on to deal, in its entirety and for its own sake, with the question of rank, which was initiated by the section on recruitment.[1]

Moreover, Chapter 62 is obviously constructed on the same plan as Chapter 60, to the ideas and vocabulary of which it refers back. It is therefore opportune to take these two chapters together, in order to sift out the idea of RB on the priesthood in relation to the cenobitic life.

We note first that only Chapter 60 possesses a corresponding chapter in RM. It is a curious thing that RM, which explicitly prescribes daily communion,[2] makes no provision for the promotion of monks to the priesthood. The abbot in RM, moreover, seems to be a layman.[3] Each Sunday the brethren process to the 'parish' church for Mass. On weekdays the abbot apparently ministers the eucharist in a community rite *extra missam*.[4].

So only Chapter 60 of RB could have been directly inspired by a text analogous to that of the Master. That text is Chapter 83 of RM. Yet it must be noted from the beginning that the place of the chapter on priests is not the same in the two rules. In RM, Chapter 83 is situated in a section relating to the reception of guests.[5] In RB, on the contrary, Chapter 60 is situated further on, in the section on recruitment, as already noted. This change in itself marks an important modification, which an attentive comparison of the two texts confirms: RM does not, strictly speaking, envisage the incorporation of priests and clerics into the community and does no more than settle the conditions of their stay as guests. On the other hand, RB certainly seems to envisage the complete integration of priests and clerics into the community, although for them as for visiting monks (Chapter 61) there is no question of a novitiate.

Apart from this exception, the two rules are in agreement as to their single fundamental attitude, which may be summarized in a word: mistrust. Both rules look upon the priest living in the monastery as a potential source of serious annoyance, against which they do their best to safeguard the abbot and his community. In Chapter 62 RB only stresses further this attitude of mistrust and reinforces the line of strict conduct prescribed with regard to priest-monks. Everything that RM and RB have to tell us about the priesthood is therefore of great homogeneity.

Such directions are not at all surprising, when we correct them with the evidence furnished by other cenobitic documents. Chapter 60, notwithstanding the silence of the *Concordia*,[6] can be compared with the *Rule of the Four Fathers*, 1.173–185, which, after prescribing for the reception of clerics with the deepest respect and paying them full liturgical honors, refuses them the authorization to live in the monastery, unless it is a case of *lapsi*, desirous of undertaking penance and seeking nothing but humility. To such as these every manner of liturgical prerogative is denied, so that they purely and simply disappear into the body of the community. The *Rule of the Four Fathers* therefore practically excludes all sacredotal or clerical presence from the monastery. By going back to the origins of cenobitism, one finds in Pachomius a less exclusive attitude but equally staunch as to principles: if he accepts priests desirious of becoming monks into his Congregation, if he even 'respects their standing', he makes no concessions to them as regards a departure from 'the constitutional rules of the brethren'.[7]

It appears that our two Rules, RM and RB, can appeal to the cenobitic tradition for their adoption of a rigorous line of conduct towards clerics received at the monastery. In the chapter on monks promoted to the priesthood, the facts of tradition, rare as they are, tend in the same direction. In order to illustrate RB 62, the citation that the *Concordia* finds is a passage of rather slight relevance from St Jerome,[8] and a small but more illuminating paragraph from the rule of Aurelian.[9] If we understand his text correctly, Aurelian affirms the exclusive right of the abbot to designate the candidates for orders, and no one may receive any holy order without his consent. This immediately reminds us of the important decision of the Third Council of Arles, which recognized this same right for the abbot of Lérins, contrary to the claims of the bishop of Fréjus.[10] But the text of Aurelian is directed not so much to bishops as to the cenobites themselves: the legislation is intended to remind them that they may not be promoted to orders without leave of their abbot. This recalls the episode in the life of Pachomius, where we see the superior of a *coenobium* disputing this point with one of his monks who is imperiously demanding to receive clerical status. Pachomius counsels the superior to yield in order to avoid the worst, and his concession has a felicitous outcome, for the monk once ordained returns to his original humble disposition.[11]

Here, two situations enable us to grasp an actual conflict between a monk and his abbot over clerical status. The two testimonies, it is true, speak only of the reception of holy orders, not of their exercise nor of the behavior of the monk in the ordinary run of cenobitic life. In these last two spheres, the testimony of RB 62 remains, so far as we know, almost alone. However, the curious passage in the *Life of St Eugendus* can be cited, where an abbot who is contemporary with St Benedict is portrayed as grappling with problems of government caused by the presence of priest-monks in the bosom of the community[12] Eugendus himself, having steadfastly refused that dignity, was not a priest. Nevertheless he intended that the faults of his monks should be corrected by their monastic superiors and by them alone. He accordingly assigned the priest-monks to occupations which kept them separated from the community. Thus they could be unaware of the faults of the brethren, and they were neither obstructed in administering the Eucharist to them nor presumptive in granting it to them before the regular session for the correction of faults.

It is perhaps of difficulties of this type that St Benedict is thinking when he puts the priest-monk on his guard against every kind of 'presumption'. In any case, RB 62 fits perfectly into a tradition, which maintains the rights of the abbot and the rule against any claim by clerical monks to emancipate themselves from their authority or to substitute themselves for it.

Fears of the disorders, which a desire for the priesthood might produce, had even in the earliest times dictated to Pachomius a line of conduct still more severe than that of St Benedict. We have seen that the coptic founder used to accept clerics desirous of embracing the cenobitic life. But for all that, he does not allow his monks to receive ordination, 'for fear that if such an opportunity were given, strife, envy and jealousy might be established in the midst of a numerous body of monks . . . only to result in the end in a splitting of the community'.[13] Both he and his successor, Horsiesios, declined ordination.[14] It is interesting to note the motive put forward by Horsiesios to justify his refusal: 'We have what is necessary for us, thanks to those who come to us.' This text leads us to believe that the pachomian congregation, under Horsiesios as superior, remained faithful to the principle laid down by its founder. The only clerics that the monasteries possessed were those who had embraced the cenobitic life at the time when they were already invested with the clerical dignity. Lay monks were not ordained, in conformity with what Pachomius had prescribed.

Defensiveness: all the documents relating to cenobitism in ancient times are agreed on this point. The priesthood is only mentioned in these texts in order to erect barricades round it, which will prevent it from extending itself outside the domain of its sacred functions, to which it claims to confine itself. Such an attitude is easily understandable, if we consider the nature of monasticism and the priesthood, and if we take an overall view of their relationships in the course of the first centuries of cenobitic experience.

Priesthood and monasticism are two different things. The former is ordained for the government of the people of God, the latter consists of a break with the present world. The purpose of priesthood is to incorporate men into Christ, through giving them the divine word and the sacraments. Monasticism is an effort to realize in solitude the perfection of union with Christ. Whereas the priest is defined by his ministerial function, the monk has no responsibility for souls, unless it be his own. His work consists not in procuring the saving word and sacraments for his neighbor, but, as far as lies in his power, in rendering these talents fruitful in himself, through ascetic practices and prayer. The combat of the priest is in the world, where he collects and defends his flock. The combat of the monk is given up to the desert, against the passions that the devil sows in his heart.

Monasticism is therefore in line with baptism. It is nothing else but a supreme effort to die with Christ and live in him, in other words to realize daily the sacramental action of baptism. It can therefore be said that monasticism is in line with the function of the laity. Not only is it not confined to clerics, but the tendency to solitude, which defines its nature, runs counter in principle to the pastoral vocation of the priest.

Monasticism is something like martyrdom. Every Christian, whether cleric or layman, may be called upon to render this supreme witness. Martyrdom is not confined to clerics but is part of the glorious duty of every baptized person. Martyrdom can have a special significance when endured by a priest, but it is true to say that it is under the title of baptized Christian that the priest confronts the martyrdom which puts an end to his role as pastor. We know that, in fact, monasticism got off theground at the time when martyrdom ceased to offer itself to every Christian as a possible way of breaking with the present world and of being perfectly united with Christ. Monasticism is presented as a substitute for martyrdom. Consequently it is not surprising that monasticism, like martyrdom, is open to every Christian and requires nothing more than the grace of baptism. There will be priest-monks, as there have been in the past, and, in great numbers, priest-martyrs, but both are called upon effectively to renounce their sacerdotal function by a gesture of voluntary sacrifice which, however, is in some sense linked on so deep a level with this same function.

The facts confirm what we have just deduced from the very essence of monasticism and of the priesthood. It does not appear that the first monks were clerics, nor even that their vocation had been brought into existence under the direct influence of the clergy. Anthony and Pachomius are laymen. Their vocation arises from an inspiration from on high, without the leaders of the people of God having contributed to it in any tangible fashion.[15] The monastic movement, even when it attracted numerous clerics to itself, remained fundamentally in line with its origins, by retaining the character of a lay movement. Authority is not conferred upon it by ordination, but by the grace of the Spirit, which is radiant in a blameless life. The spiritual Fathers form a hierarchy of graces and sanctity, which is not to be confused with the ecclesiastical hierarchy, even if sometimes, for reasons that we are going to set out, the same person is invested with both authorities.

Of course, once the essential distinction separating monasticism and the priesthood has been pointed out and has been recognized from the facts, one cannot fail to be struck by the multiplicity of examples, which have arisen between the two orders—indeed from the earliest times. It lies beyond our present scope to expound here the attitude of the priesthood in respect of the monks, the intelligent and active sympathy of certain prelates,[16] the hostility of worldly clerics,[17] the individual or collective attempts to unite monastic observances with the clerical life,[18] and the efforts to recruit clerics from among the monks.[19] According to all the evidence, monasticism has deeply influenced clerical circles, and this influence is discernible not only on the factual plane, but even on the level of ideas, where people were not slow to formulate, in different ways, theories—rightly so-called—on the relationship between the two states.[20] What is important here is rather to describe summarily the attitude of the monks towards the clergy and the clerisy. By so doing, we shall see the general framework within which the cenobitic documents analyzed above and the directions of our two rules acquire their full meaning.

True monks have always been distinguished by a profound respect for the priesthood. In this they were doing nothing but raising to the highest pitch a sentiment experienced by the entire Christian people in that age of living faith. There is a classic story, attested both by the *Life of Anthony* and by the *Historia Monachorum*,[21] of a monk already renowned for his sanctity, who requires a cleric of the very lowest rank, who is visiting him, to 'conclude the prayer' that they have made together. The RM itself bears witness to this attitude by devoting two chapters to regulating the manner in which clerics are to be received, as well as to the gifts that they send. The gifts are to be received with profoundest respect: the abbot rises, kisses the priestly gift, and recites together with those of his monk who happen to be in his company the verse *Suscepimus*, followed by the *Gloria Patri* and a prayer.[22] Priests or clerics visiting the monastery are surrounded with the same veneration. They are requested to bless the meal and monks are forbidden to give a blessing in their presence.[23]

Such respect for the priesthood was sometimes severely tested. It inevitably happened that monks would feel ill at ease in the presence of clerics, whose behavior diverged too greatly from the monastic ideal, even from simple propriety. The *Verba Seniorum* have preserved for us the echo of such scandals.[24] It even appears that the *detractatio clericorum* was a classic and well authenticated sin of monks. Jerome, who accuses the *remnuoth* of Egypt of it,[25] could, of course, have made the same accusation against himself. His disciple Sulpicius Severus offers perhaps the best or the saddest example of this sardonic literature, which maliciously emphasizes all the failings and pettinesses of the clergy.[26] This sort of anti-clericalism, moreover, is in no way aimed at the hierarchical order. It is directed at individual persons, precisely by reason of the respect, which the sacred office inspires.

However, profound respect for the priesthood inevitably led the monks, as general rule, to refuse to be invested with it. Sometimes this refusal is motivated by the fear of becoming involved in the world and committed to pastoral tasks, which would put an end to solitude and ascetic practices.[27] But even if such fear should not exist, the monk dreaded the priesthood for the simple reason that it is an honor. This manner of looking upon the clerical state as a 'dignity' or a 'grandeur' appears constantly in the ancient texts. It surged from the living and respectful faith of which we have spoken. Hence it is no surprise that mention of the priesthood in monastic writings is almost invariably framed in a context of vainglory.[28] Desire for the priesthood does not befit a monk, who makes a profession of humility. If there is a wish to ordain him, his duty is to conform to what a certain historian has wittily called the traditional rule of the preliminary refusal.[29] At this period, hardly a single case is known of a bishop-elect, who did not make the gesture of fleeing, in order to escape ordination. A monk could not but feel himself particularly obliged to adopt such an attitude, even if it were only a question of the priesthood or the diaconate, or even a minor order. It must be admitted, moreover, that quite often the stubbornness of the rebellious individual made his refusal a good deal more than a mere convention. Examples abound of monks who have successfully resisted all pressure to cause them to be ordained, or who, ordained in spite of themselves, withdrew by flight from the exercise of their function.[30]

This refusal of the priesthood was grounded on two special motives in the particular case of cenobitism. The sacred order was looked upon not only as a threat to the personal humility of the individual, but also as a danger for the community. Let us recall the fears of Pachomius: he dreads for his congregation, ' strife, envy, jealousy, in a word, division'. The same words recur when his biographer repeats the exclamation of Athanasius, after Pachomius, by his obstinacy, has successfully managed to ward off the threat of ordination.[31]

In these circumstances, the founder of the *coenobia* knew how to make prevail against the will of the pontiff the fundamental principle, upon which the authority of this new kind of church rests. Cenobitism will have lay leaders, designated not by ordination but by the grace of the Spirit, which is radiant in them.

Notwithstanding this refusal on grounds of principle, monasticism was going to be led to allot a certain place to clerics, not only in its ranks but even in its structure. This evolution was dictated by the need to provide for the sacramental requirements of the monks. The lay Christian is obliged to have recourse to the priest in order to receive the two indispensable foods for his supernatural life, the Word of God and the Eucharist. Of these two priestly benefits, it was not the word which the monks most lacked. Even though they generally showed themselves eager to receive. the teaching of the hierarchy,[32] they found in abundance the word that brings liberty close at hand from the great *pneumatikoi* in their midst.[33] On the other hand, no spiritual Father, however holy he might be, could give them the Body of Christ, unless he were a priest.

Several solutions were available to monks in search of the holy mysteries. They could approach the local clergy, if there were any close at hand,[34] or the clergy could agree to come to visit the monks in their retreat.[35] It happened too that priests withdrew into their midst[36] and exercised their ministry for them. But in default of, or along with these solutions, there was yet another which tempted the monks time and again, that is confer the priesthood on one of their own number, a monk already renowned for his holy life. By so doing, the monks were not acting differently from the Christian people, who so often at this period compelled well-known ascetics to be ordained to minister to them.[37] Nothing used to seem so natural and so opportune to a group of disciples gathered round a revered master in solitude as to have him ordained priest. In this way the man of God, already radiant with the grace of the word, became in addition the minister of the Eucharist. In the same person the sacramental source was added to the charismatic source. The type of these priest-abbots is several times attested by Palladius, by the *Historia Monachorum*, and by Cassian.[38] Moreover, there was a predetermined harmony between the role of abbot and that of priest, both being essentially pastors of souls. Motives of humility, which in principle diverted monks from the priesthood, partly lost their force, when the individual was already, in fact, exercising an actual spiritual authority analogous to that of the priest.

Monasticism also very often came to be organized round a priest-abbot, who was the center of a colony of hermits or head of an actual *coenobium*. Hilary of Arles has left us an unforgettable picture of the pastoral activity of St Honoratus, founder and priest-abbot of Lérins:[39] so great is his loving care, boundless in its insight and devotion, and so many are the virtues that can be recognized as those of the future bishop of Arles that they cause his biographer to say that the *sacerdotium* of this simple priest has already reached the highest point as regards inner sanctity and outward acts.[40] After Honoratus, Faustus of Riez, Caesarius of Arles and John of Réomé, all of whom belong in their different capacities to the history of Lérins, were likewise priests and abbots. Also we may cite St Romanus in the Jura, Fulgentius in Africa, Agapitus at Poitiers, Silvinus and Venantius at Tours, and many another priest-abbot with a reputation for sanctity, whom Gregory of Tours brings to our notice.[41]

These are prestigious names in the West, names which bear sufficient witness to the role played in cenobitism by the institution of the priest-abbot. But the Latin cenobites met with the same type of institution, which had already been actualized in those 'congregations' of hermits at Scete and to which their favourite matter never ceased to attract them. The desert of of Scete, at its great period when the eremitic life flourished there, boasted four churches, each served by a priest, a deacon and some clerics. Every hermit belonged to one of these parishes where the eucharistic liturgy was celebrated on Saturdays and Sundays, and was followed by a fraternal meal taken in the church. A large number of texts enable us to be present, as it were, in the life of these communities, in which the priest is center and head. It is he who summons the assembly, presides, judges, excommunicates, distributes alms, proclaims the word of God, and prescribes special fasts. We see the Church even playing the role of town hall or information bureau for visiting strangers. The priests of Scete were of course chosen from among the monks of exemplary character. Many an apophthegm reports their words or celebrates their virtue.[42]

The priest-abbot solution combined all the advantages, and we have just seen how it won much favor. Nevertheless it must be admitted that it does not seem to have been in force in the monastery governed by RM.[43] Nor is there anything either in RB to indicate its presence. Though attempts have been made to find allusions to St Benedict's priestly status in the second Book of the *Dialogues*,[44] it seems unlikely that St Gregory, if he had been acquainted with a fact of this kind, would not have mentioned it more clearly. He does not fail, when such a case falls due, to prepare explicitly to call the reader's attention to the priestly status of an abbot.[45] Our Rules therefore do not seem to apply to the institution of the priest-abbot, and similar cases during the century of St Benedict are not lacking.[46]

If the *coenobium* was without a priest-abbot, it normally had recourse to a priest, who had become a monk, or to a monk, who had been ordained priest. In both cases, it is easy to imagine the problems of authority, posed by this sacerdotal presence in the midst of a community of laymen under the direction of a laymen. It is to such problems that the cenobitic documents cited at the beginning of this study allude constantly. It is certain that, notwithstanding the noteworthy cases of priest-abbots, monasticism retained a keen awareness of its non-clerical essence. It never saw in the priesthood a title for governing a group of monks. The priest-abbots themselves are no exception to this law, for the priesthood hallows and completes their abbatial authority more than it furnishes grounds for it.[47] The monastic hierarchy is charismatic, not clerical; to borrow from the Master's terminology the abbot is 'doctor,' a title, which certainly implies a divine mission, recognized by the hierarchy,[48] but which is not identified with any of the holy orders. The independence of the monastic order in the choices of its heads, and their independence in governing their lay subjects are principles solemnly affirmed nearly a century earlier than St Benedict, by the Third Council of Arles.[49]

Within this historical context, the directions of RM and RB acquire their full meaning. They express in their own way the will to remain faithful to the tradition and essence of monasticism, by resisting every attempt to transfer authority to the benefit of the clerics.

In Chapter 83, RM prescribes that priests are to be received *peregrinorum loco.*[50] By that it means two things: first (vss 1–9), they shall have no power over the community, in which they will live as visitors, even though living in the monastery. They will be called *patres monasterii*, but this title is purely honorary and bestows no authority. In the same way, they shall be permitted to pronounce the collects and to make the sign of the cross. On the other hand, all interference in the government of the monastery is denied them. The abbot, though a layman, should maintain his exclusive right to govern the monastery, a right he holds from the rule itself. Next (vss 10–22), the priests shall be treated as guests in the sense that they are obliged to perform the common work. Only on this condition will they be able to have their share of the food and clothing of the monastery. Thus the rule laid down for guests is applied to them, with respect but without compromise.[51] The RM even provides for the situation in which they would refuse to submit to this rule; in that case they will be sent away, and should they offer further resistance, they will be expelled (from the monastery).

When we read Chapter 60 of RB after this, it is obvious that the situation regarding priests is no longer the same. The expressions *monasterio sociari* and *suscipi* are used with respect to them, expressions which in neighboring chapters designate the reception of a postulant into the community.[52] Then too, when they are called upon to 'observe *all the discipline* of the rule' it means something different from the simple law relating to work, imposed on guests by the RM. Determination of 'rank,' so characteristic of RB's preoccupations, likewise implies a real integration into the community. Lastly, the vow of stability, mentioned in connection with the clerics would be devoid of meaning, were the question not one of a definitive incorporation into the *coenobium*. Everything within the chapter therefore confirms what is suggested by the place assigned to it in the rule.[53] In RM priests are received only in the name of hospitality, while RB integrates them into the monastery in the name of the monastic life. This evolution is furthermore achieved without the line of conduct being substantially altered: RB takes care to maintain the priests in the obedience and humility common to all monks, just as RM had imposed on them the rule of work common to all guests. We should even say that in RB the priest submits the more to the Rule and to the abbot, the more he is integrated into the community. Thus it comes about that the liturgical prerogatives granted unreservedly by RM (vs 5) come under the control of the abbot in RB. On the abbot's authorization depends the possibility of the priest's occupying the place next to him, of blessing, and of concluding the prayers.[54]

By integrating priests into the community, RB has classed them in the category of postulants. What it prescribes for them hardly differs from what has been said in Chapter 58, except for the year of probation, from which they are apparently dispensed. This last arrangement causes them to resemble the visiting monks of Chapter 61, who like them, benefit from a higher status, if the abbot judges it right. Aligned in this manner with Chapters 58 and 61, the chapter on priests loses some of its prominence. The case of priests received at the monastery does not seem essentially different from that of lay postulants or visiting monks. We must go back to RM and other cenobitic documents, in order to become fully aware of the significance and energetic thrust of these directions.

As much may be said of Chapter 62. The case of the monk ordained priest is expressly compared with that of the other office-holders of the monastery, the deans and the provost. Like them, the priest is obliged to keep the rule and to submit himself completely to the abbot. If he is no different, in this respect, from the other officers, this comparison must not deceive us as to what is original in his own case. It is rather the unique nature of the situation of a priest, whose ministry is limited to altar functions, and who is subject in everything to a superior, who is probably a layman, that should be emphasized.

* * *

The meaning of the vocation of the priest-monk that has emerged from these two chapters has been highlighted on several occasions.[55] We believe that there is no need to insist on it. We should prefer to draw attention to the important lesson that these chapters contain, regarding the lay character of monasticism. It is particularly useful to recall this lesson at a time of growing awareness of the anomaly constituted by the general practice of ordaining monks to the priesthood. Whatever the historical roots of this situation are, it certainly creates serious difficulties for monasticism. Suffice it to mention the temptations to undertake an apostolate, the problem of studies, the abandonment of manual labor, and above all, the alien division of communities into two ill-assorted groups, in order to give an idea of the inconveniences involved.

Our rule is certainly not responsible for it. Indeed, this Rule, if we really wish to listen to its voice, which is that of the whole of an ancient monasticism, can put us on the way towards a more adequate solution than that which consists in justifying the actual situation by means of dubious theological arguments. The priesthood of monks is envisaged in RB only in two cases: when they come to the monastery already invested with the priesthood and when a need arises in the community to ensure the ministry of the altar. In other words, the Rule provides a place for priesthood only in cases of real necessity. The priest-monk, far from constituting the ideal type of monk, is conceived rather as an anomaly, fraught with danger, but inevitable, of which efforts are made to mitigate the inconveniences by means of severe warnings. In our day, in a completely changed situation, these inconveniences no longer make themselves felt, but if the practice of general ordination to the priesthood has brought about their cessation, it has also created new difficulties, which the Benedictine Rule was not able to foresee. So it is true that monasticism, on the whole, cannot renounce its lay character without casting a slur on one of the essential features of its vocation.

NOTES TO CHAPTER SIX

1. Note, however, that Chapter 62 sets no restrictions on the liturgical ministry of the priest, whereas Chapter 60 expressly subordinates it to the authority of the abbot. That is readily understandable: the monk of whom Chapter 62 is speaking has been ordained priest in order to satisfy a real need of the community, and the abbot, in causing him to be ordained, has no intention of leaving him idle. On the contrary, a priest, who enters the monastery, may find himself redundant, the community already being provided with the ministers that it needs.

2. RM Chapters 21, 22, and 80.

3. RM 83:9: *ne ipso obtentu honoris (sacerdotes) de ratiociniis uel dominatione monasterii utpote laicos abbates excludant.*

4. See our article 'Scholies sur la Règle du Maître' in RAM 44 (1968), pp 122–27. Cf. below, p 299–300.

5. This is not evident at first sight, for Chapters 80–82 which immediately precede, interrupt this section which begins at Chapter 78 and closes with Chapter 84.

6. *Conc.* 67. Only RB 60 and RM 83 are cited there.

7. *Vies Coptes*, p 237, 1. 19–25. Among the parallel passages, note the Latin *Vita*, § 24, PL 73:245d.

8. *Conc* 69, citing Jerome, Lr 125.17. In this passage, Jerome dissuades the young monk Rusticus from embracing the clerical life and invites him to enter a monastery to receive serious training there. When he has attained 'the perfect age', the decision may be taken as to whether he merits clerical status. It is a question of urban clerical life in the service of a church, and not of priesthood exercised in the bosom of a community of monks.

9. R Aur M 46,

10. Labbeus, *Concilia*, vol 4, col 1024e: *regula quae a fundatore ipsius monasterii dudum constituta est in omnibus custodita.* Possibly, in this case, the right granted to the abbot of Lérins may rest on a rule laid down by St Honoratus from the beginning of the famous monastery. One observes too that the bishop of Arles, Aeonius, adhered scrupulously to the Council decree, when he wished to ordain the young Caesarius priest: the authorization of Porcharius, abbot of Lérins, was sought and obtained (*Vita Caesarii* 1.10). This right of the abbot was to be recognized by the Council of Agde presided by Caesarius in 506: *si necesse fuerit clericum de monachis ordinari, cum consensu et uoluntate abbatis praesumat episcopus* (can 27 in Labbeus, *Concilia*, vol 4, col 1288a).

11. *Vie Coptes*, pp 241–242 (S 5, § 42). Neither this text nor the coptic parallels speak expressly of priesthood: the brother desires 'a post', the nature of which is not specified. But the Latin *Vita* (35) says: *clericatus desiderans dignitatem*. It is therefore in this sense that Latin readers understood the meaning of the episode. Denys adds a further clerical touch to the story by making the superior a priest.

12. Mabillon, *Vita sancti Eugendi* in AS OSB, vol 1, 554–559, n 14.

13. *Vies Coptes*, p 237= Denys, § 24.

14. Ibid., p 99 (Pachomius) and p 393 (Horsiesios).

15. Apart from the fact that Anthony hears the first call to the perfect life in the course of a liturgical office in a church.

16. St Athanasius will remain the model of those great bishops who accomplished so much for the expansion and influence of monasticism.

17. Such hostility is well attested in Gaul by the complaints of Sulpicius Severus, *Vita Martini*, Chapters 9 and 27; *Dial* 1.2 and 26; 3.15–16. The priscillian affair sparked off the opposition between the worldly clerics and the ascetics. The prelates who conducted the suppression of heresy tried to include in this suppression some orthodox ascetics, whose only crime was to devote themselves to study and fasting (*Chron.* 2.50, cf. *Dial* 3.11). For their part, the monks held it against the bishops, who had Priscillian put to death, that they had recourse to violence and the secular arm (*Dial.* 3.12). Previously, the welcome that the episcopacy had given the usurper, Maximus, had seemed to them a discreditable platitude (*Vita Martini* 20). The Priscillian affair will provok a real break in communion between the monk-bishop-Martin and his gallican colleagues (*Dial* 3.12:13).

18. Eusebius of Vercelli, Ambrose, Martin, Augustine, Honoratus and Hilary of Arles, and later Caesarius come to mind. Cases of bishops leading the monastic life are particularly frequent in the *Vita Fulgentii*. Cf. 9–14; 23; 26; 37–39; 43.

19. Let us quote in particular the letter of Athanasius to Dracontius (PG 25:524ff), and that of Augustine to the monks of Capraria (Lr 48). At Arles, Honoratus takes care to prepare himself a successor in the person of Hilary, a monk of Lérins, like himself. A century later, the bishop Aeonius causes Caesarius to be designated as his successor. The role played by the episcopal monasteries at Hippo, Tours and Arles, as nurseries of bishops, is well-known. Lérins became still more famous in this respect, as Eucherius already bears witness (*De laude eremi* 42), and a century later, St Caesarius (*Serm* 236. Morin, vol 2, p 894, 14–20). The impulse often came from the Christian people, who evidently preferred

this kind of bishop to worldly and scheming prelates. The vicissitudes of the episcopal succession in Arles, from 410 to about 430, are informative in this respect: a disciple of St Martin, Heros, banished through a political intrigue, succeeds the wretched Patroclus (412), who will distinguish himself by his pillaging and will perish by assassination in 426. The people of Arles then procure themselves a bishop after their own heart in the person of Honoratus, abbot of Lérins.

20. Athanasius, writing to Dracontius to persuade him to accept episcopacy, recalls the example of the prophets and apostles who knew how to pass from the desert to the apostolate. He praises the works of the sacerdotal ministry and the graces of election which recompense those who devote themselves to it. Moreover, nothing prevents the monk who has become a bishop from carrying on his ascetical efforts in his new way of life: fasting, abstinence from wine, celibacy, can be practised by a bishop. Athanasius therefore advocates the union of the monastic life and the priesthood exercised in the world. The two states are compatible. By accepting episcopacy, the monk Dracontius has everything to gain and nothing to lose.

The viewpoint changes with Ambrose (Lr 63, §§ 66–82). This time it is a question of showing the help which monastic asceticism brings to the apostolate of a bishop. His example will impart greater authority to his word, and the habit of austerity will prepare him to face persecutions. But though union of the two states is regarded from the point of view of the advantages which the episcopate derives from it and not, as with Athanasius, from the point of view of the sanctification of the monk, the theme remains fundamentally the same. After praising the bishop-monk, Ambrose passes on to a lengthy parallel between priesthood and monasticism, which finally comes down on the side of the advantage of the priesthood. The struggle of the priest in the world is rougher and more dangerous, and therefore more meritorious, while the flight of the monk, who puts himself in a place of safety, far from the world, is less glorious.

This paradox about the dilemma of monk and priest is furthermore a commonplace exploited by Augustine (*De moribus ecclesiae* 1.32) and by Sulpicius Severus (*Dial.* 1.24–26), in order to glorify clerics leading a saintly life in the world (cf. also Paulinus of Nola, Lr 24.4): the temptations of the world, to which the cleric is exposed, confer on his asceticism a distinction and a merit which surpass that of the monk. We shall observe how these authors conceive the clerical life and the monastic life as mutally opposed states, while extolling the union of asceticism and the clerical life. To sum up, it is a matter of taking certain ascetical observances of the monastic life and transplanting them to the world, to the benefit of the apostolate. In like fashion, Jerome, after having set monastic and clerical life in strong opposition (Lr 14.8–9), celebrated their union in the persons of Heliodorus and Nepotian (Lr 52 and 60), whereas Lr 125 depicts cenobitism as the best preparation for the clerical status. In the East at the same period, Chrysostom professes analogous views. Cf. the study of Louis Meyer, 'Perfection chrétienne et vie solitaire dans la pensée de saint Jean Chrysostome,' RAM 14 (1933), pp 232–262.

In the opposite sense, the *Lives* of Honoratus and of Hilary of Arles develop the theme of the superiority of the monk over the priest. The inner splendor of the former in the order of sanctity surpasses the outward splendor of the latter, in the order of the ranks of the hierarchy. Cf. *Vita Honorati* 16 and *Vita Hilarii* 12 Sulpicius Severus had previously depicted bishops humbly asking to be blessed by the monks [*Dial* 1.20]; the theme recurs in many an apophthegm, cf. for example VP 5.15.27). The Arlesian *Lives* go so far as to present the monk as the ideal of the priest, in the sense that he is the perfect embodiment of all that is expected of a priest in sanctity and apostolic influence. See *Vita Honorati* 9, 13, 16, 25 (cf. *Vita Fulgentii* 17), and *Vita Hilarii* 10, 12. All this seems aimed against the tendency in certain clerical circles to despise the monks and to flaunt their own dignity too insolently.

21. HM 1 (PL 21:394b); *Life of Anthony* 67.

22. RM 76.

23. RM 77. Cf. R 4 Pat 175–177.

24. VP 5.9.11.

25. Lr 22.34.

26. *Vita Martini* 6, 9, 20, 24, 27; *Dial* 1, §§ 2, 6, 7, 9, 21, 24, 26; 2, §§ 1, 12; 3, §§ 6, 11, 12, 15, 16. Sulpicius Severus on two occasions admits his dependence by reference to Jerome (*Dial* 1, §§ 9, 21).

27. Athanasius combats this fear in his letter to Dracontius. See above nn. 19–20. This is the sense in which Cassian tells the celebrated apophthegm, according to which a monk ought to flee equally from bishops and from women (*Inst* 11.18).

28. See for example Cassian, *Inst* 11.14–18; *Conf* 4.20; 5.12.

29. Edmond Charles Babut, *Saint Martin de Tours* (Paris, 1912).

30. Ammonas, one of the Tall Brothers, threatened with episcopal ordination, lops off his left ear to escape it. Since that does not prove adequate, he threatens to cut out his tongue, which disarms his persecutors (LH 11). For another case of refusal, see ibid., 68. For refusal to exercise a holy order received in spite of oneself, cf. VP 5.15, §§ 21, and 27 (context of humility, cf. above, n. 28).

31. *Vies Coptes*, p 238. Sarapion, bishop of Nikentori, wanted Athanasius to ordain Pachomius to the priesthood, 'in order that he may be set at the head of all the monks in my diocese' (*Vies Coptes*, p 99). In this, we perceive a living example of the passage from charismatic authority to hierarchical authority. Pachomius is the father of the congregation, which has been assembled round him. The bishop wants to give him an official mandate, springing from the priestly dignity, in order to govern the monks of a whole diocese, without consideration for their personal vocation, which has not brought all of them into the pachomian congregation.

32. Let us content ourselves with recalling the attitude of Anthony such as his biographer describes it (*Life* 68–70, cf. 89 and 91), as well as that of Pachomius (*Vies Coptes*, pp 352ff, in particular p 353, n. 8). The support furnished by the Coptic monks to Athanasius in his fight against heresy is well-known. A good example of this docile and receptive attitude towards the teaching of the hierarchy is found in the reception given by Theodore to the festal letter of Athanasius on the canon of the Scriptures in 367 (*Vies Coptes*, pp 205–207). Yet there were some notable exceptions to this rule, such as the reaction of the monks to the condemnation of the anthropomorphite heresy by Archbishop Theophilus (Cassian, *Conf* 10.2–5), or the affair of Origenism in 401–402 (Sulpicius Severus, *Dial* 1.6–7), which was still more serious.

33. Even more, the clerics themselves crowded round the important monks, in order to receive a word from their lips. Several apophthegms (VP 5.2.4 and 5.15.42) depict archbishop Theophilus seeking a word from Arsenius or from Pambo; these two, moreover, baffle the curiosity of the prelate. Anthony, as Athanasius tells us, used not to refuse the word to clerics, who asked him for it (*Life* 67). In the same way, we see Athanasius questioning Pachomius (*Vies Coptes*, p 387), and the Alexandrian deacons Faustus and Timothy inquiring of Horsiesios about the meaning of a whole series of scriptural texts (ibid., pp 395–99). All these facts imply, on the part of the clergy, the recognition of some kind of right to teach imparted by the Holy Spirit to the holy monks. Gregory the Great reports an episode, which is highly significant in this respect: Equitius, abbot of several monasteries in Valeria, urged on by an irresistible inspiration, began to preach everywhere even though he had received no commission from the ecclesiastical hierarchy. The Roman Curia became disturbed at this and had him summoned before the court, but God directly intervened to put an end to the proceedings. It is clear that Gregory, then pope, acknowledged this non-commissioned preacher to be fully in the right. The ecclesiastical authority must bow to the charisma of the word bestowed by the Spirit on a lay monk (*Dial* 1.4).

34. The *Vies Coptes* (p 96) show Pachomius and his monks going to the village church on Saturday to receive the sacraments, and receiving the local clergy in the monastery church on Sunday. Originally, before 'the number of brethren had reached the hundred mark',

and before the monastery church had been built, everything took place 'at the parish church', as we should say today. The drawback of such assemblies in which monks and seculars found themselves intermingled is indicated clearly enough in the same passage (p 96, 1.2–5): there was need to 'keep custody of the eyes', in order to guard against carnal temptation. We find a trace of the same difficulty in R Aug 10.88, and in the recommendations of Jerome to Demetriades (Lr 130.19). This is what led to the abandonment of such a system and to the construction of churches for all the monastic communities. The R Caes V is filled with allusions to the 'basilica' of the nuns and to the strict enclosure which ought to exclude seculars (36–38, 59, 73, etc.). See also Justinian, Nou 133, § 2. One reference in the *Life of John of* Réomé shows him rigorously applying a rule which forbids seculars from attending the liturgy celebrated by the monks in their church, a rule which the saintly abbot says he received 'from the holy fathers' (*Vita S. Iohannis Raeomensis* in AS, Jan. 28, n 15).

RM seems to suppose that the brethren process to the 'parish church' for Sunday Mass. There is no question of Mass celebrated in the monastery, except on the feast of the patronal saint of the chapel and for the blessing of an abbot. During the week, the abbot and brethren partake of the Eucharist daily in a community rite *extra missam*. This state of affairs seems rather archaic. In the daily communion, the absence of priests in the community, and the necessity to go out for Mass, RM appears to look rather towards the past than the future. In Gaul at almost the same time, communion is less frequent, monks are ordained priests for the service of the community, and Mass is celebrated in the monastery itself. These latter two features likewise characterize RB. See our article '*Scholies sur la Règle du Maître*', RAM 44 (1968), pp 122–37.

35. *Vies Coptes*, p 96. VP 5.9.11. HM 15.

36. See above, n. 7. We could also cite Evagrius 'the illustrious deacon', as Palladius calls him (LH 38.1), who came to the desert already invested with the diaconate.

37. Such was, for example, the case of Augustine at Hippo, and later that of Pinianus, husband of Melania the Younger. Paulinus endured the same fate at Barcelona. In fact, neither Paulinus nor Pinianus were to exercise their function in the service of the community, which had them ordained against their inclination.

38. Particularly typical are, in the writings of Palladius, the cases of Chronius (LH 47), of Elpidius (48), of Sisinnius (49), and of Dorotheus (58). Chronius took up his abode alone in the remotest desert. Some years later, 'he was judged worthy of the priesthood as a fraternity of about 200 men had assembled round him' (LH 47.2). Similarly this formula, which presents a striking summary of the transition from solitary life to abbatial responsibility and, subsequently, to the priesthood, is found elsewhere. We shall observe that Dorotheus is at the service of a group of recluses. To the same category of priest abbot belong—more or less—the two monks who both bear the name Macarius (LH 17–18), Isidore of Scete and his disciple Moses the Ethiopian (19), as well as Innocent, a priest at the Mount of Olives (44).

Priest-abbots are no less numerous in the *Historia Monachorum*. We can mention with certainty Copres (HM 9), Apelles (15), Serapion (18), Dioscorus (20), Piamoun (32) and with probability Apollonius (7) and Eulogius (14). Three of them, Eulogius, Dioscorus, and Piamoun, are depicted to us as watching over the purity of conscience of the monks who approach the sacraments (cf. also the case of Macarius of Alexandria, HM 29, whom we know from the writings of Palladius to have been a priest). But the most remarkable example of zeal for reception of the eucharist is that of Apollonius, apostle of daily communion (HM 7). An anxiety to hold Holy Communion in high esteem, in opposition to more or less Messalianistic tendencies to underestimate its utility, is very apparent in HM (cf. 2, 7, 14, 20, 29), as also in the LH (cf. 25, 26, 27). See also VP 5.18.3.

In the writings of Cassian occur the names of Isidore, Paphnutius, and Daniel, men who succeed one another at the head of one of the four churches of Scete (*Conf* 3.1; 4.1; 10.2–3; 18.15–16), of Piamoun, superior (*senior*) and priest of the anchorites of Diolcos (*Conf* 18.1), and of Pinuphius, who directed the great *coenobium* near Panephysis (*Conf*

20.1). Isidore, like Paphnutius, is described as *abbas et presbyter*, a combination of terms which indeed shows to how little distinction Cassian made between a superior of a *coenobium* and a superior of the hermits.

39. *Vita Hon.* 17–24.

40. Ibid., 25.

41. Romanus: AS, vol 3, pp 746–752; cf. § 6. Fulgentius: *Vita Fulgentii* 31. Agapitus: Mabillon, AS OSB, vol 1, p 561. Silvinus and Venantius: Greg. Tur., VP 16.1–2; cf. also 2.4; 9.1–3; 14; 15.

42. Full details of the references concerning the 'congregations' of Scete cannot be given here. Suffice it to refer to those which have been given above, n. 38. They are to be completed by all that VP 5 and the other collections of apophthegms teach us on this subject.

43. See above, n. 3.

44. Thus Ildephonsus Schuster, *St Benedict and his Times*, trans. by Gregory Roettger (St Louis, Herder, second ed 1953), idem, *Historical Notes on St Benedict's Rule for Monks*, trans. by Leonard Doyle (Hamden, Conn. Shoe String Press, 1962).

45. Lr 1.9; 5.3–4; 13.8–10. Cf. Dial. 2.35: *Seruandus diaconus atque abbas.*

46. Thus Equitius: Greg. the Gr., *Dial* 1.4, Moricca, p 31, 1. 19–20 and 22; Eugendus for his part always refused to let himself be ordained (Mabillon, *Vita Eugendi*, pp 554–559, no. 8), for fear of arousing ambition for the priesthood among the younger brethren, and of himself falling into pride; Peter, abbot of the monastery of Byzacena, does not seem to be a priest, although several of his monks are invested with the priesthood or diaconate. (Labbeus, *Concilia*, vol 4, col 1643b; 1644d; 1647a). One of those priest-monks, Fortunatus, seems however to have succeeded Peter as abbot (ibid., 1785a).

47. Reread the excerpt of LH 47.2 cited above, n. 38.

48. The bishop intervenes in order to give liturgical sanction to the designation of the abbot. Designation is in principle reserved to the abbot, but, in the case of his dying suddenly before having named the future abbot, it is the bishop who is responsible for nominating who shall designate the new abbot (RM Chs 93–94).

49. *Laica omnis monasterii congregatio ad solam et liberam abbatis proprii quam sibi ipsa elegerit ordinationem dispositionemque pertineat* (Labbeus, *Concilia*, vol 4, col 1024e). This singularly precise decree cannot be set in opposition to the much more general terms which the Council of Chalcedon employs at the same period to prescribe to the monks obedience to episcopal authority to (can 1 in Labbeus, vol 4, col 610 nor even with can 19 of the First Council of Orleans in 511: *abbates pro humilitate religionis in episcoporum potestate consistant* (Mansi, vol 8, col 356). However, we must acknowledge that this last council, like most of those held in Gaul during the sixth century, gives the impression of an active control over the monasteries by the episcopate.

50. Vs 1. The expression may be understood either of the lodging provided for priests, which would be the guesthouse, or of the status to be attributed to them. In either case, it is a question of keeping them outside the community.

51. RM 78.

52. *Sociari corpori monasterii* (61:6) and *suscipiatur congregationi sociandus* (61:8), with regard to the visiting monk, who decides upon stability in the monastery. Cf. *monasterio sociari* (60:8). *Suscipere* is used when speaking of the reception of guests (it serves seven times in this sense in Chapter 53), but also to designate the acceptance of young monks (Chapter 58). In this last sense, we find the expression *suscipiatur in congregatione* (58:14), which indeed seems reserved to the monastic profession. We find this used when there is talk of priests: *in monasterio se suscipi* (60:1).

53. See above, n. 5.

54. RB 60:4: *post abbatem stare et benedicere aut missas tenere*. This last expression, of course, signifies not 'to celebrate Mass,' as is usually meant, but *complere post orationem* (RM 77:6; cf. *orationes colligere, complere*: RM 83:5), according to the interpretation of A. Calmet, recently taken up by Basil Steidle, 'Ante unam horam refectionis. . . ,' *Studia Anselmiana* 42 (1957), p 100. For the meaning of these limitations, see above, n.1.

55. We cite only the two most recent studies: Ghislain Lafont, 'Sacerdoce claustral,' *Studia Anselmiana* 42 (1957), pp 47–72; A. M. Henry, 'Le sens du sacerdoce monastique,' *Le message des moines à notre temps*, Paris, 1958, pp 172–193.

COMPLEMENTARY NOTE

Literature concerning the relationship between priesthood and monasticism is superabundant. It goes without saying that a commentary such as the present one must refrain from citing several interesting texts dealing with this matter. Yet we should not want to close this chapter without mentioning two or three especially important documents.

On the subject of efforts made by the hierarchy to recruit clerics from among the monks (n. 20), we should like to call attention to the letter of Pope Siricius to bishop Himerius of Tarragona in 385 (c. 13, § 17, PL 13:1144). See also *Vita Fulgentii* 58.

On the subject of the defensive attitude of cenobites in respect of clerics living in monasteries (pp 291–293), few documents are as significant as the *Vita Fulgentii* 57–58. Bishop Fulgentius, returning from exile, chooses domicile at the monastery where he had formerly been monk and abbot. But he forbids himself to interfere in the government of the monastery and refers the slightest details connected with it to the abbot Felix. What is more, he draws up a written declaration according to which he repudiates all his authority in the monastery (*nihil se in illo monasterio proprium uindicare*; cf. RM 83:6). This declaration is intended to bar the way to claims which his successors to the episcopacy might make, while appealing to his example.

In its turn, the Council of Carthage in 535–536 (Labbeus, vol 4, col 1785) forbids bishops to exercise any jurisdiction in monasteries, apart from the ordination of clerics (at the request of the monks) and the dedication of chapels. This strongly worded text uses expressions which are particularly reminiscent of RM 83: *nihil sibi in eis uindicans . . . nec aliquam ordinationem quamuis leuissimam facere . . . esse enim debent monachi in abbatum potestate*.

Chapter 7

THE ORDINATION OF THE ABBOT (RB 64)

THIS CHAPTER CONSISTS OF two very distinct parts, the first of which only correspond exactly with the title. Indeed after dealing with 'the ordination of the abbot' (vss 1–6), the rule appends to these legislative arrangements a long abbatial directory which is fundamentally comparable to Chapter 2, and which is linked with the questions dealt with at the beginning of the chapter only by its opening words: *ordinatus autem abba.* Evidently the redactor's intention is to make this passage a kind of admonition addressed to the new abbot on the occasion of his ordination. We shall examine these two passages in succession.

THE ABBATIAL SUCCESSION (RB 64:1–6)

On this point RB and RM diverge considerably. Whereas the Master entrusts the designation of his successor to the former abbot, RB provides for an election by the community. This fundamental difference is accompanied by a number of lesser divergences, even in the details, where our two rules seem to be speaking the same language: for example, the role of the bishop, or that of the neighboring abbots. The truth is that in this chapter the Master's legislation has been subjected to a complete recasting, of which, on first sight, nothing of the original seems to remain. We shall therefore have to study the legal provisions of both RM and RB separately, restoring both of them to their place in the juridical setting of the first centuries of cenobitism. Finally, we shall have to try to grasp the meaning of the transformation, which the RB has caused the RM to undergo.[1]

The system of designation by the former abbot sanctioned by RM draws no support from the civil, ecclesiastical, or monastic laws of the period which have come down to us. Neither the imperial legislation, nor the councils and the letters of the popes, nor the cenobitic rules other than RM make any allusion to it.[2] Not until the year 650 do we come across conciliar evidence of such a practice: the Council of Chalon-sur-Saône, summoned at this period, (Mansi, vol 10, col 1189), while disapproving of the coexistence of two abbots in the same monastery, implicitly recognizes that the abbot himself can choose his successor, provided that this abbot-designate has no power over the temporalities of the monastery. This is, for Gaul at least, the sole document originating from ecclesiastical authority which comes to the support of this system of designation. Yet it comes at a singularly late date, especially when we consider that appointment by the previous abbot had in fact been in practice here and there for nearly three centuries.

Indeed this system is attested in numerous cases of dealing with abbatial successions, which have been reported to us by non-juridical documents. We know from the pachomian *Lives* that the dying Pachomius designated Petronius, who in his turn designated Horsiesios.[3] Similarly in Cassian, an anonymous abbot and Paphnutius, priest of Scete, themselves provide for their succession.[4] If we may believe Faustus of Riez, St Honoratus did the same when he left Lérins for Arles.[5] In the second half of the fifth century, Lupicinus, before he died, nominated the abbots of his monasteries in the Jura.[6] In the sixth century, John of Réomé, and then in the seventh Columban and Landelin in Frankish territory and Frurimian in Spain made plans in the same way for their succession in the monasteries founded or ruled by themselves.[7]

This imposing list, which could obviously be completed down to the time of Cluny,[8] shows quite well the fate, with which this system of designation originated and continued on through the centuries. In the face of these facts, the silence of the juridical texts down to the mid-seventh century is somewhat surprising. Certainly, monastic rules busy themselves only very rarely with the question of abbatial succession,[9] and their silence as regards the designation of a new abbot by his predecessor does not mean this system was excluded.[10] But we must note that the laws of Justinian, like the roman and conciliar documents prior to 650, do not recognize the right of the previous abbot to name his successor. It is to the community, as we shall see, that this right belongs. From that time onwards the question arises as to what may be the juridical grounds for abbots to act in this fashion, and for the Master to codify this practice in his rule. Must we see here, with Kassius Hallinger, the 'old' system for which that of election by the community would subsequently be substituted? This interpretation does not take full account of the facts. Indeed on the one hand, we see from the earliest times that the idea of election makes its appearance side by side with that of designation by the previous abbot.[11] On the other hand, we do not see that the 'old' system ever gave place to the new one after a clean break. Long after usage and laws made election by the brethren general, certain abbots continue to name their successors, and their biographers report these facts to us without observing that there was anything unusual about them.

What is more, it is only at a very late date that we come across the first example of at least indirect approval, given by ecclesiastical authority to the procedure of designation. Far from appearing as an archaic system which has given way to election by the assembled community, nomination by the previous abbot, on the contrary, made its appearance in the canonical texts long after the 'new' norm, which is supposed to have supplanted it.[12] This in no way means that we have to wait until the mid-seventh century before we find cases of designation by the abbot actually in office, but it does at least suggest that we should not look upon this system as the primitive type, to be followed later by the election.

It seems, then, that designation by the previous abbot had been not so much the practice of a definite period as a kind of variant on the periphery of the more common practice sanctioned by law, a variant admitted at least tacitly at every period.[13] It characterizes not so much an archaic stage of the evolution of law as a certain kind of situation, which recurred at every period. Indeed if we consider the examples cited above, we shall discover in the majority of cases a particularly prestigious abbot either as founder (for example, Pachomius, Honoratus, Lupicinus, Columban, John of Réomé, Landelin) or as renowned for his sanctity (Pinufius, Paphnutius), if not for both reasons, as was the case for all the holy founders that we have just enumerated. It can be explained without difficulty that masters such as these causes the man of their choice to be admitted to take their place. Such was the veneration of which they were the object that their monks were disposed to accept those whom they designated, even to ask them for such designation.[14] Often, it seems, the prestige of the founder transferred itself to the successor named by him, and the method of designation instituted at the first succession remained in force for a generation or two. Thus it comes about that, some months after the death of Pachomius, Petronius in turn designates Horsiesios, and in the Jura at Réomé, we witness similar series of designations.[15]

We must reckon with this psychological element if we wish to explain the persistence of such a practice on the fringe of official discipline. The particular prestige of certain abbots is, of course, what accounts most fully for the various aspects of this phenomenon. By that means it can be explained why it is better attested in the beginning, that is to say, in the period of the foundations, when the prestige of the abbots was at its greatest and again, why it reappears much later, every time that a new foundation or a distinguished figure re-creates the situation found in the beginning. Finally, this explains why the principle of these designations was never challenged prior to Theodore of Canterbury (668–690), though in one or another individual case the personality of the successor gave rise to some difficulties.[16]

It is even possible that hagiography, which is our principal source of information for the first centuries of cenobitisim, sets before us a number of instances of designation far out of proportion to the real frequency of the phenomenon in those times. The lives of the saints, by the very nature of the subject that they are treating, are pledged to gather facts of this sort, because a saintly abbot is exactly in the situation where the designation of a successor is likely to occur.[17] In this way we should explain why the phenomenon passed unnoticed by civil and ecclesiastical legislation down to a late date, since its relative infrequency, as much as the particular circumstances where it arose, caused it to be neglected. In any case, it is a very remarkable fact that no juridical document has absolutely disapproved of it,[18] although the Church spoke out several times against the parallel custom whereby a bishop designated his successor.[19]

After these remarks, which help to place the system advocated by the Master within the framework of the institutions of ancient cenobitism, it is necessary to emphasize the extent to which this question of abbatial succession is treated by him in strict continuity with the rest of his cenobitic concepts. It is not for him a straightforward article of legislation for resolving the problem of succession. It is an element in the spiritual education, which the monastic discipline desires to permeate everything. Although the Master approaches the question rather abruptly,[20] he has been preparing us for some time to hear what he is now going to propound.[21] The expedient by which he approaches the subject is the question of rank (*gradus, locus*) and of the 'second' or 'third' place after the abbot. This place constitutes an 'honor' and implies a right of succession to the abbot actually in office.[22] Now, the Master deems it essential to leave this place vacant, so that no one may be designated for the future succession. Normally it is only on the approach of death that the old abbot ought to appoint his successor.

The chief reason for this dilatory procedure is the emulation the Master wants to maintain among all the members of the community. In order that everyone may cherish the hope of attaining the enviable honor, it is necessary that no one should be installed in the peaceful and assured possession of that place. The Master hopes all the monks will vie with one another in fervor and humility under the eyes of the abbot, with a view to obtaining from him the reward of the abbacy. Thus, while waiting until the last moment to proclaim his choice, the abbot will arouse a current of emulation, which will be the most powerful of stimulants to virtue.

What should we think of this educational device? The Master is very proud of it and expounds it with complacency. The modern reader cannot believe his eyes. Is the abbot to set himself up as a ringleader and referee of this outlandish competition for honors? What else can result from such a tournament, except an exasperating display of self-love and ambition in a climate of hypocrisy? Though the abbot may hope for the progress of his community in the outward marks of virtue in consequence of such a competition, would it not be an infallible perversion of all seeking for God to turn it so explicitly towards the purely human ends, such as the abbot prefers, the honor of the second place, the abbatial succession?

To judge this disconcerting theory justly, we should remember that emulation is a very familiar theme in all ancient spirituality. From the time of the beginnings of monasticism, the *Life* of St Anthony and the sayings of the Fathers show us this concept, without leaving any stone unturned. The athletic metaphor, which is the most constant figure of speech in Christian asceticism since the time of St Paul, necessarily involved this theme, which today is so highly suspect. Even in the bosom of cenobitism, the spirit of competition is several times mentioned and recommended by authors of sterling quality;[23] RB itself will exploit this theme—with how much delicacy—in the chapter *On Good Zeal*.

And yet, when all has been said and done, the system extolled by the Master still seems to us indefensible. If the idea of provoking the brethren to a holy emulation is, from the standpoint of antiquity, perfectly legitimate, on the other hand, no ancient writer is seen to have had the unfortunate idea of associating this theme with the desire for honors and the hope of governing. There is in this association a kind of contradiction of which it is strange that the Master perceived nothing. How can emulation in humility be genuine if it has as its motive the desire for power? Who does not see how one can thus fall into the worst aberrations of Pharisaism?[24]

We could say that Gregory of Nyssa already had such dangers in mind when he denounced so insistently, in *De Instituto Christiano*, the misdeeds, resulting from the desire for human glory, which occurred in the community life of the monks. It is from God alone, says Gregory, that the ascetic should expect his reward. To seek the esteem of men would amount to the cancellation of the result of all our efforts. The deplorable *anthrôpareskia*, the perversion of the ascetical life, must be constantly repelled by an intention to please no one but the Lord.[25] For want of having put himself on his guard, the Master here ventures on to false ground. His concern to exploit to the maximum all the resources of communal life, in order to educate the cenobites, has led him astray into this dead end, where all his educational work runs the risk of foundering. Here is a profitable lesson warning us of the limits of all community education, since it is a question of the Christian education of souls. Precious as the discipline of the 'band of brothers' may be for this education, it is absolutely necessary, if it is not to fall short of its goal, that it should result in the individual speaking to God alone. No social pressure will ever make Christians, much less monks.[26].

However, this unfortunate theory is not the only reason that the Master invokes for deferring the designation of the future abbot until the last moment.[27] Another consideration tends in the same direction: provision must be made for the case of a monk of great virtue, formed elsewhere and perhaps already abbot, who would enter the monastery incognito. What would happen if it were to be perceived that this newcomer excels the already designated 'Second'? A revocation of that designation would be necessary, in order that the more perfect monk be substituted instead, *cum non est dignum ut melior sub deteriore consistet.*[28] Rigorous even to a fault, the Master's logic again enters here: the sole criterion for choosing an abbot is the personal perfection that he has attained. In order to teach the *ars sancta*, nothing more is required of him than to practise that art better than all the others. In these chapters of RM, there is never a question of the human qualities of leadership, of a charisma for directing souls, of all those Christian pastoral gifts, which RB illustrates in its admonition to the abbot.

The modern reader is surprised, besides, that no account is taken of an accepted situation with all the human experience that it contained. In our eyes, length of time in the community and intimate acquaintance with its members and its spirit are advantages, which largely compensate for inferiority in good works. That a 'better' monk be subordinated to a 'less good' one does not seem abnormal to us, provided that the latter be humanly and supernaturally fit to head the flock. Without difficulty we dissociate personal sanctity from the aptitutde for leadership. The Master appears to ignore this distinction. Faithful to the principle laid down at the beginning of the treatise on the abbot,[29] he asks nothing more of the abbatial candidate than to be 'superior' in his actions as he is in name. The chapters on abbatial succession, which might have provided him with the occasion to enrich his chapter 'on the abbot,' and to vary its tone are in fact limited to developing the single idea[30] with rigid and meagre logic.

These remarks sufficiently illustrate the close bonds linking this treatise on abbatial succession to the whole educational system outlined by RM. Once again we must note the strong cohesion of the Master's thought. All the interest of RM, and all its weakness too, lies in this logical rigor ordering the cenobitic life, in its major institutions as in its minor details, around a small number of clearly enunciated and methodically developed principles.

These chapters contain several important developments, of which it is necessary to make at least a rapid inventory, before seeing what RB does with them. First, the long and minute description of the ritual for the abbatial ordination (RM 93:1–42), of which the essential rite seems to be the handing over of the rule by the old abbot to the new one. The little discourse which accompanies this gesture could well have served to solicit the admonition *Ordinatus autem abba* . . . , which we find in RB. It is also to be noted that the entire ordination takes place in the presence of the bishop and his clergy. The role of the pontiff is certainly important. It is he who inscribes the name of the new abbot on the diptych, which will be read by the priest in the course of the Mass, celebrated immediately afterwards, and it is he who, through his prayer, 'binds into the acts of heaven' the handing over of powers enacted on earth.[31] Yet this role seems to be limited to a liturgical sanctioning of the choice of the old abbot. The Master says nothing about an examination of the candidate by the bishop, or of a ratification of the choice. He no doubt tacitly presupposes such episcopal confirmation of the election. But on reading his text, one has the impression that the bishop proceeds to the ordination, as soon as the old abbot has announced his choice, with no episcopal enquiry on the fitness of the candidate intervening between the two acts. The old abbot seems to act all alone when designating his successor.[32]

After the ordination, the Master deals at length with the conduct of the new abbot, should the former continue to live (RM 93:43–90). This development constitutes a real treatise on the 'second', called the 'provost' by RB. His attributes are spelled out precisely (vss 63–78), but the issue is, above all, one of putting this 'Caesar-elect' on guard against all haughtiness, either towards the former abbot or the brethren. The Master would have him remain entirely dependent on the one who appointed him, observing the rule and regarding himself as inferior to everyone. Threats of removal from office sanction this warning (vss 76–90).

Lastly, RM envisages the case of the abbot dying suddenly without having designated his successor (Chapter 94). This eventuality gives the legislator the opportunity expressly to disapprove election by the community, a system which would produce nothing but disorder (vss 9–10).[33] Since the former abbot has been unable to make his choice, it is the abbot of some other monastery, who will be responsible for it. Designated by the bishop, this abbot shall come to the monastery and, rule book in hand, observe the behaviour of the brethren for a month, in order to learn who is the most faithful to the rule.[34] Let us take note of this very definite resolution not to leave the choice to the brethren. The Master is not unaware of such a process of designation, but he disapproves of it.[35]

Such, in its broad outline, is the Master's legislation, where abbatial succession is concerned. Considering it as a whole, one is struck by its breadth, its clarity and its care to provide for all eventualities and to grapple with them one by one, while remaining faithful to the same principles. A treatise of this sort is, from the literary standpoint alone, unique in ancient cenobitic literature.

From the standpoint of the history of institutions, the work of the Master is hardly less original. Not that designation by the old abbot, the cornerstone of the entire system, is something unheard of in antiquity, but, although evidence for such a procedure is not lacking, no rule, as we have seen, codified such a custom, which deviates from the norm indicated by all the documents, which had the force of law down to the year 650. Nor did any rule expressly condemn the norm of election by the assembled community. All of this presents itself to the Master as a homogeneous construction, inspired in its every detail by the same educational thought, without the interference of accepted usages, which would have had to be followed, or of higher juridicial questions, to which conformity would have been obligatory. The legislator seems totally free to develop his pedagogical system according to its internal logic, with nothing to hinder him from plunging finally into what we cannot refrain from calling error or Utopia.

When we pass from RM to RB, at first we are struck by the difference in literary tone, which separates these two treatises on abbatial succession. RM deals with this question in a section, which also includes questions of rank and of the 'second place,' after the abbot; RB isolates these different questions much more clearly, and its exposition of 'the ordination of the abbot' stands as a small entity, complete in itself.[36] It is furthermore very clear that RB reduces the long treatise of the Master to a minimum: the ordination ritual disappears,[37] the case of the sudden death of the former abbot ceases to be envisaged, and purposely so. Everything is scaled down to some brief indications regarding the election of the new abbot, with no allusions to the fate of his predecessor. These indications themselves are devoid of any obvious relationship or necessary connection with the remainder of the Rule. Instead of referring the reader, as the Master does, to the abbatial treatise, to the theme of the *ars sancta* and to passages in which the question of rank has already been regulated, RB dealt with the question almost in isolation, as a new direction to be placed after the others.[38]

These observations already warn us of a change of standpoint, which our study of the institutions will enable us to establish. Whereas the Master legislates within the single perspective of his educational system, RB keeps to the terrain of customary practice, at any rate as regards the role of the community in the election. It is no longer a matter of crowning the edifice of the rule with a law of succession in harmony with the rest of the construction, but simply of providing for the best functioning of the elective system, which was in fact practised in the monasteries of that day.

There is little need to pass in review the numerous attestations of election by the community before and after the time of St Benedict, for they have been assembled by Kassius Hallinger.[39] There are only two remarks to be made in order to emphasize the antiquity and the normal character of choosing the abbot in this way. We must bear in mind first of all that the principle is attested from the origins of the pachomian congregation, though the desire of the previous superior was in fact the determining factor in these cases.[40] Although Cassian reports to us two cases of designation by the previous abbot,[41] he is also acquainted with election by the brethren, at least for the office of 'president of the deaconry.'[42] At Lérins, Honoratus seems to have prescribed as a rule from the beginning that the abbot be elected by 'the whole community of laymen', though he himself seems to have designated his replacement when he became bishop of Arles.[43]

The system of election by the assembled community is therefore as ancient as cenobitism. Its normative character, approved by civil and ecclesiastical law, is also to be stressed. The Council of Arles in about 455, that of Charthage in 536, the rule given by Caesarius of Arles to his nuns, two of Justinian's three laws, a decree of Pelagius I in 559, and finally numerous texts of Gregory the Great, in short, nearly, all the official documents that can be brought forward in this matter, bear witness to the right recognized to the community to choose its abbot. Furthermore this right is affirmed, not in opposition to designation by the predecessor (no text speaks of this latter process before the Council of Chalon in 650), but sometimes in opposition to the claims of bishops,[44] more often in conjunction with the episcopal right to examine candidates and to ordain them.[45]

In prescribing election by the community, RB shows itself to be as much lacking in originality as possible. Starting from the Master's highly personal legislation, the redactor seems to have recoiled before the singularity of this legislation, and to have ranged himself with the common norm of his times. He describes this norm in few words, as being a thing already established and well-known. His preoccupation is not to win acceptance for an unusual law, but only to provide for the efficient functioning of the widely admitted system of election.

Two directions aim at assuring the success of the election, the first being the appeal to outside control, that of the bishop and neighboring abbots or Christians.[46] It is mentioned expressly in the hypothetical situation of a bad choice made unanimously by the monks, but it ought to be understood in other cases as well: the discernment of the *pars senior* can only be the business of an outside arbiter who is none other than the bishop responsible for the ordination. In election by the brethren, RB therefore sees only a simple presentation to the bishop, as we should say today. The episcopal right to examine and approve the candidate before ordaining him is clearly implied here. On this point RB again allies itself with the whole collection of the juridical documents,[47] whereas RM, it will be recalled, passes over in silence the question of episcopal control of the election, the old abbot being thought infallible in his choice.

In addition to control by the bishop, RB prescribes election *uitae merito et sapientiae doctrina . . . etiam si ultimus fuerit in ordine congregationis.* Hallinger has clearly illuminated the meaning of this clause, which is more important and more original than it appears. In fact, custom allowed that rank should be taken into account and the election, at the same time as personal merit. Cassian already gives these two criteria with regard to election to the deaconry of Scete,[48] and the laws of Justinian insist that neither one aspect nor the other should be neglected. The formula in RB, when compared with the even clearer formula employed in connection with the deans,[49] seems, on the contrary, to rule out considerations of rank and to make personal merit the sole criterion.

This time, therefore, RB deviates from the accepted norm. One might see in this attitude a trace of RM's defiance as regards accepted practices and fixed ranks. Both rules seek to have the 'best monk' elected, without making allowance for seniority rights or offices previously held. To this end RM suppresses all precedence,[50] while RB does have an order to precedence but dissociates it from right to the succession. The same end is sought by two different paths. In maintaining the ranks suppressed by the Master, RB shows itself less radical than he. But, in excluding seniority from the criteria for the election of an abbot, RB remains faithful to the Master's intention and, together with him, deviates from the accepted custom. Hallinger has moreover shown that the stance assumed by our two rules had no further impact on the general practice, which is found again with Pelagius I, and even Gregory the Great.

All in all, as one can see, the RB legislation bears traces at the same time of ideas peculiar to the Master and of the common legislation in ancient cenobitism times. On two significant points—election by the community and episcopal control[51]—it foresakes RM to adhere to the prevailing customs. On only one point (exclusion of seniority) does it seem to have followed the Master, in reconciling this requirement with the maintenance of rank. As for the meaning of the profound modification to which RB subjects the Master's legislation by no longer entrusting the election to the previous abbot but to the brethren under the bishop's control, it seems, that we should see no more in this than conformity with the common practice of the time of St Benedict. The Master's system rests on the omnipotence of the abbot, and no doubt it mirrors the actual situation, which existed in his monastery and the personal tendencies of a spirit singularly prone to geometrical analysis. The 'democratic' element introduced by RB in the elective system marks a falling back upon a more modern conception, which prevailed whereever the abbacy was not in the hands of personalities as exceptional as those to be found at the beginning of monasticism.

THE SECOND DIRECTORY FOR THE ABBOT (RB 64: 7–22)

This passage seems to be a development of the admonition, half as long, found in RM 93:15–23. In the Master, it is a question of one element of the ordination rites of the abbot. That ceremony, as we have seen, has for its principal rite the handing-over of the rule, which the old abbot solemnly consigns to his successor, at the same time as the keys and the inventory. A brief discourse, in accordance with the Master's habit, stresses the importance of this gesture and elucidates its meaning. The former abbot proclaims the dignity and the authority of this document, which is to serve as the norm for the new superior: it is the 'law of

God' and the touchstone, by which the brethren will be judged for eternal salvation or damnation. For the abbot himself, this rule is like the inventory of the flock, according to which the shepherd will have to give an account to the Lord.[52] Consequently, the new abbot, in receiving the rule, assumes responsibility for the whole flock. From the secure state of obedience, which freed him from all care, even for his own conduct, he now becomes a pastor on whom lies the weight of the care for all: the worries, which come from the continual machinations of the devil and the worries of having to find and implement 'methods and admonitions with which to bring back to spiritual health all the wounds from which his sheep are suffering'.

One can see what may have passed from this text into the RB text that we were studying. The theme of the rule comes through, indicated briefly but forcefully at the end of RB 64 (vs 20): *et praecipue, ut praesentem regulam in omnibus conseruet.* The perspective of the divine judgment and, of the account to be rendered to the Lord is equally well indicated in RB, where it provides the introduction to the discourse (vs 7) and its conclusion (vss 21–22). Lastly, the theme of the 'methods and admonitions', by which the abbot must know how to cure his wounded sheep, is not unconnected with the rest of the RB text, and more particularly with the considerations on correction (vss 12–15).

No sooner has this parallel between RM and RB texts been established than the originality of RB in relation to RM appears in high relief. To tell the truth, this originality is such that, were we not informed elsewhere of the relations underlying the two texts, we would hardly think of seeking in RM the possible source of RB. If the RB redactor has been inspired by the Master's example in introducing a warning for the abbot at this place in the rule, it must be admitted that the appearance of the two passages, and still more their content, differs considerably.

First, their appearance. Whereas the Master places this allocution in the form of a direct discourse on the lips of the former abbot in the course of the ordination ceremony and in immediate connection with the handing-over of the rule, RB presents us with an impersonal text in the third person, a sort of treatise on abbatial duties, which connects with 'the ordination' only by the link of the introductory formula: *ordinatus autem abba . . .* (vs 7). This piece was perhaps composed separately, with no precise connection with the ordination. The relationship, which some have tried to establish between RB 64 and the ordination monitories addressed to new deacons and priests in the Roman Pontifical,[53] is of little significance.

Whether or not an abbatial ordination monitory underlies the RB text, it must be conceded that the passage as it has come down to us, in no way differs as regards its form, from the abbot's directories, which we reviewed in Chapter 2. The very place it occupies, almost at the end of the rule, reminds one of several of those directories.[54] It is especially noteworthy that RB, whose habitual purpose of abridging is particularly emphasized in the treatise on abbatial succession, here has a text twice the length of the Master's. This is what warns us of the fact that the RB passage, even if it really does depend on the Master, must in any case have a highly original meaning.

This initial impression is intensified, when the context of the RB text is examined analysis of it is not very easy, for the redactor does not obey laws of symmetry as obvious as those which, for example, govern the composition of RM 2. Yet a certain number of elements which do pair-off can be detected in this director for the abbot:

INTRODUCTION	(7)	Eschatological theme (rendering of account,
CONCLUSION	(21–22)	judgment, reward).
LIST OF FOUR POSITIVE QUALITIES	(9)	*oportet ergo eum esse . . .*
LIST OF SIX NEGATIVE QUALITIES	(16)	*non sit turbulentus . . .*
DEVELOPMENT ON CORRECTING	(12–15)	*in ipsa autem correctione sua. . .*
DEVELOPMENT ON COMMANDING	(17–19)	*in ipsis imperiis suis . . .*

The reader will have noticed that this analysis leaves out certain phrase numbers. These do, however, connect quite easily with the units, which we have extracted:

1. *Sciatque sibi oportere prodesse magis quam praeesse* (8): this phrase links both with what precedes (the liaison *cogitet . . . sciat* harks back to RB

2:6, 30; cf. 34–37) and with what follows (*oportere* foreshadows *oportet*). Transition from the general consideration of the task to the particular directions, which will follow.

2. *Et semper superexaltet misericordiam iudicio ut idem ipse consequatur. Oderit uitia, diligat fratres* (10–11). The first sentence is obviously a biblical comment on the preceding *misericordem*. We are therefore dealing with an appendix to the list of positive qualities. The second sentence is a variation on the same theme: 'hatred of vices' replaces 'judgment' and 'love of the brethren' replaces 'mercy'. The theme of charity thus introduced continues to run through the development on correction: *cum caritate* (14); *plus amari quam timeri* [15; forms with *diligat fratres* (11) a kind of enclosure framing the development on correction: love the brethren and make oneself loved by them.]—Note too in *ut idem consequatur* the theme of 'care for one's own soul' already exploited in RB 2:13–15, 39–40, perhaps reappearing in *suamque fragilitatem semper suspectus sit* (13), and certainly in the Conclusion.

3. *Et praecipue ut praesentem regulam in omnibus conseruet* (20). This mention of the rule, as we have said, may be a reminiscence of RM. It has no link with what precedes it, and ties in only very vaguely with the Conclusion. Besides its connections with the handing-over of the rule and the discourse which accompanies this ceremony in RM, the analogous petition in RB 3.11 deserves our attention (the abbot ought to do everything *cum obseruatione regulae*). Similarly, Caesarius of Arles, dealing with the election of the abbess, notes as the first of her duties: *regulam monasterii custodire* (R Caes V 61). This short phrase, which seems estranged from its context, is indeed well situated if the intent of the passage is considered, for it heralds the Conclusion.

Having thus revealed the links which attach these three isolated segments to the major elements of the text, we must now return to these elements for a closer analysis of content and for an identification of sources. There is nothing to gain by dwelling upon the Introduction and the Conclusion, whose similarity with the corresponding sections of RB 2 is evident.The two lists of qualities, on the other hand, constitute an innovation in relation to RM 2—RB 2. Were we to look for a parallel to them in RB, it is not to be sought in the treatise on the abbot, but rather in that on the cellarer (RB 31). There also are enumerated at the outset four positive and six negative qualities, which the candidate elected should possess.[55] In that list are found two of the adjectives enumerated in RB[64]: *sobrius* . . . *turbulentus*. These analogies can be explained by common reference to the Pastoral Letters, where enumerations of this sort are found on every occasion when it is a question of the qualities which a bishop (cf. the abbot), a deacon (cf. the cellarer), or 'elders' of either sex should possess. The adjective *sobrius*, in particular, recurs in the Vulgate with each enumeration,[56] and often *castum* also or some equivalent.[57] Reference to the Pastoral Letters is emphasized in RB 64:9 by the introductory formula *oportet eum esse*, which is usual in those Letters.[58]

Moreover, the portraits of the deacon and bishop in the Pastoral Letters have many a time inspired monastic writers in their directories for the abbot. Thus it is that Basil characterizes the superior by a series of terms, all of which reappear in our text: 'possessing foresight, sufficiently competent in the Word, sober, compassionate . . .'[59] The sequence of these last three epithets surely constitute a curious parallel with RB, showing once again how a common reference to the Scriptures, together with similarity of situations, leads our monastic authors quite unconsciously to speak the same language.[60] Before leaving the first list of qualities (RB 64:9), we would point out yet another parallel with the Master. The words *oportet ergo eum esse doctum lege diuina ut sciat et sit unde proferat noua et uetera* are found almost word for word in RM.[61]

As for the second list of qualities (RB 64:16), it is not only comparable, as we have already pointed out, with RB 31:1 (a text peculiar to RB), but also with RB 4:34–40 (a text originating from the Master), which similarly enumerates seven negative 'instruments' taken more or less directly from the Pastoral Letters.[62] *Non turbulentus* also recalls Is 42:4, that is, the portrayal of the Servant of Yahweh as applied to Christ by Mt 12: 18–21. This half-concealed scriptural reference ought to be emphasized, for it is probably what gives us the key to the entire list: *anxius, nimius, obstinatus, zelotipus, nimis suspiciosus*, which all lack exactly corresponding objectives in the negative lists in the Pastoral Letters, seem no more than particular aspects of the initial *turbulentus*, which they detail and on which they cash in with a good deal of psychology.[63] We are conscious here at the same time, of the influence of the Christ-portrait in Isaiah-Matthew, along with a personal experience of the torments and temptations, which beset the abbacy, and which are in reality peculiarly fitted to lead the abbot far away from the ideal tranquillity of a teacher of the Gospel.[64] The highly personal nature of this passage is stressed by the two-fold *nimis . . . nimis*, which brings us back to a theme that we have previously met (cf. above, vs 12: *nimis . . . nimis*) and betrays the basic preoccupation of the redactor throughout this abbatial directory, as we are going to see it when we study the developments of the two themes on correcting and commanding.

Ne quid nimis: such indeed is the point of the whole development on correction (vss 12–15). The two *prudenter* of vss 12 and 14 mean nothing else, and every detail of this passage has just been arranged around this concept, either illustrating or amending it (vs 14: *in quibus non dicimus*. . .). Cuthbert Butler has adequately pointed out in his *fontes* the banality of this proverb, which Christian writers absorbed from secular culture. Nor is the Master ignorant of this dictum (RM 27:25). It is therefore under the banner of popular wisdom, very much stripped of pretensions, that RB places the theme, which occupies the central place in this whole passage. However, a reference to Is 42:3 (*calamum quassatum non conterendum*) turns this common sense injunction into one which demands imitation of Christ (cf. Mt 12:20).[65]

The same basic preoccupation and the same types of references appear in the development of the theme on commands (vss 17–19). There again it is a matter of being on guard against excesses (vs 18: *plus laborare*), of 'wise moderation' (vss 17, 19), and of using 'discretion' (vss 17, 18, 19). There also the hellenic notion of the just mean, which has become popularized in public mind, is enhanced by a scriptural reference (Gen 33:13) and an appeal to the *testimonia* of the Scriptures. But here we have to leave a large place for the theme of *discretio* one of the common-places of ascetical literatture, and especially of the monastic apophthegems. Cassian devotes an entire *Conference* to this virtue, which he had previously crowned as the 'mother of virtues,'[66] and significantly, in this same *Conference 2*, an elder, a director of souls, has been asked not to 'break the bruised reed,' exactly like the abbot in RB 64:13.[67]

Thus the unity of this directory for the abbot is again affirmed. In the development on the theme of correction, as in that on commanding, the same basic theme is treated, that of 'discretion' or 'prudence', which is enemy of 'excess.' The redactor no doubt is not unaware that this lofty virtue is opposed as much to deficiency as to excess, and that it consists precisely in demanding of each what he is capable of giving, by stimulating the laxity of the negligent and moderating the ardor of the presumptuous.[68] But here it is only a question of avoiding 'excess' (*nimis. . . plus*), and the elegant formula of vs 19, in its apparent antithesis, does not rise above this unilateral standpoint: all that is asked of the abbot is that he be not *too* exigent,' in such a way that the strong may have something for which to strive, and the weak nothing from which to recoil'.[69] This last term *non refugiant* recalls the *non refugias* of the Prologue (vs 48), and we are dealing with much more than a mere encounter with words. A rereading of that entire passage in the Prologue (vss 45–49), which is an addition peculiar to RB, will show that the redactor has the same human situation in mind in both instances, that of the 'weak' or 'fearful' monk who is tempted to abandon an observance that is beyond his strength. In the Prologue it is to that monk that the exhortation to persevere in the Prologue is directly addressed, and in Chapter 64 it is the abbot who is asked to take pity on his weakness. In both, there is the same care not to burden the monk with a 'harsh and oppressive' yoke (Pr 46) and to avoid giving him excessive responsibility.[70]

Thus therefore the analysis of this directory for the abbot reveals a singular homogeneity of thought and of sources throughout its different parts. From beginning to end, the same vision inspires the redactor, that of Christ the ideal pastor, the humble servant, gentle and patient. A spirit of service, compassion, a love for men, which attracts their love in return, prudence which fears chiefly any excessive harshness both in correcting and in commanding, gentleness, peace . . . who is not aware that all these virtues are aspects of one and the same fundamental attitude? The Servant of Yahweh, the Christ of St Matthew, the Pauline Pastor, the compassionate and 'discreet' elder in Cassian, all these ideal images of the head of a Christian community blend effortlessly into a portrait of the abbot, which is profoundly simple. The predominating feature is, according to all the evidence, 'prudence' or 'discretion,' and still more precisely that part of discretion which consists in avoiding 'the too much,' (meaning too hard, too laborious, excess of zeal).

The well-known maxim 'Better to err through too much leniency than too much severity',[71] though it does not correspond literally with vs 14, would express the general tenor of this passage quite well. Does not *semper superexaltet misericordiam iudicio* (vs 10) say the same thing in different words? This quotation from Jn 2:13, which emphasizes the most important characteristic in the list of qualities taken from the Pastoral Letters and, at the same time, introduces the development on the theme of correction, could be set up as an inscription at the beginning of the whole directory, whose guiding principle it symbolizes with sufficient exactness. The anxiety to make peace, to incline towards compassion and indulgence, and to soften, which is so constantly affirmed throughout the different developments, can derive only from personal experience and from surmounting difficulties. The interest of this directory, as its very individual charm, lies in this deep homogeneity and in the tangible personal note, which it affirms.[72]

However, one important characteristic is still lacking in our analysis. We have left it aside until now, because it comes in those parts of sentences, which have appeared to us as intervening spaces between the main sections of the text or as a means of linking them up:

Prodesse magis quam praeesse (vs 8)

Oderit vitia, diligat fratres (vs 11)

These three little phrases, as Butler has observed, repeat sayings of St Augustine. Dom C. Lambot who, as we know, is little inclined to recognize RB's borrowings, would willingly see in *prodesse magis quam praeesse* 'a common saying which St Benedict does not necessarily derive' from the bishop of Hippo.[73] However, in default of well substantiated proofs, we may consider the saying as an authentic reminiscence of St Augustine, to whom it is familiar. As for the two others, Dom Lambot does not seek to question their Augustinian origin. It is rather remarkable that both of them are to be read in R Aug Chapters 11 and 15, in the same order as they are quoted here. *Oderit uitia, diligat fratres* has been recopied many times over, with slight variations, by the spiritual and literary posterity of St Augustine: *Vita Fulgentii* and Gregory the Great may be cited, not to mention Caesarius of Arles.[74] *Et studeat plus amari quam timeri* has this particularity that, while certainly a reference to St Augustine, the phrase has, if one may so style it, a pre- or extra- Augustinian history; the opposition between love and fear which a Christian superior should inspire occurs in Ambrose, in the *Vita Honorati*, and even in RM— RB 2.[75]

The theme of charity, which frames and penetrates the development of prudence in the correction (vss 11, 14, 15), therefore owes its two most striking expressions to the teacher of charity, that Augustine was. This fact does not detract from the very personal character, which we have recognized in this passage, and which is not due to an originality of expression, which would exclude reminiscence or borrowing.

To conclude, it remains for us to compare the present directory with those of RM and RB in Chapter 2, as well as with the admonition in RM 93:15–23. Certainly, it is an easy matter to find points in common between RM 2 and RB 64. Both speak of *cogitare semper* concerning the same thing, namely, the grave responsibility of the abbot and the 'account', which he will have to render to the Lord. Both ask the abbot to adapt himself to different kinds of souls, both deal with correction and its necessity, and both wish the abbot to love his own monks. But as soon as we examine the importance attached to these commonplaces and the point of view from which they are considered, we begin to perceive distinct differences. Adaptation, for example, which is indisputably a major theme of RM 2, is no more than stealthily indicated in RB 64:14 (*ut uiderit cuique expedire*). Love, in the Master, is considered from the point of view of equality, by setting it in opposition to the reception of persons and contrasting it with the educational variety of its treatments. In RM 64 it is opposed rather to a hatred of vice and to the rigors of correction.

Still more than these differences, we must observe how far the processes of composition in RM and RB diverge. No doubt RB 64 is better arranged than it seems at first glance, and we believe that we have brought to light a series of symmetrical arrangements not without a resemblance to the plan of RM 2. But this analogy in structure is precisely what lays bare differences in manners. Whereas the Master thinks in contraries (diversity-equality; word and example), which he repeats in symmetrical developments, the RB redactor pursues through the full length of his own symmetrical developments a single basic theme, which runs through the passage from beginning to end, or at least between the Introduction and the Conclusion, both of them very brief. We observed in its proper place how the methodical arrangement of RM 2 put this abbatial directory in a special place in the long series of writings of this type. As much must be said of RB 64, though partly for different reasons. The literary originality of this second directory consists in the profound unity of a single theme, dealt with in a double series of brief fragments:

	first fragment (9–15).	second fragment (16–19).
Lists of qualities	positive	negative
Developments on	correction	commanding

Each passage, as we see, includes a 'list of qualities' and a 'development'. The two passages, appreciably equal in length, thus possess the same internal structure, like the two 'passages' of RM 2. But whereas, in the Master, the constituent elements of each passage are distinct *themes*, forming an antithesis between themselves, here these elements are defined by the *style* (list of qualities, development), while the fundamental theme does not change.[76]

However, it is less important to distinguish the literary process peculiar to each author than to investigate the relationship between their respective doctrines. That of the Master, as we have seen, is especially remarkable for the work of organization and synthesis, which it applies to the themes current in directories for abbots. The ideas themselves in RM 2 are in the least original. Between these traditional ideas, of scriptural origin, and those propounded by Rb 64, there are indeed points of contact, of which we have already indicated the principal.[77] But what about the fundamental theme of RB 64, that set purpose of mercy, moderation, gentleness, discretion? Does it harmonize with the Master's directory and with the whole of RM? In other words, does RM bear the same marks, in particular that of 'discretion,' in its conception of the abbot?

In its last form the question certainly calls for an affirmative answer. To limit ourselves to the crucial matter of 'discretion,' it is unlikely *a priori* that the Master, imbued as he is with Cassian and the *Vitae Patrum*, would not have accorded the greatest consideration to this virtue. In fact, the 'adaptation' theme, which occupies so prominent a position in RM 2, already approaches the concept of discretion very closely. This theme does not appear solely in the theoretical considerations in the treatise on the abbot; it is found in the most practical parts of the rule. It is a cherished idea of the Master that the abbot ought not to ask for the same standard of perfection from everyone, and that there are degrees of observance. No sooner has RM presented the ideal norm than it provides a *relaxatio* for the imperfect, well aware what a 'diversity of grace' separates individuals.[78] But this concern, which reveals genuine discretion, quickly reduces itself to casuistic terms and scruples. If the subject is silence, there comes an exact determination of rules to be followed, according to whether a brother is perfect or imperfect. If the subject is obedience, the number of times that the abbot may repeat his order without any fault on the part of the inferior, when the latter belongs to the category of the 'imperfect' is specified.[79]

In both cases, it is remarkable that RB has not preserved such casuistic developments. It offers us something altogether different in Chapter 64: a theory of 'prudence' or 'discretion' considered solely, moreover, from the point of view of the 'too much', which is to be avoided. This theory is set out in its complete form in other RB passages,[80] and undoubtedly such insights, detached from every implementation of the rules of casuistry, are one of the merits of RB that are most appreciated. What this rule does in fact lose in precision and details it regains from the point of view of breadth and the letting in of fresh air. The abbot should be 'discreet'. How? A dangerous question, which the Master did not know how to escape. In RB, the measure of discretion is first left to the abbot's own sense of judgment, and that is all to the good, for it is the characteristic of a virtuous man to exercise a ruler's judgment precisely in such matters. Nothing should be substituted for the living wisdom of the head of the group. Thus, by the mere fact that it is shorter and has to forgo many details, RB frees itself from the burden of a system of rules which, in the Master, seems to us to be stifling by dint of its minutiae. Nevertheless it retains, and even purifies, the spirit of discretion. Chapter 64 represents this 'pure state' of discretion, which is nothing more than the Providence of God acting in the monastery through the loving reason of the abbot.

In relation to RB 2 the present abbatial directory might also seem a little lacking in harmony. For RB, in revising RM 2, suppressed (second omission) the Master's reflections on the humility of the abbot and the love, at the same time both paternal and maternal, which he must have for his sons, and replaced this whole humble and gentle passage with a severe warning on the immediate suppression of vice, using the rod, as necessity may require (second addition: RB 2 26–29). Omission and addition conspire equally to give the new redaction a less tender and even somewhat harsh aspect. Consequently this is the explanation of the impression of contrast, which certain commentators receive, when they compare RB 2 and RB 64. Dom Bernard Capelle has even spoken of a 'retractation' made by St Benedict at the end of his rule and at the end of his life, correcting in the direction of mildness, the severity of his first directory for the abbot.[81] It is certain at any rate, that Chapter 64 shows a rather different tone from that of the second addition, as may be perceived when listening to these two parts of sentences:

RB 2:26: *mox ut coeperint oriri radicitus ea ut praeualet amputet.*
RB 64:14: *prudenter et cum caritate ea amputet, ut uiderit cuique expedire, sicut iam diximus.*[82]

The context of this second quotation perhaps alludes to the first (in quibus non dicimus ut permittat nutriri uitia). The author was recollecting his energetic caution in Chapter 2 against a wait-and-see policy in the matter of the correction, but this time it would be the opposite danger that would seize his attention, that of precipitancy, of excess and, of hardness.

This interpretation, so plausible and even seductive as it appears when RB is considered in isolation, nevertheless encounters difficulties when one gives a thought to the RB 2 process of redaction, deriving from RM. In effect, one would have to admit that the same redactor emended RM by his omissions and additions in the severe sense of Chapter 2, and then corrected himself in the opposite sense in chapter 64. Or have we here an indication of a plurality of RB redactors? We noted concerning the words *non refugiant* (RB 64:19) the resemblance of this second directory for the abbot with the final addition of the Prologue. The two texts square as to their care to treat the weak gently, and in their repeated mentions of charity. The beautiful Chapter 27 of RB, on the abbot physician and good shepherd, could also be compared to Chapter 64.[83] These three such tender passages, would they not proceed from the same hand which should be distinguished from the one responsible (probably unique, as we have seen) for the second omission and second addition of Chapter 2?

In any case, whether the redactor of Chapter 64 is correcting himself or the work of someone else, the hypothesis that it is his intention to correct the severity of RB 2 should be retained as probable. Thus RB would return in some fashion to the tone originally set by the Master in this passage on humility and on the tender charity of the abbot, which RB 2 had believed ought to be suppressed (RM 2:21–25: second omission). Let us note further that RB has not merely one directory for the abbot, like RM, but two, the one with which the Rule opens and the other, which brings it to a close, for all practical purposes. This development given to the treatise on the abbot is all the more remarkable, as RB habitually abridges its source. Whereas RB in its entirety is nearly three times shorter than RM, here, in the particular chapter on the abbot, it adds to the Master's directory this Chapter 64 as appendix, which amounts to one-third of the length of Chapter 2. This fact is linked with the analogous observation made on Chapter 2: that chapter itself is already a little longer in RB than in RM. By means of this double verification we can see that RB has no fear of failing in its general policy of abridgment, when the question is as decisive as that of the abbot. The material importance given to the treatise on the superior by RB proves by itself alone that the role attributed to this personage has only increased in importance in passing from RM to RB.

However, we cannot content ourselves with comparing Chapter 64 with Chapter 2 of RM and of RB, as we have just done. We must end where we began, namely by again comparing Chapter 64 of RB with the admonition in RM 93:15–23 and, more generally, with the Master's treatise on abbatial succession (RM 92 through 94), where this admonition occurs. The harmonies and the differences existing between the RB directory and the Master's ordination monitory have been sufficiently indicated above, as much from the point of view of form as of content. What must now be emphasized is the enrichment, which the RB text represents in comparison with its source.

Twice as long as the RM passage, this RB text preserves the principal ideas of RM: responsibility in respect of the Rule and of souls, before the Lord, to whom an account will have to be rendered. But these elements, derived from the Master, are kept only in the form of a summary. The recommendation to safeguard the rule, urgent as it is (*praecipue*), does not take up more than two lines, slightly outside the framework of the plan of the text and just before the Conclusion. The theme of responsibility before God is relegated to the Introduction and the Conclusion. That of responsibility with regard to the souls, whose direction the abbot assumes, is certainly present everywhere, since the directory speaks of nothing else from beginning to end, but it is precisely on this point that we can observe the enrichment, of which we were speaking.

The Master confines himself to calling to mind the pastoral mission of the abbot in vague and general terms:

> Henceforth, be very careful; do not let yourself feel at peace, on account of ravening wolves and of the snares, which the devil will set for his flock, and when you are thinking about the processes (*artibus*) and the admonitions, by which you will be able to restore to health souls which have received wounds, or which have been brought to ruin by their own faults. Henceforth, as far as within you lies, be vigilant and careful, for until today, you have been in peace (RM 93:21–23).

In this text, as we can see, it is only a question of inviting the new abbot to take his task seriously. The task itself is described only in two words of very general meaning: *artibus et monitionibus*. The contribution made by RB consists precisely in giving a few details about these *monitiones* by insistence on the mercy and the prudence and discretion, with which the abbot ought to fulfill his role. Not only does the RB define precisely of what these *artes* (the word alludes quite clearly to the *ars sancta* of the first chapters) or these *monitiones* consist (as one finds so much in RM, which abounds in discourses by the abbot to his monks). What RB has to offer is something different but very valuable in a different way from those precise objectives, that is, insight into the 'how', the manner in which the abbot should acquit himself in his task of correction and direction.[84] The abbot has no need here for an exposition of the program of his teaching (it is set out in the chapters which follow on RB 2) nor for the educational method which allows him to instil it effectively (the whole rule is nothing else but such a method). But it is not superfluous to lay stress on some personal qualities, on some individual attitudes, and on certain dominant virtues, without which this whole fine educational system risks failing in its purpose for want of a master, who is not only holy and learned,[85] but also—above all else—truly prudent.

In this sense RB 64 may be considered as a development—and what an enriching development—of RM 93:15–23. Not satisfied with warning the abbot of his responsibility by calling to mind his task as physician of souls, the RB redactor has further wished to help him to shoulder this responsibility and to fulfil this task, by showing him the qualities that he ought to possess and to develop, and by giving him counsel on how to govern.

Lastly, RB 64 equally marks a considerable progress with regard to the entire treatise on abbatial succession (RM 82 through 94). The Master, it will be remembered, envisaged no other qualification for the role, except moral 'superiority', especially in that fundamental monastic virtue, humility.[86] To sift out the 'best monk from his flock, the monk who is most observant of the rule, the most humble monk of all,' such must be the sole preoccupation of the Great Elector, that is, the old abbot. It is really a question of literally putting into practice the dictum of the Gospel: in order to be first, put yourself in the last place. It is also a question of providing the cenobitic school with a master, who knows by experience what he has to teach, and who practises what he preaches. Lastly, it is a matter of conforming to the hierarchy of worth established by the grace of God and by the free effort of each individual, 'for it is not suitable that one who is better be subject to one who is less good'.

These considerations are certainly not without interest, and we may conclude from them that a certain spiritual superiority is necessary for the abbot to carry out his role authentically, in order that he may be truly a master, who has something to give, which his disciples do not possess. A certain difference of level between abbot and monks is indispensable, in order to establish and maintain between them a current flowing from the former to the latter. But it would be a slight over-simplification of the problem, if one confined oneself to this valid principle. Personal merit and superiority in virtue are indeed necessary, but not sufficient. Even if the Master is right to remind us that without such effective superiority on the part of the abbot, the *coenobium* will vegetate and stagnate for lack of spiritual exchanges, we can regret on the other hand that he left other data of the problem in the background.

Sanctity is not enough where the direction of others is concerned, and above all the direction of a community, intent as it presumably is upon the one thing necessary. Moreover the Master has incidentally recognized the truth of this when he observes in another part of his rule, *oportet abbatem multum esse de lege structum*.[87] Here is, on the very avowal of the Master, a quality distinct from the monastic virtues, a capacity created through knowledge, which the abbot must possess in order to heal souls.[88] We meet it again at the top of the list of qualities in RB 64, *oportet eum esse doctum lege diuina*, but the RB redactor does not stop there. To this first quality he adds three other virtues especially necessary for a superior. He has laid particular stress on one of them, mercy, and then developed its aspects: charity and a sense of proportion in the exercise of correction. This notion of a sense of proportion, of moderation and of prudence has seemed so important to him that he has again added a list of defects to avoid and a development on discretion, both of which only then enhance different aspects of the same virtue.

All this forms a portrait of the Christian pastor which is singularly richer and more subtle, let us say even *truer*, than the schema proposed by the Master. The essential word, lacking in the Master, that of 'prudence' or 'discretion,' is here uttered in a context which has no other purpose than to clarify it and to make the most of it. That is an appreciable enrichment. We should entertain a lively sentiment of gratitude to the RB for having transformed, as it has, the treatise on abbatial succession that it found in the Master, whether by effacing every trace of the strange 'race for honors,' or by deliberately adding, contrary to its habits of abridgment, this fine directory for the abbot.[89]

NOTES TO CHAPTER SEVEN

1. The most recent study on abbatial election is that by Kassius Halinger, 'Papst Gregor der Grosse und der Hl. Benedikt', *Studia Anselmiana* 42 (1957), pp 309–317. References to all previous works may be found there. This remarkable study has furnished us with much useful evidence, which we have at times corrected or completed, in particular where it concerns the Pachomians and Cassian. Among the works utilized by Hallinger, see especially the fundamental study by Suso Brechter, 'Die Bestellung des Abtes nach der Regel des Hl. Benedikts', *Studien und Mitteilungen zur Geschichte des benediktinischen Ordens* 58 (1940), pp 44–58.

2. Kassius Hallinger (cf. preceding note) sees evidences of this system in the *Vita Fulgentii* 8 (read 15) and 29, as well as in the *Regula Vigilii* (= R Or) 3. These two documents do not, in fact, directly concern abbatial succession. The *Vita*, in the two passages cited, speaks of government by two. This curious system is described in considerable detail in the first passage: Felix and Fulgentius are both very young at the beginning of their association. They share power, one occupying himself with material things, the other with the instruction of the brethren, and they render mutual obedience. This collegial régime has little in common with the relationship between an elderly abbot and his future successor and seems to have been conceived apart from any idea of succession, though in fact it could have repercussions on it. As for the R Or, it deals with the establishment of a *praepositus* by the abbot, with the assent of the brethren. There again, no relation to abbatial succession is indicated. So we prefer not to make use of this text to trace the history of a usage, for which it does not produce any clear evidence.

3. *Vies Coptes*, pp 48 and 272. In both cases, the dying superior begins by asking the brethren to choose his successor themselves. Then the brethren refuse, and the dying man designates his choice. There is the same procedure when Horsiesios makes Theodore his deputy (ibid., p 245). These texts, as we see, do not provide evidence only for designation by the predecessor; they witness at the same time to the recognized right of the brethren to elect their future superior for themselves. Hence there is need to modify Hallinger's affirmation (ibid., p. 309): '*dieser älteste Wahlmodus findet sich bei den ersten Pachomianern.*' In reality, the two methods of election appear at the same time, the one exercised *de facto* the other acknowledge, *de iure*.

4. Cassian, *Inst* 4.28 (an egyptian abbot gives himself as his successor the heroic Patermutius), and *Conf* 4.1 (the priest-abbot Paphnutius, *optans sibimet successorem dignissimum prouidere*, causes Daniel to be ordained priest). The system of election by the brethren is, on the other hand, attested for the deacons of Scete (*Conf* 21:1–9).

5. Faustus, *Hom. de S. Maximo* in Schott, *Bibliotheca Maxima Patrum* (Lyons, 1677), 655ab. For the same purpose, Faustus recalls Elijah abandoning his mantle to Elisha and Moses entrusting the people of God to Joshua. The typology is significant: Honoratus, like Elijah and Moses, recognized his right to designate his successor. Yet it may be that, at this period, Honoratus had prescribed that the abbots of Lérins should be elected by the community. This is what the canon of the Third Council of Arles (*c.* 455) appears to say; cf. Labbeus, vol 4, col 1024E: *abbatis proprii quem sibi ipsa (congregatio) elegerit . . . regula quae a fundatore ipsius monasterii dudum constituta est in omnibus custodita*. Once again, the two systems for choosing an abbot are proved to be contemporary. Honoratus himself designates his successor, but assigns the right of election to the community for the future, and this notwithstanding episcopal claims. It is not certain, however, that the two clauses that we have compared with our quotation do in fact have a bearing on each other in the mind of the Council.

6. *Vita Lupicini* 12, *Acta Sanctorum*, vol 9, 21 March, p 266 (second half of the fifth century).

7. For John of Réomé see below, n. 15. For Columban, see Henri Leclercq, "*Elections abbatiales*", DACL, col 2616. For Landelin (late seventh century) see Mabillon, *Acta Sanctorum OSB*, vol 2, pp 875–76. On Frunimian, a Spanish abbot contemporary with Braulio of Saragossa, see below n. 18.

8. See Hallinger, "Papst Gregor der Grosse und der Hl. Benedikt", p 309.

9. The only two texts that one can cite are Basil, LR 43.1 (election by the superiors of other fraternities) and R Caes V 61 ("unanimous" election by the community of nuns).

10. It will be remembered that, for Hallinger, R Or 3 (nomination of the *praepositus* by the abbot with the assent of the brethren) is a case of this type. Cf. above, n. 2.

11. See above, nn. 3–4.

12. The Council of Chalon, the twelfth canon of which authorizes the abbot to choose his successor, is dated from about 650 (Mansi, vol 10, col 1189). Other documents from the seventh century (LT 13 of Braulio of Saragossa and Canon 46 of Theodore of Canterbury) are cited below, n.18. Although unfavorable to designation by the predecessor, they do attest the contemporary practice of this system, which does not seem previously to have attracted the attention of ecclesiastical authority. On the other hand, juridical texts from the fifth and sixth centuries attesting election by the assembled community are not lacking: below, nn.43–45.

13. Let us recall the contrast between the conduct of Honoratus designating Maximus to replace him, and the "rule" of election by the community which the Council of Arles seems to attribute to him (cf. n. 4).

14. Thus the Pachomians, when consulted by their dying superior, avoid the issue and entreat the old superior to designate the new one (cf. n. 3).

15. Here is the reply of the brethren to Petronius: "After God and our father, we acknowledge no one besides yourself; it was to you, moreover, that we were entrusted by our dying father" (*Vies Coptes*, p 272). Here we vividly perceive the process, according to which the first successor, the benefiting from the prestige of having been chosen by the "father," in turn finds himself in a position to dictate his choice. In the Jura, Lupicinus' successor in his turn designates Eugendus to succeed him. Cf. *Vita Eugendi*, Mabillon, AS OSB, vol 1, p 555. At Réomé, we find a series of designations by the predecessor, following the example of the first abbot. Cf. François Masai, *À Cluny* (Dijon: Imprimerie Bernigaud & Privat, 1950), p 197. Is there any need to say that one cannot draw from this fact any conclusion as to the presence of RM at Réomé, contrary to what Masai believes? The abbots of Réomé had no need of a rule in order to proceed to such designations since an ancient usage, which had never at any time been rejected, authorized the abbot to act thus when he felt capable of it.

16. We are well aware of the crisis which resulted from the nomination of Horsieseios by Petronius. Apparently Horsiesios was relatively young, and consequently lacked the authority which would have permitted him to rule over 'elders.' See the study by J. Chitty, 'Chronology of the Pachomian Foundations', *Studia Patristica*, vol 2, pp 380–85. Rather similar difficulties were raised in the case of Eugendus (cf. n. 15).

17. What is more, when the successor is himself an exceptional personality, the former abbot likes to give himself the credit for having appointed him to the abbatial office. Such is the case of Patermutius and Daniel, the two abbots instituted by their predecessors, on the evidence of Cassian (see above, n. 4), and of Eugendus (n. 15). Here again, hagiography tends to multiply examples of this type. The case of Fulgentius, whom the abbot Felix takes as his associate by reason of his superior merit and uncommon knowledge, is of the same nature (cf. n.2).

18. One even finds an allusion to the recommendation of an old abbot as constituting one of the valid credentials of a particular candidate for the abbacy in a letter of Gregory the Great (Lr 12.34, PL 77:1233b). Then too, canon 12 of the Council of Chalon, about 650 (Mansi, vol 10, col 1189), recognizes the legitimacy of the designation of an abbot by his predecessor, while denying the abbot-elect the powers of government before the demise of the old abbot. Cf. Can 12 with can 4; the latter, in like fashion, forbids the holding of office by two bishops in a single city, without however alluding to a right of successorial designation which the old bishop might have had. Braulio of Saragossa, in his Lr 13 (PL 80:659–660) written between 631 and 651, shows himself to be not very favorable to the designation of an abbot by his predecessor. But he does not attack the principle of this designation. what he holds against his correspondent is rather his wish to abandon his abbatial office and also his lack of trust in Providence by being too anxious about the future; let Frunimian attend solely to governing well during his lifetime, leaving to God the care of providing for his replacement after his death! Finally, Braulio's most severe reproach against the abbot is that he wishes to impose on the brethren a superior whom he alone had designated and whom they do not want; by acting in this way, he violates the well-known adage: *inuitis neminem debere praeponi*. Braulio therefore implicitly admits that the abbot in office could have designated his successor, provided that this was done with the agreement of the brethren. The position of the legislator is still the same in the Canon of Theodore of Canterbury (668–690): an abbot is forbidden to give his monastery to anyone *sine uoluntate monachorum*. Certainly, the accent here clearly falls on the right of the community to elect (*ipsi eligant sibi abbatem*), but the final words of the text suggest that designation by the predecessor is not excluded, if it receives the assent of the monks. See d'Achery, *Spicilegium* (Paris, 1669), vol 9, p 56, can 46.

19. See Leclercq, '*Elections épiscopales*' col 2623–2629. Such defensive tactics did not, moreover, prevent the abuse from continuing. It is known that in the time of Augustine, the see of Milevis was filled in this fashion, and that Augustine himself took care to appoint his co-adjutor whom he moreover caused to be acclaimed by the people. At Rome the right of the Pontiff to intervene in the designation of his successor seems to be attested by the

decree of the Roman Council of 498 under Symmachus, as also by the conduct of Felix IV, who designated Boniface in 530. Let us also cite the *Vita Caesarii* 1.12: Bishop Aeonius campaigns for Caesarius, whom he wants to have as his successor. All these facts show to what extent, in those times when elections occasioned so many difficulties, the bishops, like the abbots, were careful to assure to their flock a good pastor and a smoothly enacted succession.

20. RM juxtaposes Chapter 92 (no 'second!') with Chapter 91 (the son of a nobleman), that is, it passes without any transition from the section on recruitment to that on abbatial succession. The idea of renewal, either of the community through recruitment or of the abbacy through succession, no doubt serves as the link between the two sections, but this link is not made explicit.

21. Cf. RM 22:8–13.

22. This implication is apparent right from the first sentence of Chapter 92 (vs 1). It goes without saying for the Master as for his readers: he who is second to the abbot is his future successor.

23. See HM Prol and Chapter 7 (PL 21:389, 412c); *Vita Honorati* 9–10; Eusebius, *Hom.* 43 (=Faustus), PL 50:856b; R Caes M 19. Note in this last text the conclusion *ut laetetur Deus et angeli eius*. Here is what distinguishes these sane uses of the theme of rivalry from the aberrant theory of the Master. In the first case, the competition takes place under the eyes of God and for him alone; the Master, on the contrary, appoints a *man*—the abbot —as judge of the outcome, and makes his human appreciation (granted that he is the representative of God) the stake of the contest, together with the prospect of a *temporal* honor and of a *terrestrial* authority as the victor's reward.

24. Besides, is it not setting the problem of the succession badly to conceive the abbatial office as belonging by right to the most virtuous monk, as the Master does; would it not be a question of distinguishing who is the most capable monk, which is not quite the same thing?

25. Gregory of Nyssa, *De Instituto Christiano*, pp 50, 76, etc. See the remarks of Jaeger in *Two Rediscovered Works*, p 114.

26. However, we must take account of a certain realism on the part of the ancients: they were perhaps less sensitive than we as regards the autonomy of conscience, and more inclined to make use of social pressure as a means for obtaining a minimum of virtue. The disillusioned reflections of the Master (RM 92:46–47) could be illustrated by the *Vita Fulgentii* 14: *ut qui nolebat esse humilis propter pietatem, disceret humilis esse propter hereditatem.*

27. RM 92:54–65. Masai (art. cit., see note 13) bases an argument on this passage to prove that Moutiers-Saint-Jean was in contact with RM. In reality, the theme of the fugitive abbot who tries to pass himself off as a postulant is commonplace in the *Lives of the Fathers*, exploited notably by Cassian (*Inst* 4.30–31). Both RM and the *Vita* of John of Réomé refer to these famous examples, and the common theme does not create any bond of dependence between them.

28. RM 92:65.

29. RM 2:1 *nomen maioris factis implere*. The chapters on succession constantly allude to this principle; the abbot ought *effectually* be *maior* (92:28), *superior* (92:72), *melior* (92:76, 82).

30. The Master causes this 'superiority'. which he demands of the abbot, to consist of humility above all. Here again, the treatise on succession does no more than repeat the treatise on the abbot (cf. RM 2:22–25 with 93:43–55, 71–73). Basically, all the reflections of the Master on the qualities of a pastor consist in taking very seriously, even literally, Mt 18:4: *qui uult esse inter uos fortior sit talis* (like a child), and Lk 14:11 - Mt 20:27: *qui uult interuos esse fortior sit uester ultimus . . . qui se humiliat exaltabitur*. In view of the fact that

he must teach others an 'art' which consists above all of humility, the abbot ought essentially to be the most humble of all. Even the *qui uult* of the Gospel text has influenced the Master's thought, making him consider as normal the competition for honors in humility.

31. RM 92:36–37. Cf. a second prayer by the bishop, vs 43.

32. It is also the old abbot who has the chief role in the ordination (cf. RM 93:12–13: handing over of the rule, the keys and the inventory; handing over of the *pallium*). Note that to eradicate the name of the dismissed second in command from the diptychs, *quiuis sacerdos rogatus ab abbate* is enough, without the abbot being obliged to refer to the bishop himself who effected the inscription. This detail well shows the abbot's freedom of action. He has recourse to the bishop only for liturgical acts beyond his competence as a layman, and the bishop, in these acts, is only an officiant who carries out the wishes of the abbot. Note finally, in the same sense, that in the case of a sudden death, the bishop is limited to nominating the abbot who shall make the choice, while not himself directly intervening in the matter. All this seems to be the application of the theory propounded in Chapter 83: the clergy should not exert any sway over the government of the community.

33. Such a result could be expected in a monastery where the abbot organizes and sustains the competition for honors.

34. This procedure reminds one of Basil, Lr 43.2, where the nomination of the superior devolves upon the superiors of the other fraternities. Cf. also the role of the bishops of a province in episcopal elections. Sidonius Apollinaris even tells how, as bishop of Clermont, he was charged by the people of Bourges to designate all by himself the bishop of that city, in the course of a difficult election (Lr 7.5). The procedure is the same as that which is established here by the Master, and the motive is identical: episcopacy and abbacy are fiercely coveted. Contemporary testimonies abound as to the large number of candidates for the episcopate, and on the lively competitions in which they engaged.

35. On the contrary, *Vita Fulgentii* 15 and R Or 3 (see n. 2) note the asssent given by the brethren to the choice made by the abbot. The Master's determination not to consult the opinion of the brethren can be explained by the disorders which consultations of this sort would bring about in the competitive atmosphere which then existed (see n. 2). In practice, the rule of election of the bishop by the people, theoretically maintained, underwent more than one modification. Cf. Leclercq, '*Elections épiscopales*', DACL. Apparently the Master boldly codified for his monastery what circumstances had simply required to be done, without this being too clearly avowed. The disorders of which he speaks may be compared to the intrigues that Gregory the Great unmasked in one of his Sicilian monasteries (Lr 5.6: the nuns of St Martin at Palermo).

36. In RB the question of rank is postponed to Chapter 63, and that of the 'second' to Chapter 65.

37. Save for the warning to the new abbot (RM 93:15–23), which probably survives in RB 64:7–22.

38. The single reminiscence of a previous passage is that of vs 2, which reproduces RB 21:4 almost literally.

39. Hallinger, *art. cit.* (n. 2 above), pp 310ff.

40. Cf. n. 3.

41. Cf. n. 4.

42. Cassian, *Conf* 21.1–9.

43. Cf. n. 5. Still, in the fifth century, we find another case of election by the community at St Martin of Tours (Greg. Tur., VP 16.1).

44. This is the case with the Councils of Arles and of Carthage.

45. Thus the three laws of Justinian, the decretal of Pelagius I, and the letters of Gregory the Great. The idea of having the assembled community elect their abbot would seem all the more normal as the bishop was traditionally elected by the people.

46. On episcopal control, see nn. 45,47. Where neighboring abbots are concerned, we should mention the Council of Carthage in 536 (Labbeus, vol 4, col 1785c), which entrusts *abbatum aliorum concilio siue iudicio* with the task of resolving the differences which could arise among members of the community on the subject of the election. This decree comes as close as possible to RB 64: the abbots play the role of arbitrators or a court of appeal, and not that of electors by right as in Basil (Lr 43.2) and RM (Chapter 94). As for the 'Christians of the neighborhood', their intervention is mentioned in the correspondence of Pelagius I (see Hallinger, p 311 and n 242).

47. Leclercq (*'Elections épiscopales'*, DACL col 2614) seems to us to have taken a wrong turning by setting RB in opposition to the Councils of Arles (455) and of Carthage (536), where the episcopal control of the election is concerned. In reality, the two councils do not exclude this control, but simply limit themselves to affirming the right of the monks to elect, which the bishops had been tempted to forget.

48. Cassian, *Con* 21.1: *is prouehitur*) quem cunctorum seniorum coetus aetatis praerogatius et fidei atque uirtutum testimonio excellentiorem sublimioremque censuerit. This text should be added to the dossier compiled by Hallinger (*art. cit.*, pp 313–17).

49. RB 21:4:*et non elegantur per ordinem sed secundum uitae meritum et sapientiae doctrinam.* This text goes further than RB 64:12 (*etiam si ultimus fuerit in ordine congregationis*), where the repudiation of the *ordo* is not clearly affirmed. Were we in possession of the RB 64:2 text alone, we should be right to interpret it in the sense of the *cuiuscumque gradus sit* of Justinian (*Corpus Juris Ciuilis* 1.3.47) and of the Gregorian expressions cited by Hallinger, that is, as the affirmation of the criterion of personal merit, *without excluding* the criterion of seniority. Even when compared with RB 21:4, the text remains open to this interpretation. Yet the parallelism of expressions employed in RB 21 and 64 invites us to understand the second text in the same sense as the first, that is, *excluding* the consideration of rank.

50. There ought not to be a *secundus* or *tertius* after the abbot (Chapter 92).If, after the 'Second' has been designated, someone 'better' should come along, the existing precedence must be abolished, to the advantage of the new-comer (ibid.), and the same procedure takes place if the 'Second' falls into disrepute (Chapter 93). Thus the 'Second,' who has been created only by accident (when the abbot, contrary to all expectations, continues to live), remains insecure; he is by no means irremovable. The anomaly occasioned by his appointment is compensated by the threat hanging over him and by the obligation that the rule imposes on him to consider himself the least of all.

51. Let us recall that RM *does not formally exclude* episcopal control, but does not in fact assign it any role in the procedure indicated. Certainly RB, by mentioning such control without any possible doubt, adheres more closely then RM to the texts cited in n. 45 in line with the right of supervision recognized to bishops by the fourth Canon of the Council of Chalcedon (451).

52. *Brebe gregis* (RM 93:19) is to be understood in a metaphorical sense, and signifies the rule. It is not a question of the inventory, called *brebem rerum* (93:13).

53. Thus Suso Brechter, cited by Herwegen, *Sinn und Geist*, p 379. The latter enumerates everything which can in fact be invoked as parallel: *cogitet, onus, oportet*. It is not very much really, particularly as *cogitet* recurs in RB 2:34, and *oportet* refers in both cases to the Pastoral Letters. In reality, ordination monitories in the Roman Pontifical differ greatly from RB 64 by their abundance of allegorical exegeses which symbolically interpret the name and the functions of each Order, as also by the corresponding scriptural types. Nothing of the soft is found in this directory for the abbot.

54. Thus R Aug 15, R 4 Pat 205–225, R Fer 37.

55. RB 31:1. The fourth positive quality (*timens Deum*) is relegated to a position after the list of negative qualities. A new list of negative qualities is given further on (RB 31:11–12). Besides these analogies in the enumeration of qualities necessary for the incumbent, note the parallelism of the expressions: *qui bene ministrauerit* (RB 31:8) and *dum bene ministrauerit* (RB 64:21).

It will be observed that in RB 31 these words make up part of a scriptural quotation (1 Tim 3:13), whereas in RB 64 they do not belong to the scriptural context (Mt 24:47), and may be considered as a reminiscence either of St Paul or of the chapter on the cellarer.

56. 1 Tim 3:2; Tt 1:8–9; 2:2, 5.

57. 1 Tim 4:12; Tt 2:5 (the two adjectives *castas, sobrias* succeed one another as in RB); cf. 1 Tim 3:2 (*pudicum*); Tt 2:2 (id.); 1:8 (*continentem*).

58. 1 Tim 3:2; Tt 1:7. The other two RB 64 epithets (*doctum . . . misericordem*) may also refer to Pauline enumerations which give the following equivalents: *doctorem*, 1 Tim 3:2 (= *didaktion*); *bene docentes* (Tt 2:4; cf. a lengthy circumlocution in Titus 1:9); *benignum* (Tt 1:8; 2:5). However, *doctum lege diuina* is a reference primarily to Mt 13:52, as the following words show.

59. Basil, GR 35.1. 'Possessing foresight' (*prooratikon*) is found again under the form *prouidus* in RB 64:17. The two adjectives 'possessing foresight, compassionate' likewise figure in the Basilian directory of GR 43.2. As for RB, it recommends *prouidentia* to the abbot on three other occasions (RB 3:6; 41:4; 55:8).

60. Let us recall that Gr 35 and 43 lacked any correspondence in R Bas. Now, this is the sole Basilian text which was accessible to Latin readers. See another point of contact between RB and Greek Basil: Chapter 3, vol. 1, p. 164 & n.10. Besides Basil, one may also cite R Or 1, where a list of qualities inspired by the Pastoral Letters is found, but without a precise point of contact with RB.

61. RM 15:35: *unde oportet abbatem multum esse de lege structum ut aut testimoniis omnia doceat aut pertinentia ad locum legenda consignet.*

62. In the corresponding text of the Master (RM 3:39–44), we find only six instruments (*detractorem* is missing).

63. The special importance of *non turbulentus* at the top of the list can be ascertained from the fact that this expression is already met in RB 31:1. It is very probable that the portrait of the Servant of Yahweh underlies this passage, if we note that this same description of the Servant (and of Christ) is already used in the development of the theme on correction (RB 64:13: *calamum quassatum non conterendum*). In this fact we put our finger on the continuity of thought extending through the diversity of stylistic forms (development-list of qualities).

64. RB 65:22 will put the new abbot on his guard against *zeli flamma*. This passage has every appearance of being an observation based on living experience. In the same way, *quia nunquam requiescit* sounds like the echo of an experience. Once again we find ourselves brought back to RB 31, which closes with analogous recommendations, echoes of the same experiences: *aequo animo . . . nemo perturbetur neque contristetur* (RB 31:17, 19).

65. We have already called attention (n. 63) to the bond existing between this development on the theme of correction and the list of negative qualities which follows it; both passages refer to Is 42:3–4. This bond is strengthened by the presence in both of *nimis*, twice repeated. In passing from one mode of expression to the other (development-list of qualities), the redactor never ceases to pursue the same theme.

66. Cassian, *Conf* 2.4.

67. Idem, *Conf* 2.13. The two developments (on correcting and on orders) therefore exhibit a common reference to Cassian's *Conference* 2, just as the first development and the list of negative qualities both refer to Is 42. let us emphasize again the homogeneity of the text throughout its different parts. The redactor is constantly moving in the same mental atmos-

phere, which is the Christ-portrait in Isaiah-Matthew, interpreted in the sense of the 'mercy' which every director of souls ought to have for brothers in distress, according to the doctrine of *Conference* 2 of Cassian (2.13). According to the same *Conference*, it is above all necessary to cultivate 'discretion,' mother of virtues (*Conf* 2.4), which enables one to avoid all 'excess' (*nimietas*: *Conf* 2:16), and especially excess of rigor (*Conf* 2.17).

68. A complete formula of discretion, excluding negligence as much as excess, is given by RB 41:5 in terms which quite closely recall those that we read here: *sic omnia temperet. . . . Cf. another complete formula in Pr* 46-49, *where restrictius* balances *nihil asperum*. Here (RB 64: 14), the reservation *in quibus non dicimus ut permittat nutriri uitia* itself proves that the full and exact doctrine on discretion remains present in the mind of the redactor. Only, he is much more occupied with issuing an alert against excessive rigor than against excessive indulgence. In this respect it is to be obseved that *nimis* and *nimius*, in this chapter, envisage solely excessive *rigor*, whereas in Cassian *nimietas* designates both extremes (*utraque nimietas*: *Conf* 2.16). Yet Cassian was already affirming that too much severity is even more pernicious than negligence (*Conf* 2.17), which corresponds with the tendency of RB 64. Cf. above, Chapter 5, n. 69.

69. A stylistic relationship links this formula *ut sit quod* (vs 19) with that which we read above, *et sit unde* (vs 9). The second recurs in Gregory the Great Lr 7.43 (902c): *si talia loca sunt ut sit ibi subsistere ualeant*. Cf. RB 39:3: *et si fuerit unde poma* . . . (RM 26:1: *quodcumque fuerit*).

70. Note also, in this Prologue addition, the theme of charity (vss 47 and 49), which recalls RB 64 (vss 11, 14, 15).

71. The saying goes back at least to St Odilo, abbot of Cluny, as Ménard indicates in a note on the *Concordia* (PL 103:756d), but I believe it to be much older. It is possible that we can find it already in Hildemar, *Expositio*, p 352 (= Paul the Deacon, *Commentarium*, p 284), and possibly it is even found in a *Vita* prior to St Benedict (Ambrose, Augustine, Caesarius?). See a very similar axiom in the Byzantine *Typika*, according to Irénée Hausherr, *Direction Spirituelle en orient autrefois* (Rome: Pontifical Institute of Oriental Studies, 1944), p 142 and 4.

72. While speaking in a 'personal tone,' we have not forgotten the very traditional character of this directory. One acutely perceives it when reading Hausherr, *Direction Spirituelle*, pp 56–105 (intellectual and moral qualities required of a spiritual father), where all the RB 64 notations are to be found abundantly illustrated, without the author apparently having had our text in mind. 'Charity and discernment' are the two words which summarize the tradition (ibid., p 63).

73. C. Lambot, 'L'influence de Saint Augustin sur la Règle de Saint Benoît', *Rev. Lit. et monastique* 14 (1929), p 327, no 1. The word as such is not found in the R Aug, but in other works of Augustine. Yet the R Aug says almost the same thing when speaking of the superior (R Aug 15, 194–96: *Non se existimet potestate dominante, sed caritate seruiente felicem. Honore coram uobis praelatus sit uobis, timore coram Deo substratus sit pedibus uestris*).

74. R Caes V 24 (*sororum*, as here *fratres*); VF 53 (*homines*, as in Augustine. Note that the RB citation is closer to Caesarius than to Augustine or the *Vita Fulgentii*). In Gregory the Great, the reminiscence is less precise: *ut personas diligas et uitia persequaris* (Lr 11.12). See again a text of Ferreolus of Uzès in the following note.

75. Ambrose, *De Off.* 2.38: [David] *diligi a subiectis quam timeri maluit. Vita Honorati* 28:*studebat amore potius regere quam timore dominari*. R Fer 37 says curiously: *faciens se ab omnibus, eo quod uitia oderit, plus amari*. A double reminiscence in these words is perceptible: R Aug 11, cited by RB 64:11 (*uitia oderit*) and R Aug 15, cited by RB 64:15 (*plus amari*). It is impossible to say whether R Aug or RB served as the inspiration for Feriolus here. RM 2 and RB 2 have something analogous: *miscens terroribus blandimenta, dirum magistri pium patris ostendat affectum*. Likewise R Fer 37, just before the words we quoted above: *blandimento uocet, terrore castiget*.

76. There is obviously no need to exaggerate the homogeneous character of RB 64. The

first list of qualities opens with three traits (*doctum, sobrium castum*) which are not connected with the fundamental theme of which we are speaking, at least not directly. Nevertheless, this list finishes with *misericordem*, which is specially glossed, and introduces the theme. In any case, on the level of ideas, there is no *antithesis* between this list of qualities and what follows. That is the important fact, which contrasts with the RM 2 manner of composition. As for the final mention of the rule, it too is alien to the theme of the passage, we ought to look upon it as a trace of RM 93:15–23 (handing over of the rule). From the stylistic point of view, as well as from the point of view of ideas, this recommendation of the rule is a kind of erratic block.

77. Besides those rapprochements already mentioned, note the affinity between RM 2:26–28 (the humility of the abbot) and RB 64:8 (*prodesse magis quam praeesse*).

78. RM 9:48–50 (silence) and 7:10–21 (obedience).

79. Cf. preceding note. The same minutiae in the fasting regulations for those on journeys: everything is provided for (RM 61).

80. Cf. above, n. 68.

81. Bernard Capelle, 'Aux origines de la Règle de St. Benoît' RTAM 11 (1939), p 384. This explanation is rejected by Herwegen, *Sinn und Geist*, p 381.

82. These last words seem to allude to 2:26–27 and to 2:21–32 (variety of procedures for correcting).

83. In particular RB 64:8: *prodesse magis quam praeesse*, RB 27:6: *nouerit se infirmarum curam suscepisse animarum, non super sanas tyrannidem*. The last word recurs in RB 65:2, *adsumentes sibi tyrannidem*. Now, 65 forms a single unit with RB 64. Note too that the theme of the Good Shepherd, utilized by RB 27, is already found in RM 14:7.

84. We partially catch up again here with an opinion of Herwegen, *Sinn und Geist*, pp 381–82). He believes that RB 64 sets forth the *quomodo* of the abbatial office, whereas RB 2 propounds its *quid*. This explanation, which appears to account for the RB 2 - RB 64 doublet, does not prove satisfactory as regards the first directory for the abbot: in fact RB 2 does already treat the *quomodo* as much as the *quid*. But it must be retained that RB 64 does descend further into the interior of the soul of the abbot, and assumes a more subjective standpoint. Here, we resume the same distinction in order to characterize RB 64 by relation to RM 93 and the whole of RM.

85. Let us remember that *doctum lege diuina* (RB 64:9) is a characteristic already found in the Master (see above, n. 61).

86. See nn. 28–30.

87. RM 15:35 (cf. n. 61).

88. Certainly every monk ought to be zealous to learn the Scriptures by heart (cf. RM 50: 10–15, 62–69, etc.), but that is not to say that all are sufficiently gifted with a memory and an intelligence to attain the degree of culture necessary for an abbot. Perhaps the Master is thinking of this intellectual attainment when he requires the abbot to be preoccupied with the *artes et monitiones* which he will need (RM 93:22).

89. Moreover, these two modifications have a mutual connection. In both cases, RB relinquishes the theme of 'superiority' as an essential qualification for a candidate to the abbacy. This theme nevertheless remains latent (cf. RB 64:2: *uitae merito*, and Chapter 2).

Chapter 8

THE ABBOT'S LIEUTENANT (RB 65)

IN THIS CHAPTER the *Concordia* offers a series of sixteen texts, on which modern commentators do not fail to draw. Yet there is no need for a lengthy examination, in order to realize that several of these texts relate to something quite different from the Benedictine 'provost', that is to say, from the abbot's 'Second in command'.[1] Such an inference, which might be revised in the works of some commentator who puts too much trust in the *Concordia*,[2] warns us from the very first that it is necessary to define the precise meaning of *praepositus* in the monastic tradition. A linguistic enquiry must precede our study of the function of the *praepositus*. Furthermore, this preliminary investigation will furnish us with some data that will be useful for determining the meaning of the attitudes taken by RM on this question.

THE TERM *PRAEPOSITUS*

In RB, *praepositus* in the singular exclusively designates the superior, who comes immediately under the abbot, the second-in-command of the community. Furthermore, the word appears with this meaning only in Chapter 65, which deals with the question *ex professo*, and in a note slipped in at the end of the chapter on deans.[3] As to *praepositi* in the plural, we find it twice in RB. According to Hallinger, it would then designate the deans, in conformity with the pre-Benedictine usage attested in particular by RM.[4] One might also think of a more general meaning: 'the superiors, the officers', for this is the meaning in Caesarius of Arles and other authors, who knew nothing of the decanal system.[5] But I prefer to believe that, in these two RB passages, *praepositi* (plural) must be understood in the sense of *praepositus* (singular), that is to say, as of the second-in-command, the abbot's lieutenant. Of course, RB 36:10 says the same thing: *cellarariis aut servitoribus*, in the plural. Now there is only one infirmarian (cf. 36:7, though 36:4 gives the plural), and likewise only one *cellararius*. In this passage, RB is therefore designating the successive holder of the offices of infirmarian and cellarer; these offices are not held by more than one religious at a time. The same is probably true for *praepositi* (plural) in the two passages that we are examining.[6] Be that as it may, the meaning of *praepositus* in the singular is sufficiently clear to enable us to discover its place in the semantic history of the word.

What first strikes us in this history is that originally *praepositus* in no way signified the second-in-command. From its etymology it naturally suggested not the second place but the first. In fact, it is apparently with this meaning of 'head' that it has been used in civil and ecclesiastical language.[7] Originally, the same was true of it in monastic terminology. The *praepositus* is a leader, either at the top or (more frequently) in a subordinate position; in any case he is the first in the group entrusted to him, and not the second-in-command. This latter function is called by another name, *Secundus*.

This terminology appears very clearly in St Jerome, who is the first to establish it. In 384, when he is composing Lr 22, he employs *praepositus* as a synonym for *decanus*, who is also called *parens*.[8] Twenty years later, when translating the R Pac, it is again in order to designate the head of the house that he uses *praepositus*.[9] The factual meaning is evident, when the full expression *praepositus domus* occurs. When *praepositus* stands alone, we believe that it also designates the head of the house. Nevertheless it is possible that in certain cases, a detailed examination of which would exceed the limits of the present study, the word covers the head of the monastery, that is, the man who governs all the houses united in the same place, and whom Jerome normally calls *princeps monasterii, pater monasterii*. The last meaning could be due either to a conscious plan on the part of the translator or to an error in interpretation on his side. In any case, whether it be a question of the head of the monastery or of the head of the house, this personage is the leader of his group. His assistant is denominated as *secundus*.[10] Finally, when he is writing Lr 25 in the year 411, Jerome speaks of *praepositus monasterii* to designate the local superior, the abbot.[11] The little sentence, in which this expression appears, deserves quotation, for we shall find it again on several occasions in later documents, together with other excerpts from this famous letter of Jerome:[12] *praepositum monasterii timeat ut dominum, diligat ut parentem.* If Jerome is here designating the abbot by this term, which is exceptional in his writings, it is no doubt because he cannot call him *pater monasterii* or *pater* as he did previously, on account of the idea expressed by the final words of the sentence, since he is recommending Rusticus to love his superior 'like a father', Jerome could not have given this superior his usual title of *pater* without being clumsy. Thus he writes *praepositum,* which shows even better than the facts previously cited how suitable this term originally was for signifying purely and simply 'the first place.'

Cassian's terminology is identical, but for this one difference: the 'Second-in-command' never appears in the *Institutes* or *Conferences*, as Cassian seems to know nothing of this functionary. Notwithstanding the silence of Petschenig's Index, we have pointed out four examples of *praepositus* in the sense of 'dean',[13] and two in the sense of 'abbot' in *Inst* 5:27 and *Conf* 18:7.[14] Clearly then, for Cassian, as for Jerome, *praepositus* simply suggests superiority, the highest rank.[15]

As for St Augustine, it is possible to hesitate at first. The use of *praepositus* as a synonym for *decanus* in *De moribus ecclesiae* 1.31.67, is not at all typical, since Augustine is only following Lr 22 of Jerome. But what causes difficulty is the use of *praepositus* in the R Aug. Is it a question of a real superior, or, as Steidle suggests,[16] of the representative of the real superior, who would be the *presbyter*, priest or bishop, perhaps Augustine himself? Let us state the question more precisely: there is no doubt that, according to R Aug, the *praepositus* is subordinate to the *presbyter*. We may ask, however, if it is this subordination, which is signified in the mind of Augustine and of his readers by the term *praepositus* itself—the term which already indicates the post of second-in-command—or whether the *praepositus* is truly the monastic superior, the master of the house, to whom the *presbyter* would issue orders from outside, as one who held ecclesiastical rather than monastic authority.

This last interpretation seems to us much nearer to the facts. The *presbyter* never appears alone in the R Aug, but always in the company of the *praepositus* whom he caps, so to speak, with his higher authority. On the other hand, the *praepositus* time and again intervenes alone, obviously performing the function of a superior.[17] It is he who is designated by the synonymous expression *ipse qui uobis praeest* in R Aug 15.193–194, which introduces the directory for the superior.[18] Elsewhere Augustine seems to be unaware of the name *abbas*:[19] *praepositus* is used in his writings as the title of the head of the monastic community. We ought not, therefore, to pay any attention to the interpretations of R Aug 15 given by R Caes V 35 and R Tar 23, both of which—apparently independently—substitute for *presbyter* the characteristic term for the monastic superior (*mater* in Caesarius, *abbas* in the R Tar), thus making the *praepositus* a genuine abbot's lieutenant, a 'second-in-command' in RB. For Augustine, the *praepositus* is still 'the man who takes the first place'—even though his lay status makes him subordinate to a priest —who settles difficult cases once and for all. Nothing indicates that the word has lost some of its force, on account of the fact of this subordination, although such a situation could have contributed to the altered meaning, which we shall establish in the later terminology.

To sum up, the first generation of Latin monastic writers employs *praepositus* with the meaning of head or 'the man who takes the first place'.[20] In Jerome, it is a question of his being head of a group within the community, the superior of the community being normally called *pater*; yet on occasion *praepositus* may even be applied to the superior of the monastery. We meet these same two accepted meanings again in Cassian: the *praepositus* is a dean, but the term can replace *abbas*, which is the proper name for the head of the community. In Augustine, *praepositus* no longer means dean, except in *De moribus ecclesiae*, which derives from Jerome; in the R Aug it is a question of his being the head of the monastery, the genuine superior, though subordinate to a priest; Augustine does not use any other term, such as *abbas*, to designate him.[21] In all these sources, *praepositus* signifies 'the man who takes the first place'. As for the second-in-command, neither Cassian nor Augustine makes any mention of him, and Jerome calls him only *secundus*.

As opposed to these early data, the terminology current in the sixth century exhibits a marked difference. In that terminology *praepositus* means the second-in-command, the abbot's lieutenant. This meaning has already appeared in a narrative by Gregory of Tours (VP 18.1), obviously composed at the end of the century, but which relates events, which happened during the reign of Alaric (485–507).[22] Caesarius of Arles,[23] Aurelian,[24] and Ferreolus,[25] all speak in the same way of the *praeposita* or *praepositus* as a unique officer for the whole monastery, coming immediately after the *abbatissa* or the *abbas*, and eventually succeeding the latter. It is also in this sense, it seems that we must understand what the biographer of Fulgentius has to tell us on the subject of the *frater qui praepositi gerebat officium* (*Vita Fulgentii* 52) in his monastery in Sardinia at the time of St Benedict. As we see, RB is well placed in this first half of the sixth century, when a good number of testimonies from various sources furnish the same meaning of *praepositus* = the second-in-command.

For the last half of the century, we may cite, in addition to Ferreolus, whom we have previously mentioned, Gregory of Tours[26] and Pope St Gregory the Great. It happens that the latter on occasion calls the second-in-command *secundus*,[27] but this is no more than an exceptional synonym for *praepositus* the term employed, furthermore, to designate the abbot's lieutenant.[28] In the seventh century, Isidore of Seville and Fructuosus of Braga will uniformly employ *praepositus* in the same sense; for the function of dean, which turns up again in both these authors, the term used is *decanus*, as in RB.

From the beginning of the sixth century, therefore, there appears a constant practice of calling the second-in-command of the *abbas praepositus*. The terminology as regards the two highest grades of the of the cenobitic hierarchy shows a great regularity of usage: *abbas* and *praepositus* seem as firmly in possession of their meanings as 'abbot' and 'prior' are with us today. About *praepositus* in the singular there can be neither hesitation nor possible ambiguity of expression; in the plural *praepositi* is still often employed, as in the preceding period, to designate 'the superiors' taken as a whole, that is, the abbot and his subordinate officers.

We therefore find ourselves faced with two different meanings of *praepositus* in monastic language, one, which is affirmed in the oldest documents, the other, which has prevailed since the beginning of the sixth century. Before investigating the causes which could have produced this evolution, we must examine, one by one, some texts which are difficult to interpret, on account of either the uncertainty of their readings or their date of composition, or their composite character.

The *Ordo monasterii*, appended to the R Aug, provides us with two instances of *praepositus* in the singular (6.25 and 7.28). In the first case, one has the primary impression of finding oneself before the 'second-in-command' after the superior, the latter apparently being designated in the same sentence by the word *pater*. If this impression were correct we should have to admit that from before the time of Caesarius (R Caes V draws on OM), and perhaps from the first half of the fifth century, *praepositus* had the meaning of 'second-in-command', which prevailed in the subsequent century. The OM, annexed to R Aug, would thus belong, from the point of view of terminology, not to the group, to which R Aug belongs and to which it is appended but to that of the later documents, which make use of it. However, OM 7.28 assigns to the *praepositus* the role role of seeing that the brethren lack nothing during meals, a role which in Cassian belongs to the dean.[30] On the other hand, we could understand *praepositus* in 6.25 as a synonym for *pater*, which preceded it; the author would employ both terms to designate the same personage, the superior.[31] These doubts are not easily dispelled, on account of the extreme conciseness of the document.

As for the R 4 Pat, a fundamental study by Anscari Mundó has just made it possible for us to include this text in the present historical survey of the word *praepositus*.[32] The oldest recension of this rule, dating from the second half of the fifth century, gave to the superior the title *is qui praeest*, in basilian fashion, a reading found in the text of St Benedict of Aniane printed by Holste-Brockie and by Migne. An Italian recension, of which the sole manuscript witness for us is Par. Lat. 12205, has changed *is qui praeest* into *praepositus*. So it is clear that in the milieu where manuscript P of RM was copied, *praepositus* still retained its old meaning of 'superior', an inference that we shall soon make by examining RM itself. The same manuscript designates the second-in-command by the periphrasis *qui post eum est in ordine* (1.179–180), whereas the primitive text carries the reading of *secundum*.[33] This last fact shows that R 4 Pat was composed in a milieu, which was not as yet unaware of the recent meaning of *praepositus* = the second-in-command, which accords perfectly with the date of composition proposed by Mundó.

With the *Regula Macarii* we are concerned with a composite document in which *praepositus* offers us two clear and distinct meanings: in Chapter 7, a simple repetition of Lr 125 of Jerome, the *praepositus monasterii* is none other than the superior, as we have said above. He is also called *senior* (Chapters 4 and 12) and *qui praeest* (Chapter 18). Chapter 27, on the contrary, draws a distinction between *abbas* and *praepositus*, without being able to say whether the latter is leader of a group (a species of dean) or the abbot's lieutenant over the whole community.

We must carefully take into consideration this same composite character, when we examine the *Regula Orientalis*. For want of paying attention to it, the *Concordia* and Kassius Hallinger (p 302, § 4) have confused the distinctive meanings of *praepositus* in this rule. First, the R Or is a cento of Pachomian texts: the *praepositus* in these passages borrowed from R Pac is head of a house. Such is notably the case with the long catalogue of faults (R Or 17 # R Pac Inst 18), which we reviewed in the directories of the superior and which, notwithstanding the *Concordia* and Hallinger, teach us scarcely anything about the idea which the author of R Or had of the *praepositus*, in the Benedictine sense of the term.

On the other hand, some important indications can be gathered from the parts peculiar to R Or. Chapter 3, of course, presents a genuine lieutenant of the abbot, installed by him with the consent of the brethren, presiding over all the activity of the monastery, and enjoying full power in the absence of the abbot. Few texts so clearly designate the second-in-command. Now, this personage is called *ille qui . . . fratribus praepositus est* and *senior monasterii qui fratribus praepositus est*. It is curious that in the other parts peculiar to the R Or and notably in the long sequence consisting of Chapters 22 to 30, this *praepositus* is never again mentioned.[34] On the other hand, we may also wonder whether he is distinct from the two *seniores* described in Chapter 2. However that may be, we must especially note that, even in Chapter 3, he is designated by a periphrasis, in which *praepositus* is treated as a participle and not as a substantive. If therefore R Or is already acquainted with *praepositus* in the sense of abbot's lieutenant, the acceptance of such a meaning is not yet so familiar that one could use the word purely and simply as a noun: an explanatory periphrasis is required. It may be that we have been present here at the birth of the more recent meaning, with which the text continues to juxtapose the old meaning in the passages borrowed from R Pac.

As for the two little *Rules of the Fathers* (R Pat 2 and R Pat 3), the article by Mundó, to which reference has been made above, shows both of them as dependent at one and the same time on the R Pat £ and the R Mac.[35] The R Pat ° twice mentions a *praepositus* (Pref and Chapter 1), who is subordinate to the *sacerdos*, rather as in R Aug. There is no reason for seeing in this personage the second-in-command of the abbot,[36] since the *abbas* is never named. This *praepositus* must be rather the chief superior, the man who is called *qui praeest* in Chapter 7. It was thus that *Par. Lat.* 12634, which substitutes *abbas* for *praepositus*, understood it. The R

Pat 2 therefore bears witness to the acceptance of the old meaning of *praepositus*. Now this rule appears to date from the end of the fifth century or the beginning of the sixth. On the other hand, the R Pat 3, which must be slightly later than the Council of Agde in 506, calls the superior *abbas* and designates a subordinate officer, who is perhaps the second-in-command of the abbot, as *praepositus*, as the expression *abbas vel praepositus* suggests (Chapters 6 and 9), but perhaps also as the head of a *decania*. There is the same uncertainty here, as in the parts peculiar to R Mac.

So then, while R Pat 4 and R pat 2 remain faithful to the old terminology, it is possible that OM, R Mac, and R Pat 3 set a new meaning before us. In R Or, this meaning is certain, but it is still wrapped up in an explanatory periphrasis and linked with survivals of the word in its old meaning. Between the two groups, which are defined clearly by their characteristics, and which we distinguished at the beginning, we find this third group lying between them from the point of view of time as well as of terminology. When we have mentioned a Latin fragment from the records of the Council of Chalcedon,[37] as well as the rules of Columban, which on this point, as on many others, are linked with antiquity, without bearing the imprint of the development of Latin monasticism, we shall have collected the principal indications, which are going to allow us to place RM and RB in the setting of this history of the term *praepositus*.

As we have already noticed, RB belongs to the recent group, assigned to the sixth century. As for the Master, he is completely unaware of *praepositus* in the sense of the abbot's second-in-command over the whole community. This office, which inspires in him the prejudices, of which we are already aware, has for its title *secundus* or *secundarius*, or again, after his abbatial 'ordination', *nouus abba*. As for the *praepositi*, they are in RM the two brothers set over each group of ten monks. These two group-leaders seem to be real colleagues, between whom an order of precedence and authority seems scarcely to exist: they share the responsibility.[39] Their group is called a *decada*. These data appear to take us back to a pre-sixth century period before *praepositus* came to be applied to the abbot's lieutenant. The Master's usage is comparable to Lr 22.35 of Jerome and the *De moribus ecclesiae* of Augustine, where *praepositus* serves to explain *decanus*, as well as to Cassian, *Inst* 4.7–10, where *praepositus* replaces the absent word *decanus*.[40] The novelty in relation to those authors is that the Master speaks of two *praepositi* and not just one. We think immediately of the pachomian institution of the seond-in-command of a house, who doubles for the *praepositus domus*. However, the Master does not seem to be thinking of this precedent, and his terminology does not include *secundus* in that sense. It seems rather that, in his concern to assure a continual supervision of the *decania*, 41 the Master has duplicated the *praepositus* by a colleague of the same rank without thinking of establishing a hierarchy between them. These two *praepositi* are therefore chiefs on an equal footing. The meaning of *praepositus* in RM is indeed in conformity with the original use of the term.[42]

Thus, if we consider only this semantic detail, RM seems to belong to an earlier period than RB. The latter has corrected the Master's terminology by reserving to the abbot's lieutenant the title *praepositus*, which became current in this sense in the sixth century, and by giving to the heads of the *decaniae* (are there one or two per group?) the title *decani*, which in Jerome was presented as a synonym for *praepositus*.

A second proof becomes possible, if we observe the destiny of *secundus*. This term, one can surmise, has known the opposite fate from that of *praepositus*. At first it was alone in designating the 'second,' as was normal (recall the terminology of *Pachomiana Latina*, to which we called attention above), it was eclipsed in the West by *praepositus* when the latter lost the meaning of chief and assumed that of lieutenant. *Secundus* is still found in one R 4 Pat recension,[43] but henceforth it appears only sporadically, as a synonym for its rival *praepositus*, which triumphs from now on. It is thus that Gregory the Great speaks on one exceptional occasion of the *secundus* of the foundation in Terracina.[44] Also we may cite an isolated mention by St Columban,[45] and in the eighth century a passage in the *Ordo Romanus* 15, § 145. As for the texts of Justinian, although it cannot be said they speak of the second,[46] it is certain that their manner of numbering the community elders recalls the terminology we have studied, inasmuch as they ignore *praepositus* as a designation from him who comes after the abbot.

With Justinian, however, we find ourselves as much in oriental territory as on Latin soil.[47] Now, in the East, the substitution of *praepositus* for *secundus* never arose, for the good reason that *praepositus* is a Latin word, and that its equivalent *proëstôs* has continued, on an equal footing with other terms, to designate the superior.[48] The equivalents for *secundus* have therefore continued to designate the second, the abbot's lieutenant. Although Basil has as yet no proper name to characterize this function (LR 45 speaks only of a *heteros* to be associated with the superior), Palladius mentions, in the pachomian milieu, a *deuteros*[49] assisting the Father of the monastery, which confirms the indications of *Pachomiana Latina* on the *secundus*. Theodoret makes use of equivalent periphrases[50] which recure with variations in Theodore the Studite.[51] According to De Meester, these expressions have remained valid in Byzantine monasticism down to our own day.[52] The East has therefore adhered faithfully to a terminology which, in the west, became almost totally effaced, as *praepositus* came to apply to the 'second.'

As we can see, RM displays a certain archaic character in relation to RB (which ignores *secundus*), when it calls the abbot's assistant *secundus* or *secundarius*; and it does that not in passing or as an exception, but habitually.[53] This usage corresponds with that of *praepositus* for designating not the 'second' but the head of the *decania* both cases, RM shows itself earlier in date than RB. It belongs to the intermediate category, and more precisely to the least developed documents of this category, those which preserve the old terminology. Furthermore it is not possible, on the basis of these data, to compile an accurate chronological table.

There remains to be answered a question which must have occurred more than once to the reader: how did *praepositus* come to mean the 'second?' A double series of hypotheses should be considered. The first takes *praepositus* in the sense of superior of the monastery as its point of departure, the other takes *praepositus* in the sense of head of the house or the *decania*.

1. As 'head of the monastery,' *praepositus* competed from earliest times with several equivalents: *princeps, pater, maior, senior,* to cite only the principal ones. *Abbas* especially very quickly took priority in the West over every other name for the superior. The term, in the sense of head of a *coenobium*, is already current in Sulpicius Severus and Cassian, and the oldest Western counciliar text which discusses monastic issues (Council of Arles, *c.* 455) calls the abbot of Lérins *abbas*, as though it were a question of this title being official from that time onwards. In the sixth century, *abbas,* without eliminating all its competitors, is nevertheless the

term which is by far the most common. This promotion of *abbas* as the official title meant that the term *praepositus* was set free for other use.

On the other hand, it is possible that the situation of the *praepositus* in the R Aug, where he is subordinate to the priest, contributed to the evollution of the expansion. Let us recall how Caesarius of Arles and R Tar utilized R Aug. At a period when the superior was no longer officially called anything except *abbas* and when his authority had been recognized as exempt from the intervention of the ecclesiastical hierarchy,[54] it became natural to substitute the name *abbas* for the augustinian *presbyter*. As a result, the *praepositus*, who for Augustine was the real superior, came to figure as a subordinate officer. Since Caesarius was as ignorant of the decanal system as was R Aug, this dignitary, whose name is in the singular, seemed from then on to designate the second-ranking superior of the entire community. Such is at least one of the causes which could have become operative in the development that we are trying to explain.

2. As 'head of the house' or of the *decania*, the *praepositus* was already subordinate to the superior of the moanstery. It was adequate when the community was too small to divide into several *decaniae*, or when the decanal system was not practised, as can be observed, for example, in the parts peculiar to R Or, that the term should be applied, in the singular, to a single subordinate officer for the whole community, that is to say, to the abbot's 'second in command'. On the other hand, where the decanal system did exist, tradition offered a term quite close in meaning as a substitute for *praepositus*: *decanus*.

These hypotheses are of interest not only for suggesting how *praepositus* could have proceeded towards its more recent sense of 'Second'. In addition, they emphasize a fact, of which it is important to be aware before we bring this semantic study to an end: a close connection exists between the two senses of *praepositus*, which we have distinguished. Although by virtue of its etymology and its originally accepted meaning, the word indicates superiority, this superiority can itself be subjected to a still higher authority; and in fact, *praepositus* in the sense of subordinate superior is at least as frequent among the first monastic generation as that of the supreme head. Inversely, the 'Second' is not only the first of the abbot's subjects: he is an officer and a 'head', even though he is not 'set over' a distinct group, but over the whole community, of which the abbot is the superior. This meaning of the word appears clearly in R Or 3, which is, of course, the earliest evidence for *praepositus* in the sense of 'second': this personage is designated there by the periphrasis *qui fratribus praepositus est*, in which his authority is stressed.

There would therefore be no need to harden, by setting them in opposition to each other, the distinctions, which we have drawn and which our exposition has perhaps delineated too sharply, for the sake of greater clarity.[55] There remain however, sufficient differences between the two meanings of the word, and these two different meanings can be assigned quite clearly to separate periods, which it is possible to define, in order that one may be in a position to place RM and RB in relation to each other, according to the terminology which they use in dealing with the question.

THE FUNCTION OF THE *PRAEPOSITUS*

The foregoing semantic study has permited us to pick out the texts, which really do bear upon the Benedictine 'provost,' that is, the abbot's lieutenant, whether he is called *praepositus* or *secundus*. It remains to draw upon this documentation to construct a history of his office and place the legislation of RB 65 within this history.

By way of introduction, we need to form as precise an idea as possible of the RB doctrine in this chapter, by comparing it with that of its immediate source, which is the RM. In the preceding chapter we presented the motives which have been set forth by the Master for categorically rejecting the Second. Two points from among those considerations deserve emphasis: first, the fear that the Master has of seeing his Second eaten up with haughtiness and pride and transgressing the precepts of the rule.[56] Secondly, it is necessary to note the intimate bond which, in the Master's mind, unites the office of Second to the abbatial succession: if the abbot is to avoid creating a Second, the reason is precisely because he would thereby be designating his successor. And if finally, in Chapter 93, the Master nonetheless envisages the existence of an abbot's lieutenant, it is occasioned solely by the anticipation of a fortuitous event, which could occur in the procedure for appointing a successor. On the supposition that the abbot, having designated upon his deathbed the heir to his power and having had him 'ordained' by the bishop, comes to regain his health and continue to live, it becomes necessary to regulate the destiny of the new abbot and his relationship with the *prior et uerus abbas*. In this way there came to be inserted, in the treatise on succession, a treatise on the Second.[57] But this is no more than the unwanted consequence of an untoward event. The Second is introduced in RM only through a chance episode in the procedure for appointing a successor; and it is already as abbot that he exercises his office. In today's canonical language he would be called quite precisely, 'coadjutor abbot,' were it not for the fact that the Master takes good care to maintain him in absolute dependence on the old abbot and gives the latter every right to depose him, should he become displeased with him.

One sees, consequently, how RB stands in relation to this legislation. It is at once both very close and quite distant. The two rules are in agreement as regards the same basic attitude of misgiving towards the Second, an attitude based on the same motives: one suspects that the abbot's lieutenant will succumb to arrogance, disobedience to the rule, and independence in relation to the abbot. The Master and St Benedict still agree in the link that they establish between the treatise on the second and that on abbatial succession. But on this point, we already encounter a divergence: whereas the Master looks upon the Second as the designated successor of the abbot, RB considers the provostship for its own sake, independently of any to the succession right.[58] Although in RB the question of the provost is associated with the ordination of the abbot, the bond is altogether different from that in RM. The legislator wants to check the custom which allows the bishop and neighboring abbots to ordain at the same time and *ex aequo* the abbot and the provost. Here we have an entirely new consideration for which the RM had made no provision. The Master never indeed envisaged that the Second might be designated by anyone other than the abbot. On the contrary, RB opposes a prevalent custom, which imposes on the abbot a provost ordained by the same authorities who had ordained him. Thus RM connects the Second with the abbatial succession, because it sees in him the future abbot, whereas RB does so because it fears that the provost might be ordained on an equal footing with the new abbot.

Another difference, clearer still: the Master is opposed to the designation of a Second as long as the abbot is not at the point of death. The situation of a permanent Second under an abbot, who governs the monastery, does not arise save in an abnormal case. There is a Second, only by accident and then he is an abbot-elect. On the other hand, RB envisages, though with some reluctance, the creation of a provost, while the abbot is in good health and without any reference to his death.

In other words, unlike RM, RB admits an abbot's lieutenant who owes his existence not to a chance episode in the succession but to reasons of expediency: *si aut locus expetit, aut congregatio petierit . . . et abbas judicauerit expedire* (RB 65:14). The categorical refusal of the Master is therefore, reduced in RB to a semi-platonic wish: *si potest fieri* (vs. 12). The redactor is resigned to the establishment of the office of provost, which he would have preferred to avoid, and he takes measures at least to restrict the havoc that it could cause. At the period and in the milieu in which RB is set, the rejection of the provost is no longer possible. The RB redactor has had to come to terms with circumstances, which make him a quasi-necessity: *si locus expetit* (vs 14), and also with the wishes of the lower ranks, *aut congregatio petierit* (ibid.). These two expressions inevitably remind one of the *secundum modum congregationis aut positionem loci*, which determines, in RB 35:4, the concession of reinforcements for the weekly kitchen helpers. As in the last passage, the issue here probably turns on the greater number of the community, with the increase of work, which it imposes on both superiors and cooks. The abbot, too, should be granted reinforcements so that he may ensure better service in the interest of the brethren.

Note in passing how the brethren voice their demand: here again is a feature unknown to the Master, accustomed as he was to regulating everything by his own authority. Without compromising the independence of the abbot, who remains sole judge in this matter just as in those handled in council, this petition by the community does at least show that he has to reckon still more with the wish of his subjects; the legislator's will is no longer the sole determining factor.[59]

The principle of government solely through the mediation of the deans, which the Master upheld so strongly, and the maxim *ut dum pluribus committitur unus non superbiat*, which expresses his thought so exactly (RB 65:13), are therefore disparaged. Although just as anxious as the Master to safeguard the abbatial prerogative, the RB redactor had to yield on this point and be satisfied with waging war against an abuse unknown to RM: ordination of the provost *ex aequo* together with his abbot. The fact that he had to envisage such an anomaly and combat it with such vigor is a new indication that the prestige of the abbot is nolonger quite the same as in the milieu of the Master.[60] The battles between abbot and provost point in the same direction. The Master knew of dissensions just as serious, as we may gather from the words *scandala . . . partibus*,[61] but according to him, they arise only while the abbatial throne is vacant, when the monks are left with the responsibility of electing the abbot, and not, as here, between an abbot and his lieutenant.

Finally, we can notice, in the same sense, the express mention of the 'council of the brethren who fear God' (vs 15; this probably means the 'elders' of the limited council described at the end of RB 3). Certainly the institution of the council, at least in its plenary form, is well known to the Master, from whom RB borrowed it. But mention of it here comes as a double surprise for the reader familiar with RM: first, because it concerns the council in its restricted form, which is peculiar to RB; secondly because the object of deliberation is the designation of the Second, a matter which is entirely reserved to the abbot in RM (the Master even wishes that this designation should be made by surprise in such a way that no one could suspect on whom the choice of the abbot will settle). Therefore this clause on the council also marks a divergence from RM in the sense that the preponderant position of the abbot meets with more competition. Not that the RB redactor is less jealous of the abbot's authority; but the situation of the first superior is no longer so strong, and the legislator has to take note of this state of affairs either by rejecting practices of which he has been a witness (*ordination ex aequo*; battles between abbot and provost) or by reluctantly yielding to a tendency too powerful to be suppressed (establishment of the *praepositura*), or finally by accepting without protest interventions arising from the lower ranks of the brethren and unknown to the Master (community petition and council of elders).

It is not until the end of the RB chapter that the same flexibility is shown (RB 65:16–22). One's first impression is to believe that one hears a simple echo of RM 93:69–90, where the same line of conduct had been laid down for the second-in-command, with similar threats of deposition. Moreover, it is of minor importance that RB specifies in *usque quater* (vs 18) the number of warnings which the abbot ought to address to the culprit, and adds the *correptio disciplinae regularis* (vs 19) before proceeding to the deposition. But it is significant that the deposed provost is immediately replaced by 'someone who is worthy of the office' (vs 20.Thus the *praepositura* does not remain vacant and the unfortunate experience will have offered no pretext for abolishing the office, so true is it that there can no longer be any question of dispensing with it. The Master, for his part, was careful not to provide on the spot a replacement for the deposed second-in-command. Faithful to his principles, he profited from the deposition of the office-holder to leave a vacancy until the abbot should again be in danger of death, which would render it necessary once again to designate his successor (RM 93:83).

As for the provost removed from office, RB goes so far as to anticipate that he will not be 'wise and obedient', and that in consequence, he will have to be expelled from the monastery. This eventuality has not even been foreseen by the Master either: once he is deposed, he no longer speaks of the second-in-command. One may detect in this ultimate reversal of fortune, added by RB, an indication of difficulties more serious than those that were in RM, probably because the abbot is less assured of being obeyed.[62] Lastly, the abbot is invited to bear in mind the judgment of God, 'for fear lest the flame of envy or jealousy sear his soul' (RB 65: 22). This caution, which had already been sounded in the preceding chapter (RB 64:16), is likewise missing in the Master. The latter is hardly accustomed to envisage faults on the part of the abbot or provosts. The mention that we find here in RB reveals therefore in its own fashion a diminution of the prestige of the abbot. The importance of the provost is henceforth sufficient to be able to arouse not only fears that he will attempt to assert his independence (something that the Master had already foreseen), but also pangs of jealousy towards him on the part of the abbot; and the legislator has not such a high opinion of the abbot that he takes account of his fears and does not depict his superior as liable to sink so low.[63]

Such are the features which differentiate the legislation of RB when it is compared with that of RM. The major fact, which deserves emphasis, is the acceptance by RB of the *praepositura*, that is of a real office of lieutenant to the abbot as distinct from all prospect of the succession. This institutional fact corresponds with the linguistic fact, to which we have previously called attention: RB itself goes along with the usage of giving *praepositus* the meaning of Second rather than of dean, which was known only to the Master. Thus, on the level of institutions as well as of terminology, the RB enables us to be present at the advent of the 'provost'.

Having analyzed the respective doctrines of RM and RB on the abbot's lieutenant, it remains for us to take a comprehensive view of the history of this office, so as to see it in the perspectives of our two rules. This we shall do by applying ourselves first to the ordination of the provost (by whom is he instituted?) and then to the functions which devolve upon him.

The first question is the only one which interests the RB redactor. He devotes almost half his chapter to it (vss 3–11, 14–15), opposing with all his might the custom of ordaining the provost *ex aequo* together with the abbot. Can we rediscover examples of such a practice in history? Steidle recalls here, not without reason, the mode of designating officers in the Pachomian congregation.[64] In fact it was the superior general, who appointed brethren to all the offices in each of the monasteries of the congregation[65] and, at least so far as Pachomius' own monastery is concerned, we know that he designated the head of the house and his Second together.[66] In all likelihood the Second in command of the head of each monastery was appointed similarly, *ex aequo* with his abbot. Here then we have attested from the beginnings a certain form of the abuse of which the RB complains.

But we shall meet it still more clearly in the milieu of Gregory the Great. He—what irony!—attributes to St Benedict in person the simultaneous nomination of the abbot of Terracina and of his Second.[67] On this point, the commentators have not failed to look for a reconciliation by supposing, for example, that the foundation at Terracina dated back to a period when the saint had not yet known the distressing experiences which have been summarized in RB 65. Whatever the worth of these hypotheses, it is certain that Gregory reports the deed as something self-evident, and at least two other passages in his correspondence show him acting in almost the same way.

In Lr 11.48, he gives as abbot of 'his' monastery at Palermo the priest Domitius, giving him 'for his comfort' a *praepositus* named Lucifer. The purpose of this joint appointment is to replace the abbot Bonus and the provost Catellus in these offices, both of whom had also been designated by the same authority, that of the abbot Urbicus, Gregory's official agent for his Sicilian foundations. Neither Urbicus nor Gregory seem to have given a thought to the opinion of the local abbot when they assigned him a provost by their authority. In any case, it is indeed from outside the monastery and by the same persons who have named the abbot that this provost has received investiture.

A similar departure from the norm of RB 65 is encountered in Lr 5.6: in another Palermo monastery: the abbot, Gregory by name, who had to be deposed because of 'the almost complete ruin of his community,' finds himself authorized to resume his office after a long period of penitence; but since his 'negligence' is still a cause for wariness, the pope orders Urbicus to provide a monk *qui ei praepositus fiat, ut quod istius incuria negligitur, illius sollicitudine seruetur*. Thus this abbot of Palermo sees himself in double harness with a provost imposed on him by an outside authority and for the avowed purpose of counterbalancing him.

All these examples drawn from the writings of Gregory the Great bring us face to face with the abuse denounced by the RB. Yet it is not necessary, in his view, that this practice should be imposed everywhere. When the pope has no particular reason to intervene, he limits himself to sending a subject whom the local abbot himself will institute (Lr 3.3), or else he contents himself with encouraging the abbot to appoint a provost, leaving him to choose a capable man from his community (Lr 7.10). This last solution, defended so strenuously by the RB, is in fact that which is attested by the greatest number of documents, which have come down to us. Let us cite Basil (Gr 45.1: nomination by the superior, with the advice of wise brethren), R Or 3 (the abbot 'ordains' with the assent of all the brethren), and Gregory of Tours, who depicts the abbot Ursus establishing provosts in his foundations in Berry and Touraine.[68] Other Western rules do not specify *who* appoints the provost, but one may believe that it is the abbot, in the same way as he does the other officers of the monastery, without there being any need to state something which is explicitly self-evident. We may therefore take what we read in R Or as being the common norm.

Thus RB, in claiming for the abbot the right to designate his provost, is probably only affirming a traditional rule, which has been disparaged as a result of some relatively recent abuses, the abnormal nature of which is keenly felt. Herwegen exaggerates when he represents St Benedict as 'fully conscious of breaking with a tradition which is at the same time a well established institution, and blazing a new trail . . . He has by his own authority withdrawn nomination of the prior from episcopal control and from the influence of neighboring abbots, and thereby greatly strengthened the authority of the abbot within the confines of his own monastery.'[69] This would be to attribute to the RB legislation an originality and a reformative power, which is contradicted both by the existence of the precedents, to which we have referred above, and by the persistence of the contrary usage at the time of Gregory the Great.

In reality RB has not introduced an innovation on this point, and its protests against ordination *ex aequo* had, so far as we know, no repercussions in Gregorian circles. Rather than isolate the RB legislation and magnify its importance, it seems more reasonable to look upon it as one step in the proceedings instituted between the abbacy and the ecclesiastical authority on the subject of the government of monasteries—proceedings which began as early as the middle of the fifth century and continued indefinitely beyond the time of St Benedict. When Benedict lays down the principle: *in abbatis pendere arbitrio ordinationem monasterii sui* (vs 11), he may indeed be speaking in his own name (*nos uidimus expedire*, ibid.) and citing motives gleaned from his own experience (*propter pacis caritatisque custodiam*), but he is doing nothing more than repeating almost word for word the decree of the Council of Arles (c. 455), which we have cited several times already: *laica omnis monasterii congregatio ad solam et liberam abbatis proprii . . . ordinationem . . . pertineat.*[70] This clash between the authority of abbots and of clergy, of which the rather monotonous vicissitudes can be followed in the minutes of the Council of Carthage (525 and 536), the *Vita Fulgentii*, and the correspondence of Gregory himself, has to take, in the particular environment of the RB redactor, the form envisaged here: the bishop took advantage of the occasion, which the abbatial ordination offered, to ordain the provost at the same time and thus assure himself of greater authority in the house.

This abuse, as we have said, seems to be quite recent and, it should perhaps be added, quite local in its scope, since we find no trace of it (with regard to episcopal intervention) before RB. Significantly RM, which energetically contests all 'sacerdotal' encroachment upon the domain of the abbot (Chapter 83), and especially concerning the monastic 'ordination', makes no allusion in this respect to the office of Second. It is in the period between the RM and the RB redactions that the events occurred, which RB so deplores. The abuse developed during and after the time of St Benedict to such an extent that it no longer caused any scruples for St Gregory, at least when it was a matter of his personal intervention in the appointment of a provost. We shall return to the causes of such interventions, which would have come to be regarded as normal.

It is therefore likely that, in the RB redactor's milieu, the ordination of the provost was the particular point upon which the episcopal claim to rule the monastery concentrated. In this light, the redaction of the RB resembles all those of which we have spoken when analyzing Chapters 60 and 62, and the affirmations of the exclusive right of the abbot to designate his provost is but a particular case of the general principle laid down by the Councils of Arles and Carthage, and by Gregory himself (when it is an issue of the encroachments of the bishops of Ravenna, for example).[71]

However, we must admit that this interpretation is not obvious. Here, RB does not reprove the *sacerdos* (vs 3) for any intention to dominate. To tell the truth, we are not told why the bishop acts like this; the redactor is satisfied with denouncing the practice, without casting any light on its causes and its significance. Moreover, the bishop is not the only guilty party; the abbots previously mentioned in RB 64:4 participate with him in the ordination of the Provost, which constitutes an abuse. These facts urge us not to use the hypothesis suggested above, except with considerable reservations.

What seems in any case to arise from this abuse described by RB is the importance accruing to the provost at this period. If this personage regarded himself as 'a second abbot' (vs 2), it is for the most part because such indeed, in the eyes of those who ordained him, is his status in the monastery. The role that he actually enjoys in the community life is so considerable that one does not think of having made serious provision for the government of the house, so long as he has not been installed alongside the abbot. The right to ordain the abbot has been extended to the ordination of the provost, only because the latter, in some respect, played the part of an abbot-colleague, indispensable for the running of the monastery.

Moreover, we are aware of the situation of the 'second abbot' not only through RM, where it is presented only by chance, but also through an allusion, which Cassiodorous makes, to the two abbots of Vivarium,[72] and above all, through two very explicit passages of the *Vita Fulgentii.*[73] Thus, at the time of St Benedict, a dual system of government was sometimes practised in the monasteries of Africa. Though perfect harmony seems to have reigned between the two young abbots, Felix and Fulgentius, one occupying himself chiefly with practical matters, the other with instructing the brethren, and vying with one another in their obedience to each other. All the same, Fulgentius was ultimately called to the abbacy by Felix himself, with the assent of the brethren, according to a procedure, which the RB redactor would not have censured, and we may conjecture how examples such as these could provide dangerous suggestions for certain provosts.

It is not by chance that the same *Vita Fulgentii* reports to us, a little further on,[74] the difficulties that this abbot-bishop had with his provost in his sardinian community. In this life of a contemporary of St Benedict we sharply perceive the tendency, which then existed, to 'duplicate' the abbacy, and the temptations to insubordination resulting from it for the provost. But this will appear clearer still when we have answered our second question: what are the powers of the provost?

In this respect, two series of functions fulfilled by the Second are to be distinguished: on the one hand he shares the abbot's powers, and on the other, he has certain functions of his own. Moreover, this distinction falls far short of being rigorous and easy to put into effect. What we shall call 'his own functions' are perhaps nothing more, in many cases, than a part of the abbatial responsibility, which the abbot has delegated once and for all to his lieutenant. Also it is far from being the case that all the texts bear witness to these two series of functions at the same time. Let us nevertheless try, with the help of this classification, to trace the history of his function.

For Basil, the Second (who has as yet no name, not even that of Second) appears uniquely as a substitute for the superior in his absences. Such absences, Basil tells us, are frequent either for reasons of illness, or for the necessity to travel, or for quite another motive. Basil is particularly anxious to avoid such absences causing a turn towards a 'democracy'. Someone must be a substitute for the superior in 'the care of the brethren', that is to say, someone responsible for the ministry of the word, either within the fraternity or among the guests, in such a way that this function is not left to the indiscreet zeal and anarchical initiative of any stray person.

In the Pachomian milieu, this role of replacement for the absent abbotis again well attested.[75] But one speaks still more often of 'collaboration', and of 'service',[76] things which ought to be understood to be as much certain functions shared together with the abbot and exercised conjointly with him,[77] as special prerogatives, which seem to devolve upon the Second alone, without involving the head of the monastery.[78]

We would here call attention to a rather surprising fact: Cassian never speaks of the Second. Should we infer that this function did not exist in the egyptian monasteries that he visited towards the close of the fourth century? We have, however, for the same period, the testimony of Palladius, who twice speaks of the Second of the monastery.[79] It is therefore probable that Cassian's silence is an omission: the role played by the Second was too closely involved with that of the abbot for the author of the *Institutes* and *Conferences* to have felt the need to make distinct mention of it in works, which make no claim to depict the organization of the egyptian *coenobia* in all its details.

An analogous reason no doubt explains the absence of the Second in Jerome's description of the cenobites (Lr 22.35). Nor does Jerome make any further mention of the Second in the new description which he composed in 404, in his preface to the rule of Pachomius. Yet he surely knew of the existence of this office during that period, since it appears ten times in the rule. There are therefore reasons of a literary order—care not to weigh down the exposition by mentioning a function judged—rightly—to be of secondary importance—which account for the very strong probability for the absence of the Second in Cassian and Jerome. Perhaps we should attach greater significance to the case of the Acoemetae, in which Hallinger notes the same absence.[80]

In other words, it seems to us difficult to assert, on the basis of the silence of the texts, that there were no Seconds in all the monasteries of Egypt and Syria. The example of the preface to the pachomian rule, where this silence certainly indicates an omission, should make us extremely circumspect in our interpretation of other documents, which exhibit the same lacuna. The only conclusion, which seems to present itself, in this case, is that the function of the Second attracted little attention either because the abbot was scarcely ever absent or because the powers peculiar to the Second were little developed. In fact, the powers described in the pachomian rule are quite insignificant,[81] although here it is only the question of Second in the house. The rule is completely silent on the Second in command of the entire monastery, though the *Vies*

Grecques and his existence is vouched for not only by Palladius, but even by the *Liber Orsiesii,*[82] a Latin work belonging to the same group of records as the rule. These remarks would tend to prove that the Second was a personage, who was somewhat in eclipse in these circles.

Yet there is one very remarkable instance where a Second displayed an activity of considerable importance: it is that of Theodore, first under Pachomius, and then, in a different manner, under Horsiesios. Before his disgrace, Theodore had become a real deputy to Pachomius, entrusted with the most important commissions, such as catechizing, the visitation of monasteries and the care of souls. We know how the thought of succeeding Pachomius was suggested to him by the brethren and became the occasion of his downfall. Under Horsiesios, though in fact it was he who was really governing the congregation, he constantly took care to maintain the attitude of the simple Second to the ejected superior. Such are the unforgettable examples which illustrate, from the time when cenobitism began, the greatness and the dangers of this office.

Not every Second had Theodore's sanctity nor every abbot that of Pachomius or Horsiesios. We also have to wait to rediscover in each new generation, the trials, rendered worse by sin, that these holy men had to endure. In fact, abbots and provosts often had strained relationships, if we are to believe their hagiographies and the monastic rules. Now is the time to say a word about it, before proceeding with our history of the office of the Second. We have already called attention to the special mention in the *Vita Fulgentii* of the obedience, which the abbot demands of his provost, 'even of his provost', as the text says, as if the thing were not self-evident. In the previous century, Theodoret was witness to the insults undergone by an abbot at the hands of his Second, a characteristic that he reports in praise of the victim and his unchangeable patience, but which would have made the Master and St Benedict frown.[83] Furthermore, their rules are not the only ones to require deference and submission from the provost in respect of the abbot. This refrain recurs in at least four other rules before and after St Benedict: R Or 3, R Fer 17, 2 R Fruc 11 and R Wal 2.

Gregory the Great joins in this chorus, but it is to throw in a note which is unexpected and in one respect, discordant. Two anecdotes in the *Dialogues* cause us to be present at passages of arms between abbot and provost, in which it is the latter, curiously enough, who is the sympathetic and edifying character, whereas the abbot shows himself as irascible and foolish.[84] But even more than this reversal of roles, which serves to discredit the abbacy and exalt the provostship,[85] we must observe the evidence given by Gregory in this passage as to the function of the Second. In the first narrative, the provost Libertinus is depicted three times as the man in charge of the affairs of the community, to defend its interests in the outside world. This seems to be his main occupation. It carries him as far as Ravenna, the distant capital, and puts him in touch with 'very many distinguished people, who esteem him highly'.[86] It is probably owing to his business trips that Felix Curvus, provost of the same monastery of Fondi after Libertinus, was a personality well-known not only to Gregory but also to the deacon Peter.[87] A no less interesting series of pieces of evidence is furnished by the second narrative. In it we see the provost Nonnosus not only washing the lamps in the chapel—really very humble work—but also occupied in the management of the monastery garden and above all, intervening decisively to prevent the monks from going to work outside the monastery during the season of the olive harvest. This last example is very interesting, for it shows the nature and extent of the provost's authority in matters of work and even of monastic discipline. The irascible abbot of Soracte (Gregory passes over his name in silence; charity or ignorance?) had given the order to go harvesting; Nonnosus, who was more prudent, as Gregory says, took the liberty of giving a contrary order, and it was his order that prevailed.

What are we to think of 'the first Benedictine pope', who quietly tells us these things? It is clear that at Soracte the real clerk of works and the true spiritual father of the brethren is not the abbot but the provost; and this is no doubt due to the personal sanctity of Nonnosus, which is thrown into relief by the proximity of an abbot of mediocre quality, and also to the authority of the office of provost. Let us remember Gregory's correspondence, especially that with the provost of Palermo, who had been imposed in this office upon an abbot who was little to be relied upon, *ut quod istius incuria negligitur, illius sollicitudine seruetur*.[88] Furthermore, in this Palermo affair, Gregory had entrusted a former provost, Urbicus, with the responsibility of selecting the new provost, and this detail seems to indicate that the pope accorded full powers to a second, when it was a question of so serious a matter as taking a monk in one monastery and making him superior elsewhere.

Gregory's esteem for the provost and the importance which he attaches to this office are indirectly evident from the other instance, in which we saw him designate simultaneously the abbot and his Second.[89] No less significant in this respect are the proposals, which he makes to the abbots of Syracuse and Rimini, to urge them to give themselves provosts.[90] The pope makes it a duty for those over-burdened superiors to associate themselves with so indispensable a collaborator. Certainly we do not know exactly why the abbots of Syracuse and Rimini were so hesitant to give themselves provosts. But it is at least likely that these abbots shared the fears of the RB redactor and preferred an excess of work to the help of a collaborator who might prove troublesome. It has not perhaps received adequate notice that these two letters of Gregory suppose on the part of their recipients an attitude of misgiving towards the provost which is in line with that of St Benedict.[91] Even at the end of the sixth century, some abbots believed that they could and should do without a Second, and it was necessary for the pope to help them surmount such prejudices. Facts such as these are to be added to the record of the difficulties between abbots and provosts.

One now sees that the little episode in the *Dialogues*, from which we began, is more than a minor fact, bearing upon the character of the individuals who held the offices of abbot and provost in the monastery of Soracte. It illustrates, besides the sanctity of Nonnosus, the importance of the provostship in the eyes of Gregory and his contemporaries. This personage has assumed so much authority that abbatial power must reckon with him. In case of conflict, there is no guarantee that the abbot must prevail against him, nor that he could count on the support of public opinion. From that situation, no doubt, springs the reluctance of certain abbots to appoint a provost. But on this point surrounding pressure is too strong for the abbots to keep the post of Second vacant. They can consider themselves lucky if they still have the possibility of at least choosing and ordaining their provost themselves.

Having surveyed the texts, which tell us of the difficulties which arose between the abbot and his lieutenant, let us resume the history of the *praepositura* where we left off, namely in Egypt during the first century of cenobitic experience. Palladius has already furnished us with a valuable testimony as to the existence of the *Deuteros*, about which Cassian's silence could have caused us to have doubts. But the same author has also something to teach us about the role of this personage. According to LH 32.4, the *Deuteros* is closely associated with the superior of the monastery in governing the brethren, supervising them, and distributing them among the various 'classes' or houses. In LH 32.8, we see him entrusted with business trips to Alexandria.

These brief indications confirm the distinction that we made at the outset. The Second is at the same time both the abbot's intimate collaborator, sharing in his tasks, and a reliable person, entrusted with such and such a function of his own, which the abbot hands over to him completely. The R Or implies as much in a formula as broad as one could wish: *omnem ad se curam de disciplina fratrum et diligentiam monasterii reuocabit, habens potestatem abbate absente faciendi omnia quae abbas praesens facit.* We should very much like to know whether the second half of the sentence explains the first or whether it adds a new thought, in other words, whether *omnem curam . . . et diligentiam monasterii* designates the role of the provost only in the absence of the abbot, or indeed even when he is present. At any rate, the formula regarding the substitution for the absent abbot is quite clear, and tells us what we are going to find in RM.

In the hypothetical situation, where a 'second abbot' would come to be created, RM assures him that in addition to the honors of the second place in community, he will have the power to 'receive (guests?) in the place of the absent abbot, to correct the faults of the brethren, to excommunicate'. However, the excommunicated brother, can receive to himself the right to make amends in person to the abbot on his return,[92] though he remains effectively excommunicated up to that time. In short, the second abbot is in everything the 'deputy' of the first, as the abbot is of Christ: *in omnibus absentis agat uices abbatis* (RM 93:68). The Master therefore explicitly envisages only the function of the substitution of the abbot when he is away on a journey (*ambulantis*). When the abbot is present, the Second seems no longer to have a role to play, which is understandable, if one thinks of the small size of the community for which the Master is legislating and of the part which the abbot plays in all the duties of the common life.

With Caesarius of Arles there appears a feature, which is going to assume greater and greater importance and contribute in large measure to the development of the *praepositura*. The abbess is an overworked person: she has the care not only for souls, and the continual worry of looking after the material goods of the monastery, but also the relationship with people in the world (an obligation emphasized by the proximity of the city). Visitors have to be welcomed and letters answered (R Caes V 27). Often enough, says Caesarius, the abbess will be in the parlor when an object addressed to one of the sisters happens to arrive from outside. On such occasions, the object must then be brought to the *praeposita* (R Caes V 43). This function of representing the community to those outside the monastery has such importance that it is mentioned as one of the two essential duties of the abbess, the other being 'to watch over the rule' (R Caes V 61).

Under such conditions, the *praeposita* will often have to act as substitute for her superior, as we have just seen in the case of objects received. She ought also to relieve the abbess of a part of her task, and Caesarius entrusts her particularly with the direction of the clothing department (R Caes V 27: *lanificium*). As for Caesarius's rule for monks, in its brevity it has only a very little to offer on the subject. Note, however, the phrase *arguente abbate aut praeposito* (R Caes M 11), which is itself destined to become current in seventh-century rules to indicate the part which the provost takes in nearly all the functions and prerogatives of the abbot. The same formula *sine abbate aut praeposito* reappears in Aurelian to indicate the substitution of the abbot by the provost (R Aur M 54).

Before leaving the two bishops of Arles, let us point out the moving injunction, which they both address to the two superiors of the monastery, recommending to them the care of the sick (R Caes V 42), the maintenance of the rule (R Caes V 47), and diligence in providing the brethren with all that they need (R Aur M 16). These formulas of injunction are interesting in that they show the provost or provostess closely associated with the responsibility of the office of superior. In RB expressions of this sort are to be sought in vain, the abbot being the sole person 'responsible for all the deficiencies of his disciples,' as St Benedict says precisely in connection with the care of the sick (RB 36:10).[93]

The *Regula Fereoli* never mentions the provost except in the little chapter which treats of him *ex professo* (R Fer 17). In this text his function is described uniquely from the standpoint of the 'solace' that it should-bring the abbot. The provost is instituted *pro solatio abbatis*, and we recognize here this term of *solatium* which, in RB, several times designates the additional help afforded to an overworked brother, when the community is numerous and service to it is heavy. It is therefore a question, according to Ferreolus, of 'rendering the office (of the abbacy) less weighty through a division of work, which distributes the daily cares between two persons.' The same thought leads Ferreolus to give to the two superiors as assistant a *formarius* or sub-prior, a personage who already figured in Caesarius's rule for virgins (R Caes V 42). Although this chapter assumes that the provost takes part continually in the work of the abbot, one never finds in R Fer the phrase *abbas aut praepositus* nor even, as we have said, a single occasional mention of the provost. Nor is there the further question in Chapter 17 of a field, which is his special responsibility. Such sobriety is all the more remarkable, as Fereolus is chronologically very close to the seventh-century legislators, in whose works the provostship assumes a singular importance and is described in great detail.

With the *Regula Tarnatensis*, Isidore of Seville, and Fructuosus of Braga, we are in the presence of a mine of extremely rich information. Initially, a striking fact is the frequency with which the formula *abbas aut praepositus* recurs. There is hardly any function of the abbot, for which no provision is made for his replacement by the provost on occasion. Moreover, each rule assigns to the *praepositus* certain special powers. In R Tar, he seems to be clerk of works, and it is he who is in charge of the sales.[95]

Isidore in his turn enumerates no less than eight sectors for which he is responsible: *sollicitudo monachorum, actio causarum, cura possessionum, satio agrorum, plantatio curaque uinearum, diligentia gregum, constructio aedificiorum, opus carpentariorum siue fabrorum*; all in all, the provost is a real manager, concerned simultaneously with personnel, with matters in dispute, and with an ensemble of agricultural services: tillages, vineyards, live-stock, and lastly buildings, timber, and metals. As if that were not enough, Isidore adds a little further on, in a formula which reminds one of the *omnem diligentiam monasterii* of R Or, that the provost is, in addition, head of all the other main departments of the monastic administration: the *sacrarium* (sacristy, linen room, wash-house, etc.), the lodge and the guest house, the kitchen and storeroom, with their numerous dependencies, the garden, the bakery and tool-shed.[96].

These picturesque lists allow us to catch a glimpse of a complex administrative machine, a singularly heavy temporality, which gives a foretaste of the great medieval abbeys. The provost is the head of this little world, a sort of general steward. If the abbot reserves to himself the right to nominate the office-holders (*omnia a patre monasterii ordinata*), it is the provost who directs the administration (*ad curam praepositi pertinebunt*[97]). Like the steward in the egyptian monasteries, it is he who receives all the work of the brethren and presents it to the abbot.[98] Mention is made even of his supervision, in company with the elders, of the expenditure ordered by the abbot.[99] One sees how his responsibility overflows the bounds of a simple deputy for an abbot, who is absent or otherwise occupied. Furthermore, he himself, is sometimes obliged to absent himself, which does not surprise us.[100]

The two rules of Fructuosus of Braga enter into less detail on the subject of management of temporalities, but the indications that they give are still more suggestive than those of Isidore. We see the provost distributing manual work to the deans each day after prime, and we immediately think of RM, where the same scene is described, but where the abbot in person and not his lieutenant makes the distribution.[101] What quite clearly indicates that the provost is the real clerk of works is that Fructuosus shows him, a few minutes later, heading the column of monks who set off for work and intoning the psalm which they recite as they march. Throughout this entire passage there is no mention of the abbot. He evidently does not intervene; he is not even present. The immediate superior of the deans, the man with whom they normally deal, is the provost, 'their provost,' as Fructuosus says. The *praepositus* again appears in his role as chief of the deans at the weekly chapter of faults: he must see that the *decaniae* are assembled and that nobody is missing. The abbot presides at the exercise, but he makes his appearance only when the community has been gathered together through the provost's efforts.[102]

The distance which separates abbot and brethren is still more striking in the description of the dormitory: there also, the abbot seems absent and it is the provost who 'occupies the center of the dormitory', exercises surveillance and wakes up before the brethren, in order to be present when they get up, after having given his blessing to the callers. Now, it is remarkable that this description corresponds almost point for point with that which the Master gives in the chapter on going to bed, with the sole difference that it is the abbot, and not the provost, who fulfills all these acts.[103] Between the Master and Fructuosus, a gulf seems to have been opened between abbot and community, with the provost stepping in to fill the gap. Instead of presiding over work, sleep, and every moment of life, the abbot lives on one side, absorbed by administrative tasks, while his Second exercises the effective direction of the community.

What then are the occupations which prevent the abbot from living the common life? He has to receive guests and take his meals with them, leaving to the provost the responsibility of habitually presiding in the refectory[104] (by the way let us note this analogy with RB: the influx of guests and the resultant necessity of making provision for someone to preside at the table of the brethren, are probably among the reasons alluded to by RB 65:14 when it says: *si locus expetit*). The abbot ought also, at least according to the *Regula communis* (2 R Fruc 10), to attend a monthly synod of abbots. Other journeys also seem to be on his program in such a way that the legislator takes the trouble to give him a detailed reminder of his obligations in the matter of prayer, when he is outside the monastery. When at home, it is made a duty for him to assist at the conventual offices, which makes one wonder to what extent this personage lives in accordance with the rule.[105] His presence in choir is so uncertain that the faculty to authorize outings is given *praeposito siue decano*.[106]

So the abbot is a personage, who is often absent and always overworked. The *Regula communis* several times betrays its anxiety to spare him. It insists that the provost effectively lighten the burden which his superior shoulders: *ut abbas nullum laborem habeat . . . omni intentione sollicitudinem gerat*. Except for the monthly synods and meals taken with guests, both of which are functions reserved to the abbot, the provost should ensure that the abbot is relieved all along the line. Fructuosus does not want the abbot to be distracted by the distribution of alms: the provost shall be charged with it.[107] Similarly, in matters of correction, the provost ought judge for himself as much as possible, presenting only really difficult cases to the abbot.[108] We have come a long way from RB's reticences! The Second, instead of being considered dangerous and superfluous, is insistently requested to concern himself with everything. Care of the sick, for which RB rendered the abbot responsible in the last resort, and extended by Caesarius to the *praeposita*, becomes with Fructuosus the business 'of the cellarer and the provost', with no mention of the abbot.[109] On this point as on so many others, the abbot is in practice withdrawn from daily life, giving place to his lieutenant. These data permit us to appreciate at their full value the unrestricted formulas by which Fructuosus defines the provostship: *in potestate habeant praepositi omnem regulam monasterii . . . omnem monasterii substantiam accipiant dispensandam.*[110] We have, of course, come across an equally general definition in the *Regula Orientalis*, but that rule is far from exhibiting a detailed justification of such a principle, as is the case with Fructuosus. For him, it is entirely true that the provost enjoys full power, save for remaining subject to the abbot and rendering him an account of each month's expenditure.[111] As with Isidore, though in different respects, the provost even exerts a sort of control over the abbot, either in providing him with his needs in matters of food and clothing,[112] or even—what is more noteworthy—by addressing remonstrances to him in the name of the brethren when they believe themselves unjustly treated.[113] After that, there is no reason to be surprised that the very same qualities are required of the provost as of the abbot,[114] and that a lengthy common directory is addressed to both of them![115]

A final point should be raised before leaving these highly instructive documents. Among the abbot's special duties, Fructuosus mentions insistently the study of the Fathers and vigilance against heresies.[116] Possibly the *lectio* required by this doctrinal function is one of the factors which keeps the abbot apart from the community, true especially where work is concerned. Ferreolus was already taking pains to assure the abbot of the leisure necessary for reading, demanding all the same that he work with the brethren 'as often as he has no book in his hands.'[117] In Fructuosus we go one step further: henceforth the abbot seems to be no longer present at work, where his second replaces him entirely.

To conclude this survey of monastic rules, we would finally cite the rule of Waldebert of Luxeuil, another seventh-century figure. The *praepositura* certainly does not stand in the same high relief as in the work of Fructuosus, and several passages even seem to lend *praeposita* the watered-down (or ancient?) meaning of 'group leader' or 'work directress'.[118] But here, as in Isidore and Fructuosus, the phrase *abbatissa uel praeposita* occurs throughout. A lengthy directory for the *praeposita* follows that for the abbess at the beginning of the rule, and the provostess plays the same intermediary role between abbess and sisters as Fructuosus had ascribed to her masculine counterpart: is it not plainly stated that 'no nun ought present her needs directly to the abbess, but all will relay their requests through the *praeposita*'?[119]

Thus, the provostship seems, on the whole, to have followed an ascending curve. Its effective importance and prestige appear forth in all their clarity after the time of St Benedict, in the writings of Gregory, Isidore, and Fructuosus. Correspondingly, we notice a certain giving way in the abbatial function, either because it loses something of its sovereign authority inside the monastery or its total independence outside of it, or because the abbot, through a process of estrangement, retreats somewhat from the common life, in order to dwell in an isolated and less accessible region. We are then led to enquire what causes could have stimulated this growth on the *praepositura* in the gap left by the retreat of the abbot. Two series of causes seem to have contributed to this evolution: the personal deficiencies of abbots and the growing weight of the tasks incumbent upon them.

The best witness to the faults committed by abbots is surely Gregory the Great. When he introduces us on two occasions in the First Book of the *Dialogues* to two abbots of scarcely edifying character, he may perhaps be referring to past events, but he may indeed also be thinking of the many sad stories which are strewn throughout his correspondence! It is only too evident to anyone who examines those letters that contemporary monasticism knew its degradations and that many an abbot was not equal to the nobility of his task.[120] But let us not paint too dark a picture. By its very nature, the correspondence of a pope informs us particularly about the abuses, which must be repressed by his authority, while numerous edifying and happy monasteries pass unnoticed. Nevertheless, it is a fact that Gregory had, time and again, to correct people in monasteries, especially abbots. This fact could not have failed to influence his attitude towards abbots and their seconds.

What then did the pope do when faced with a deficient superior? When the man had shown himself unsuitable even before his election, Gregory did not hesitate to annul it and prescribe a new ordination,[121] which matches the desires expressed in RB. But when an abbot regularly ordained committed a grave fault or allowed one to be committed, the pope did not seem so ready to pursue the same line of conduct. We observe this in the affair of the three errant abbots, of which the question is raised in Lr 5.3–4. Two were priests and the third a deacon. Now, though Gregory was absolutely opposed to their reinstatement in holy orders, whether priesthood or diaconate, he displayed, on the contrary, a surprising latitude as regards their monastic situation. It will be possible after a period of penitence to grant to one 'the first place among the monks' in some monastery chosen by the bishop, to set the second in the first place in his own monastery, and lastly, in the case of the priest-abbot Saturninus, Gregory positively ordered that he resume the government of his monasteries in Gorgonia and Capraria 'notwithstanding any opposition'. The reason he gave leaves us wondering: 'his fall itself will dispose him to greater prudence and he will henceforth watch more carefully over those entrusted to him'.

From this we see that the pope's demands for the abbacy are much less than for holy orders. Apart from the extraordinary case of Saturninus, the cases of his two colleagues are no less instructive in their own way. The expressions, which Gregory employs to define their situation are not absolutely clear: *priorem inter alios monachos . . . standi locum obtinebit; eum ante alios . . . monachos ordinate*. These formulas could no doubt be understood of the abbatial authority itself. However, comparison with what is said about Saturninus, as well as the pope's reservations *ubi tu tamen decreueris . . . ut praeuideritis*, make one think rather of an honorary rank granted out of consideration for the abbatial dignity, but without its powers.

The analogous solution that we saw employed in the case of an abbot of Palermo comes to mind.[122] After a long penance, he is authorized to return to his monastery and resume his place (*necesse est eum . . . loco suo constituere*). This place was not therefore remaining vacant. During the 'long penance', no one had thought of choosing a successor to this unworthy abbot, but now he will be given a coadjutor, and this will be precisely the *praepositus* imposed by outside authority and charged officially to 'watch over with his solicitude whatever the abbot in his carelessness will have overlooked.' In this affair we put our finger upon the incidence of personal failings in an abbot on the diminution of the abbacy. One can imagine, without difficulty, as Gregory gives us to understand, clearly enough, what the authority of such failed abbots could be when they were nominally re-established in office. A singular situation: we have some difficulty in conceiving the reasons, which prompted the pope to act in such fashion. Possibly abbatial elections and ordinations were acts upon which it seemed hard to go back. Or, on the contrary, are we to see in Gregory's conduct a mediocre estimate of the abbacy, considering it as an office, which could easily be reduced to a position of honorary precedence?

Perhaps the pope's attitude partakes of both these viewpoints. In any case, it is evident that, in so far as he takes into consideration the *personal* dignity which continued to be attached to these fallen abbots, Gregory ruins the prestige of the abbatial *office*. Had he been really anxious to maintain the authority of this office, he would have been watchful, before all else, to confer the abbacy only on men capable of maintaining its prestige and effectively exercising its rights. Now, he has a different solution: he re-establishes the unworthy abbot in his office of primacy, while at the same time giving him a double in the person of a Second, who is in fact intended to take his place.

Perhaps the pope had his reasons for preferring this method of government, which gave the actual direction of the monastery to a subordinate appointed by him and easily controllable, even removable. The confidence shown towards the *praepositus* is no doubt to be explained by the disappointments met with in the abbots. The downfalls of too many abbots seemed like a collapse of the abbatial system. Gregory had to take the side of these mediocre superiors, the results of the choice by subjects, who were even more mediocre, yet who were invested with a life-long dignity, which made them difficult to remove. The *praepositus* seemed the best remedy for this state of affairs. Emanating from an external authority that had greater weight in the estimation of the community and more pliable in the hands of the one who appointed him, the provost's office represented the best chance for reform and regularity.

Consequently, we can understand why Gregory favored this charge.[123] The *praepositus* gained in the esteem of the pope and no doubt in that of many of his contemporaries as the failings of certain abbots made them aware of the limits of the abbatial system.

However, Gregory's correspondence suggests another process whereby the evolution that we are describing was effected. To the personal shortcomings of the abbots must be added, as we have said, the growing burden of the office of abbot. Moreover, the two series of causes are intertwined. Why is Abbot John of Syracuse so negligent at *lectio*, thereby setting a bad example, copied only too readily by his monks? Why else, if not because of the legal proceedings, which often summon him out of the monastery? Let him then appoint two indispensable collaborators: within the monastery, a provost, and outside it a procurator to plead in his stead![124] The first will help him to watch over the brethren, the second will dispense him from going out.

Thus the pope testifies to the detrimental effects of overwork, from which certain abbots suffer. They need to be recalled to their essential task: reading, prayer and watching over the souls, who have been entrusted to them. We may believe that we hear in such counsels an echo of the warnings addressed by Caesarius to an abbess[125] and by RB to the abbot.[126] Let us note in addition the sharing of functions between procurator and provost. The latter is no longer, as in *Dial* 1.2, the man responsible for external affairs; it is inside the monastery that he is to help the abbot. Elsewhere Gregory defines his office: *circa cellae ordinationem fratrumque custodiam nec non in lucrandis animabus*.[127] Seemingly, then, by Gregory's time, the solution, consisting of entrusting court proceedings and external relations to the provost is superseded. It is still found, nevertheless, in the rule of Isidore, who mentions among the prerogatives of the provost the *actio causarum*. But in the pope's view, such dealings are more suited to seculars than to monks, and we see him twice taking measures either to secure for the abbot the assistance of a lay agent, or for withdrawing from business affairs certain monastic superiors, who find themselves embarrassed by litigation that exceeds their competence.[128] *In saecularibus causis omnino inexpertus est*, he notes on this occasion, in recommending the abbot Caesarius.

Even if the particularly thorny topic of legal proceedings is disregarded, it remains for the abbot to have to face many 'mundane' obligations, using this word in its least pejorative sense. At the beginning of cenobitism, as Basil informs us, the superior of the Cappadocian fraternities is often absent, sometimes for reasons of health, but usually for business purposes. The possibility of the superior's absences is foreseen even in the little monastery for which RM is destined, where the abbot does, however, live in continual contact with his monks. These outings by the superior are Basil's sole motive for installing a Second, and RM assigns to the latter no other function than that of acting as substitute for the absent abbot. If in these small communities the absence of the superior has so marked a repercussion on the lieutenant's function, one can guess what proportions this phenomenon could have attained in large monasteries. Along with the numerical importance of the community, the temporal responsibilities too continue to expand, the absences of the superior increase, and the provost plays an ever more considerable role. Let us remember the rule of Fructuosus.

But 'the world' not only obliges the abbot to go out. It also comes to the monastery in the person of its guests, and again it is the abbot who must receive them at table. In RM, where guests do not seem numerous, their presence does not separate the abbot from the brethren, since he receives guests in the common refectory, even if it entails the modification the program of readings during their stay. But in RB and Fructuosus, their influx renders it necessary to make them take their meals separately, which obliges the abbot to have a separate kitchen. As for the nuns, though Caesarius formally forbids the abbess to receive at table anyone who may be staying at her monastery,[129] visits to the parlor nevertheless remain one of her principal occupations. The connection, which Caesarius himself establishes between these occupations and the provostship, comes to mind here. Although RB and Fructuosus do not expressly notice it, such a connection probably did exist between the absence of the abbot at the common table and the role played by the provost as president of this same table.

Analogous remarks can be made in the area of work. It was possible for the abbot to distribute the daily tasks to the two dozen monks who peopled the monastery of the Master. This became increasingly difficult, where a more numerous community and heavier and more complex temporalities demanded a specially qualified organizer or one with a good deal of time at his disposal. That is no doubt why the function passes into the hands of the provost in the rule of Fructuosus. What is more, it is well-known that the Master had the wisdom to forbid the direct exploitation of the land belonging to the monks. They will give it to laymen to farm. Isidore, on the other hand, though he also refuses to authorize the monks to work with their hands in their fields, has such work performed not by farmers but by servants, placed under the orders of a monk. Thus, responsibility for directing the work is in principle incumbent on the abbot. He evidently must delegate this duty to one of his religious, and it is the provost, whom we find at the head of the agrarian enterprise, as of the rest of a good number of manual tasks (R Is 19). Here also, the increase in the temporal functions of the abbot has obliged him to divest himself of a part of his responsibilities and entrust them to his Second.

Lastly, it seems that with the passage of time the abbot has lost something of his autonomy in the administrative sphere (buying, selling, expenditure. . .). That was pointed out when we studied the chapter on the council. If we recall it here, the reason is precisely because it is the provost who, according to R Is, ought, together with the elders, to control the expenditure ordered by the abbot.

To sum up, the double series of causes we have studied amounts to the following fact: the abbot is unable to shoulder his full obligations by himself. The personal deficiencies of men and the increasing weight and complexity of the tasks, were what led more than anything else to the recognition of this fact, with the result that the provost came to exercise an increasingly effective participation in the abbatial function, either by substituting for the absent abbot or by managing a domain of his own which went on expanding. This sharing of prerogatives received varied expression. But such participation proved necessary everywhere, the authority of the abbot over everyone and everything being safeguarded, at least in principle.

Finally, we have arrived at something not unlike the collegial system, which Fulgentius and Felix had the originality and sagacity to institute between themselves in their little monastery in Africa. But instead of two abbots, who render mutual obedience to each other, there was a provost who was obedient, at least *de iure* to the sole abbot. Instead of having one man responsible for the spiritual matters and the other for temporal, as was the case with Fulgentius and Felix, the abbot and provost seem rather to have exercised their authority in the two domains simultaneously; the chief superior retained the double responsibility for souls and for material goods, while he relied heavily upon his assistant as much for the exercise of surveillance over the brethren as for the administration of the monastic patrimony.

The history of the *praepositura*, which we have just traced, now permits us to understand in all their aspects the positions taken by the Master and St Benedict. First, these two legislators range themselves with the numerous witnesses to a tension, which often set abbots and provosts in opposition to one another. Like the majority of the same witnesses, they side with the abbot and demand complete submission from the provost. Nothing original here. On the other hand the exclusion of the Second, formally decreed by the Master and desired in principle by St Benedict, is a characteristic without parallel, which puts our two authors in a class apart. The truth is, the Second seems to have always been present from earliest times, notwithstanding the silence of certain texts, and, though his behaviour has sometimes been criticized, his existence has nowhere been disputed. The Master's originality is confirmed by his desire to eliminate the Second. At least a partial return to the traditional office of abbot's lieutenant is represented by RB. Such reversion to the traditional position is the mark of a mind less free to assert personal preferences and more dependent on the collective mentality. It is caused at the same time by the greater size of the community, which is no doubt not limited to the Master's two decuries, and which obliges the superior to engage help.

Our two rules therefore present themselves as 'abbatial reactions' to the difficulties created by the provost. These difficulties were in the very nature of things. In general, abbots reacted more moderately, simply demanding obedience from the Second. The Master and St Benedict carry the reaction to its extreme. This vigor arose from the especially grave threats existing in St Benedict's environment, which only became particularized at a later date, as the work of Gregory the Great authentically testifies. It was inevitable that the temptations inherent in the office of Second would become more pronounced insofar as the test of time would reveal the distance between the ideal of the abbacy and its actualization in men with human failings. Not only did such discoveries, by diminishing the prestige of the abbots, bring to birth thoughts of independence in their lieutenants, but also there was no lack of wise men, in whose eyes a good provost appeared to be the appropriate remedy for a mediocre or unworthy abbot. Thence sprang the abuse of *ex aequo* nomination, whereby, it was believed, better government of the community would be assured by at once placing at the abbot's side his indispensable collaborator, who would eventually be his corrector.

RB is traditional, albeit reluctant, where the acceptance of the *praepositura* is concerned. It is no less traditional when it asserts for the abbot his right to nominate his own provost and when it demands complete obedience from the latter. For the omnipotence of the abbot is a fundamental and constant principle of cenobitism, even more than the presence of a Second at his side. St Benedict's protestations do not appear to have exercised a general and immediate influence, to which, moreover, the very limited authority of the legislator would not allow him to lay claim. Nevertheless the traditional ideas, which found expression in St Benedict's protestations, finally succeeded in imposing themselves, from which a crisis resulted that was far from coming to an end in the Gregorian milieu. In the seventh century the office of provost took on a remarkable new lease of life by means of a kind of retreat by the abbot, who was overburdened by his work by his job, but we hear no more about conflicts and equally serious infringements.

This, it seems, is the historical meaning of the present chapter of RB. It prolongs the Master's reaction against the office of Second, but without rigorously sustaining it. We detect in St Benedict the same nostalgia for an impossible past, the same resignation to the inevitable present, which is perceptible in other passages of the rule, that on wine, for example. His attitude is prudent; it is one which conforms with the general custom and accommodates itself to the needs of the times, while not failing to safeguard what is essential.

NOTES TO CHAPTER EIGHT

1. *Concordia*, Chapter 27 (before the chapter on deans, RB 21). In §§10, 11 and 12, the *pr* is the Pachomian 'head of the house'. Likewise in §8 (R Or 17 = R Pac Inst 18, cited in § 10). §14 reproduces R Aug 14, 180–87, which is addressed to all offices indiscriminately, without focusing particularly on the 'second' or even naming him. §5 reproduces R Tar 11, which concerns the procurators, an office distinct from that of provost.

2. Basil Steidle cites (p 318) R Pac 158 (*Inst* 17) of which we spoke in the preceding note (*Conc* 27, §10). Kassius Hallinger, 'Papst Gregor der Grosse und der Hl. Benedikt,' *Studia Anselmiana* 42 (1957), p 302, bases an argument on R Or 17 (*Conc* §8. See preceding note). We feel bound to declare here how much we owe, in the present chapter, as in the foregoing, to this remarkable study by Hallinger (pp 296–305).

3. RB 21:7.

4. RB 62:7; 71:3. See Hallinger, p 296 and n 205.

5. Faustus, *Hom* 3 (Eus 37), PL 50:839c; *Hom* 8 (Eus 42), ibid., 852a, etc.; R Caes V 35: *uos quae praepositae estis*. Caesarius, Lr 2, PL 67:1132a: *contra praepositas*; R Aur M 37 and R 4 Pat 22, quoting Heb 13:17; Gregory the Great, *Hom in Eu* 17.13. Note that in RB 62:7 (*regulam decanis uel praepositis constitutam*), *pr*. can hardly be a synonym for *decanis*. *Pr* means either the second (generic plural) or all the monastery officers taken together. Benno Linderbauer proposes the first of these meanings. The latter is supported by the texts that we have indicated. Gregorio Penco too seems to rally to the latter meaning (*superiori*. . . *incaricati*).

6. Another striking example of vacillation between plural and singular is found in Chapter 35, concerning the kitchen helpers. According to 35:12–15, there seem to be several such helpers at a time (there were two in RM); yet RB twice designates them by the singular (35:7–11, 16–18). Here again, it appears probable that a single officer-holder performs the service each week. The plural in 35:12–15 designates the *successive* office-holders.

7. Blaise, *s.v.*: 'especially the bishop'. When *pr.*designates the priest or deacon, it is in as much as they are heads, and not as subordinated to the bishop. See also Hallinger, p 296.

8. Jerome, Lr 22.35.

9. See Boon, *Pachomiana Latina*, Index, *s.v. praepositus*.

10. Ibid., *s.v. secundus*. In R Pac, it is always a question of the house Second. *Lib. Ors.* alone distinguishes the latter (18) from the Second for the entire monastery (14). For this last meaning, see the corresponding testimony of Palladius, LH 32.4, 8.

11. Lr 125.15. We use the term abbot in order to make ourselves clearly understood. But in this passage Jerome says *pater, maior*, and not *abbas*. This last term is exceptional with him. It is not found, to our knowledge, except in the *Vita Malchi*, in which it has perhaps a 'Syrian' and picturesque color. The commentary by Jerome on Gal 4:6 is often cited to prove that he does employ *abbas*, but this text most probably refers to the usage of *pater*, which is constant in Jerome (see Lr 22.35 and the *Pach. Lat.*). Cf the parallel commentary on Mt 23:8. *Abbas*, which is already current in Sulpicius Severus (*Dial* 1.10, etc.), is therefore not familiar to Jerome.

12. R Mac 7; R Col M 10 (Walker, 140, 27).

13. *Inst* 4.10 (Petschenig, pp 53, 25 and 54, 13). *Inst* 4.27 (Petschenig, p 66, 4). *Conf* 20.1.

14. Delatte (on RB 65) makes reference to these last two texts. Note, however, that in *Inst* 5.27, *pr* is a simple participle. In *Conf* 18.7, on the other hand, the term is in the plural: *coenobiorum praepositi*. It may therefore be a question of all the monastery officers (cf. above, n. 5). However, since the sentence is entirely in the plural, and since the context speaks only of the *abbas*, it is likely that Cassian is here thinking of abbots only.

15. Cf. *Conf* 18.14, where *pr.* = the director of a hospice for widows dependent on the bishop.

16. Steidle, p 318, quoting R Aug 15. 188. The *presbyter* appears as the ultimate person to whom one may appeal in R Aug 15. 192; 11.108, 119. The words *cuius est apud uos maior auctoritas* (R Aug 15. 192–193) are like an echo of Lr 226, in which a contested lay superior made an appeal to the priest *ad maiorem auctoritatem*.

17. R Aug 11.104; 12.143; 13.145, 149, 157; 5.6.

18. Same synonymy, in *De correptione et gratia*, between *qui nobis praesunt* (5), and *praepositis suis* (46).

19. Lr 48 (to the monks of Capraria); Lr 214–215 (to the monks of Hadrumetum). In both cases, the address gives no characteristic title to the superior, who at Capraria is a priest, and at Hadrumetum a layman. Lr 210 is addressed *matri Felicitati*. The same lady is likewise called *mater* in Lr 211.4. In *Enar. in Ps* 99:11 (CC 39:1399, 1. 28–29), Augustine calls the superior *quisquis talibus locis forte praeest*. In Lr 64.3, the *praepositi monasteriorum* are the superiors of the monasteries of Africa (citation of the Council of Carthage in 401).

21. Besides *qui praeest* (R Aug 15.19, cf. n. 19), Augustine is acquainted with *pater* (*De moribus ecclesiae* 1.31.67; Augustine here depends on Jerome), and *mater* (see n 79). But in Lr 211.4, in which we read *mater*, the ordinary term for designating the superior is *praeposita*. Curiously, the priest Rusticus, spiritual father of the community, is likewise called *praepositus*. This fact would suffice to demonstrate that *praepositus*, in Augustine, still retains its full value of 'head,' since the priest, here called *praep.*, is the detainer of the supreme authority in the R Aug.

22. *Pr.* has the same meaning of 'second' in other narratives by Gregory of Tours: VP 14; *Hist Franc* 10.15; *Glor Conf* 80. In this last text, as in VP 18.1, it is a question of *pr* who govern the monastery in the absence of the abbot, the latter having made a foundation elsewhere and residing in his new community.

23. R Caes 25; 35; 40; 42; 44; 47. This last passage is particularly clear: when Caesarius speaks of *praepositam sanctae congregationis*, there is little doubt that the immediate assistant of the abbess is meant. The *pr.* also appears in R Caes M 11.

24. R Aur M 26; 54 (= R Caes V 42).

25. R Fer 17. Ferreolus also speaks here of a *formarium* (cf. R Caes V 42), a sort of 'third' or sub-prior.

26. See Above, n 22.

27. *Dial* 2.22. This title is comparable to that of *tertius a loco abbatis* (Lr 3.23).

28. See Hallinger, pp 296–305; the same author cites for attention (p 296, 8) alongside of this current sense of *pr.* = the second, four passages in the correspondence, where this name would apply to the abbot. This would demand careful verification (the parentheses, which follow those references in several cases, suggest a less precise meaning). In any case, in *Dial* 2.8 (Moricca 92, 23), the *statuti praepositi* really do seem to be abbots (cf. *Dial* 2.4, Moricca 86, 5: *ab abbate suo*; Moricca 87,4: *pater monasterii* (cf. 87, 10 and 16); *Dial* 2.3, Moricca 85, 1: *statutis patribus*). It seems, then, that *pr* which in the monastic terminology of Gregory regularly means Second, could occasionally designate the first. The plural, however, in *Dial* 2.8 (the only text I myself have been able to verify) may be interpreted in the general sense of 'superiors', a sense that we pointed out elsewhere (see n. 5 above, and n. 29).

29. R Caes V 35; R Aur M 37 (citing Heb 13:17); Gregory the Great, *Dial.* 2.8 (see preceding note). Cf. n. 5.

30. Cassian, *Inst* 4.17 (Petschenig, p 58, 23–25). OM 7.28 is utilized by Caesarius (R Caes V 18), who writes: *quae mensae praeest* in place of *praepositus*. For at the time of Caesarius, the *praeposita*, having become the 'second', probably did not preside over any one table in particular. Seemingly, then, there is a lack of agreement between the OM terminology and that of Caesarius, an indication that the *pr.* of OM 7.28 is not yet 'the second', but either the superior of the whole community or a group chief. Later in the sixth century, on the contrary, R Tar 8 maintains *praepositus* in this function of table surveillance. For at this epoch the *praepositus* is the true head of the community, the abbot often being absent, as will be seen notably in Fructuosus of Braga (cf. 1 R Fruc 19: the abbot dines with the guests, as is already the case in RB 53).

31. Cf. R Aug 15.188, where nearly all the words of this sentence are already found assembled. Now, R Aug speaks in this spot of a *pr.* who is the superior.

32. Anscari Mundó, 'Les anciens synodes abbatiaux et les 'Regulae SS. Patrum,'' *Studia Anselmiana* 44 (1959), pp 107–125.

33. R 4 Pat, 14, PL 103:440b.

34. R Or 29 speaks only of those who *ad omnes errores emendandos praepositi sunt*: a text classifiable in the dossier of *praepositi* (plural) = the superiors (cf. nn. 5, 28, 29).

35. See n. 32.

36. Hallinger, *art. cit.*, p 302, §2.

37. Schwartz, *Concilia*, II 5 (p 131, 29). This *Breuiarium Liberati* was composed in Latin after 555, but utilizes sources contemporary with the council (451). *Praepositura* there designates an abbatial charge in Egypt.

38. Once only in Columban (*Ep* 4.2) does *pr.* seem to signify the second (cf. Walker, p 153, n 1). In every other case Walker translates 'immediate superior', that is, group-chief. R Col M 10 (Walker, 140, 27), in which it is a question of the abbot, is borrowed from Jerome. The second, in the rules, does not appear except once, and it is under his old name of *secundus*: R Col C 8 (Walker, 152, 24).

39. Most often the Master speaks of them in the plural. Note, however, RM 22:1–2 (communion of *the* provost at the head of his *decania*; 13:44, 51, 55, 23:20.

40. Cassian gives the following equivalents: *Inst* 4.7 (Petschenig, 52, 15): *senior qui decem iunioribus praeest*; 4.8 (passim): *senior*; 4.17: *eum qui suae decaniae praeest*. Note the first of these equivalents: for Cassian, as previously for Augustine, the provost is the eleventh man for a group of 10, whereas Jerome seems to be thinking of the tenth man for a group of 9. The Master, in 'superimposing' two brothers to each group of 10 (making a dozen in all; cf. Gregory the Great, *Dial* 2.3) falls in line with Cassian. But the term *decada* used by RM is neither that of Jerome (*decuria*) nor of Cassian (*decania*).

41. RM 11:35–36 and *passim*.

42. Note that the Master's terminology concerning the cenobitic hierarchy, is that of Cassian: *abbas* for the head of the community, *praepositus* (and not *decanus*) for the decurion, with the 'second' to the abbot for the whole community normally being omitted.

43. See n. 33.

44. *Dial* 2.22.

45. R Col C 8 (Walker, 152, 24).

46. Hallinger, p 302, §1. Actually, he whom RM calls 'the Second' is designated in *Nou.* 5.9 by the periphrasis: *qui post primum est*. He whom Justinian calls *qui post illum secundus est* is the *Tertius* of RM, etc. Same phraseology in *Cod.* 1.3.47: *primum post defunctum, et qui post illum est.*

47. 'Latin language sources, or at least sources of Latin inspiration', says J. Pargoire, concerning imperial legislation (cited by Hausherr, *Direction Spirituelle*, p 36.

48. See Placid de Meester, *De Monachico Statu iuxta Disciplinam Byzantinam* (Vatican City: Polyglot Press, 1942), p 203. Whereas *proëstôs* and its numerous synonyms, along with *hegumenos* (all terms translated by *praepositus*) are current names for the superior in the Orient, *abbas* won only a very limited acceptance (de Meester, p 202. According to Pargoire [see n 47], it would be due to Latin influence that it was adopted by Justinian). It seems certain that the generalization of *abbas* in the west played a decisive role in the evolution of *praepositus*.

49. LH 32.8; the same personage had shortly before (32.4) been called *deutereuôn*.

50. HR 4. PG 82:1347: *ta deutera periepôn*; *ta deuteraia ekhôn*. In the preceding chapter (HR 3, col 1339), we read of a certain Sabinus who is 'the third of the monastery, not the first'.

51. PG 99:1781: *ta deuteraia pheronta*; (*prosôpon*) *deuterou*.

52. De Meester, p 265. The East did not therefore elaborate a special term to designate 'the Second,' but was satisfied with the numerical ordering. The West, on the contrary, entitled him *pr.*, a name left free due to the generalization of *abbas* (cf. n 48).

53. *Secundarius*: RM 22:9; 92:1, 37, 54, 61, 64; 93;59,61; 94:2; *Secundus*: RM 92:38 (adj.), 46 (noun).

54. Third Council of Arles (about 455) in Labbeus, *Concilia*, vol 4, col 1023–1024; a

privilege of Hormisdas in favor of the nuns of Arles founded by Caesarius (PL 67:1286b); councils of Carthage in 525 and 536; *Vita Fulgentii* 58. It is evidently not a matter of 'exemption' in the precise sense of modern canon law, but of a real autonomy.

55. All the meanings of *pr.* which we have reviewed can be related to a single definition, such as is given by Cagnat for the administrative language (Daremberg-Saglio, vol 4, p 623): 'the representative of a superior power at the head of a collectivity or of a service.' The two elements of this definition (*representative . . . at the head*) are detectable in all the acceptations of *pr.* in the monastic terminology. In the case of the superior of the community, the superior authority *represented* can be either the superior general among the Pachomians, or the ecclesiastical authority who has 'ordained' the *pr.* (R Aug, etc.), or finally Christ, true superior of the whole Christian community (cf. R Aug 15.188–189). In the case of the 'second,' it is by mandate of the abbot that the *pr.* has authority over the whole community, *at the head of which* he finds himself especially when the abbot is absent. In like manner the chief of a group is the *representative* of the abbot for his particular group.

56. RM 92:2, 37, 46: *elatum*. Such fear is even more apparent in the recommendations addressed to the 'new abbot', when the recovery of the old one has reduced the former to the position of Second. Cf. RM 93: 49–51, 74–75. In the same line, the Master also fears temptations to independence toward the abbot (93:69–73).

57. RM 93:43–90.

58. Cf. RB 64:1–2.

59. The expression *rationabiliter cum humilitate* is found again in RB 31:7 and 61:4. This last passage is of major interest for the understanding of our text: the abbot is there urged to give due consideration to the remonstrances proffered by a visiting monk. The similarity of situation is noteworthy: in both, RB shows the same care to regulate the relations of the abbot with those—visitors or subjects—who offer him their counsels. These should no doubt be 'reasonable and humble', but the abbot, for his part, has the duty to pay attention to their request and to comply with it, if it proves to be just. These encouragements directed at the abbot are to be linked with RB 3:6: *sicut discipulos conuenit oboedire magistro, ita et ipsum condecet prouide et juste cuncta disponere*, in which, as we have seen, the final words aimed at the abbot are in addition peculiar to RB, the Master being occupied at this point only with the disciples' duty to obey. In these three RB notations the same concern can be observed—a concern that the Master scarcely knew—to dispose the abbot to listen to the opinions rising from below (cf. above, Chapter 3, Vol. 1, p 176, n. 26).

60. The Master had already rebelled against any clerical meddling in the *ordinatio* of the monastery (RM 83) and laid claim to the exclusive right of the abbot in this domain.

61. Compare RB 64:1–2 (*scandala*) and 9 (*dum adulantur partibus*) with RM 94:5 (*studiosa partibus pugna scandali*).

62. The peripeteia of expulsion is missing in the chapter on the deans (RB 21), of which the parallelism with the chapter on the provost is evident and even explicit. On the other hand, it is found in RB 62 concerning the rebel priest (cf. also the case of the visiting monk who is sent away, RB 61:7–8).

63. A very similar warning is read previously in RB 63:3 and 55:22. The Master puts the abbot on his guard against favoritism in the directory, which concerns him (RM 2), but in the course of the rule does not refer again to the faults which he is liable to commit on such or such an occasion.

64. Steidle, *The Rule*, p 319, in the French edition.

65. Jerome, *Pach. Lat.*, *Praef.* 8 (p 8, 16–18).

66. Bo 26 and parallels (*Vies Coptes*, p 97).

67. Called *secundus* and *praepositus* (*Dial* 2.22).

68. VP 18.1 These provosts were in fact superiors, for Ursus, who remained abbot of these

different monasteries, resided at Loches, from which he sent orders to his provosts, when such was the case (ibid., 2). An analogous fact is narrated in *Glor Conf* 80. Cf. also the situation of the provost Pretiosus in the monastery of Gregory the Great himself (*Dial* 2.57). The case of provosts such as these who function as first superiors under a more or less distant abbot is to be set in relation with the texts, which attest the prestige of provostship at the same period.

69. *Sinn und Geist*, pp 385, 388–89.

70. Labbeus, vol 4, col 1024e.

71. *Letters* 5.1; 7.43; 8.15. See also the privilege accorded to an abbess of Marseilles (*Lr.* 7.12).

72. Cassiodorus, *Inst* 32.1. Various explanations of this text have been put forward. But the singular *gregem uobis creditum* does indeed seem to indicate that Chalcedonius and Gerontius both governed the same community.

73. *Vita Fulgentii* 15 and 29 (see above, Chapter 7, n. 2). In the next century, the twelfth canon of the Council of Chalon, *c.* 650 (Mansi, vol 10, col 1189) informs us that the system of the dual abbacy was sometimes practised in Gaul and gave rise to some intolerable abuses: *ut duo abbates in uno monasterio esse non debeant, ne sub obtentu potestatis simultas inter monachos et scandala generentur*. What follows in this canon shows that the root of the disorder was sometimes the selection of an abbot-successor by the abbot in office. The council seems to consider this procedure legitimate, but denies the abbot-elect any power over the *facultates* of the monastery (cf. above, Chapter 7, n. 12). Cf. canon 4 of the same council, which prohibits the dual episcopate in the same city, for the same reasons. With this seventh-century Gallican testimony we have come a long way from the idyll described by the *Vita Fulgentii*! Dual abbacy had a long existence, but by the seventh century the system had shown the full extent of its evils.

74. VF 52.

75. G 1.28; R Pac Leg 6. In Leg 9, it is question of a 'busy' head of the house.

76. G 1.28; Bo 26.

77. R Pac Praec 82 and 96 (removing thorns from a brother's foot); *Leg* 5 (imposing a penance); *Leg* 1 (setting the example while working); *Leg* 15 (keeping superfluous clothing in storage). In all these cases the characteristic formula will be noted: *praepositus domus et secundus*.

78. R Pac Praec 65 (receiving the footwear); 70 (receiving the *lebitonaria*); 101 (keeping the *codices*).

79. See n. 10 above.

80. Hallinger, p 302, §6.

81. See n. 78.—In the same sense, note *Praec* 115: in the event of absence of the head of the house, the head of another house (and not the Second) will fill in for him in everything, notably in catechetical duties. This prescription no doubt reflects a state prior to that which is assumed by the *Leg* 6 (see n. 5). At the beginning, the Second did not seem capable of supplying or the *praepositus domus*. This function of deputyship was not attributed to him until a later date.

82. *Lib. Ors.* 14. — Cf. *Ep. Theod.* (Boon, 106, 6).

83. Theodoret, Hr 4 (cf. Steidle, p 319, French edition).

84. *Dial.* 1.2, 7.

85. It does not seem, however, that Gregory wishes to disparage the abbacy. The *Dialogues* are full of holy abbots, beginning with St Benedict. Moreover, it is necessary to take account of a certain frankness of tone, to which we are no longer accustomed and which per-

mits speaking very simply of personal failings without harming the prestige of the office. Thus the unseemly story of bishop Andrew of Fondi (*Dial* 3:7) does not impair the reputation of the episcopate.

86. *Dial* 1.2 (Moricca, 24, 23–24).

87. *Dial* 1.3 (Moricca, 25, 11).

88. Lr 5.6.

89. Lr 11.48.

90. Lr 3.3 and 7.10. Gregory's instances contrast with the reticences of RB, as Hallinger has emphasized. Yet it would be a mistake to exaggerate the opposition between St Benedict and his presumed disciple, for RB itself does concede that local circumstances render necessary the institution of the provost, and Gregory only establishes this necessity, in the cases submitted to him, without declaring such to be the general law.

91. Probable in the case of Lr 7.10, this remark seems to some extent weakened, in what concerns Lr 3.3, by the fact that abbot John of Syracuse demanded of Gregory permission to ordain the monk Boniface provost of his monastery. Yet this very demand surprises the pope, who had sent Boniface precisely for that purpose, and he seems to reproach John for the incomprehensible delay which followed the arrival of the future provost. Although we are reduced to conjecturing the meaning behind the attitude of John, what we have postulated remains likely: the abbot deferred the ordination of his provost until the moment when, at dagger's point, he pretends to have waited for the express authorization from the pope and begs the latter to excuse his delay.

92. Behavior semilar to that which R Col C 8 censures (Walker, 152, 12). Cr. R Col C 7 (Walker, 150, 31).

93. The formula in R Caes V 42 mentions, besides the abbess and *praeposita*, two other dignitaries: *primiceria uel formaria* (no doubt the same person) and the infirmarian. Ferreolus too speaks of a *formarius refularis* who is third in the community, after the abbot and provost, and who corresponds with our modern sub-prior (R Fer 17). it is understandable that the staff of the abbot was larger in these communities of Arles and Uzès, which do not seem to have know the decanal system.

94. R Tar 10, 12, 19. Cf. 14 and 23. The *Regula Tarnatensis* actually belongs to the middle of the sixth century. See F Villegas, 'La Regula monasterii Tarnantensis. Texte, source et datation', in *Revue Bénédictine* 84 (1974), p 7–65; A. de Vogüé, *Autour de Saint Benoît*, Bellefontaine 1975 (Vie Monastique 4), p 15–28.

95. R Tar 1. It is a question of some flocks belonging to a postulant. In RM, it is the abbot himself who is charged with similar operations (RM 87:38–40; 91:50).

96. R Is 19.

97. These words, we believe, refer to the ensemble of offices described in the chapter, and not only to the tools spoken of in the preceding sentence.

98. R Is 6. Cf. Jerome, Lr 22.35.

99. R Is 18. See our Chapter 3.

100. R Is 22.

101. 1 R Fruc 6. Cf. RM 50:18–23.

102. 2 R Fruc 13.

103. 1 R Fruc 3. Cf. RM 29:3; 32:4–6.

104. 1 R Fruc 19. Cf. 2 R Fruc 10.

105. 2 R Fruc 10. Note, however, that the provost is likewise asked to be present at the offices (1 R Fruc 20). Might the Second be in the process of losing the habit of regular attendence, like his superior? Cf. 1 R Fruc 19.

106. 1 R Fruc 20.

107. 2 R Fruc 11. RM 16:34–5, on the contrary, forbids the cellarer to distribute alms without the abbot's authorization, at any rate when the latter is not absent. Cf. R Bas 98–99.

108. 2 R Fruc 12.

109. 2 R Fruc 7.

110. 2 R Fruc 11. See an expression of the same kind in Gregory, Lr 7.10 (n. 127).

111. 2 R Fruc 11.

112. Ibid.

113. See the *Pactum* (Brockie, p 219).

114. 2 R Fruc 11.

115. 1 R Fruc 20.

116. 2 R Fruc 10.

117. R Fer 30. Gregory sometimes shows us the abbot working in the fields with his brethren (*Dial* 1.4; 2.32). More often the abbot is not found at the work site (*Dial* 2.9; 2.11: he is at prayer; 2.31: he is reading; 2.31: he is on his way to prayer; 2.14–15: he is seated. The first two cases are specially notable, where the brethren are at work without their abbot).

118. R Wal 2 (*praepositae tam seniores quam juniores*); 12 (end); perhaps also 11.

119. R Wal 22.

120. See in particular Lr 3.3; 11.12; cf. 6.56; 11.48. The faults most often cited are ownership of private property (1.42; 11.48); instability (1.42, 50; 2.28; 4.42; 10.22–23); lack of judgment regarding the admission of new recruits (10.26); especially sinful relationships with women (1.42, 50; 2, 28; 4.42; 10.22–23) Frequently offences are spoken of only in veiled or general terms (1.51, 52; 3.3; 5.5, 6; 13.46).

121. Lr 3.23.

122. Lr 5.6

123. Gregory occasionally preferred that a monastery be governed by a provost and not by an abbot: the former was easier to correct or to remove from office. Cf. Lr 9.12 and 10.24.

124. Lr 3.3

125. Caesarius, *Ep Hortatoria*, PL 67:1136c.

126. RB 2:33–36 (third addition).

127. Lr 7.10.

128. Lr 1.69 and 7.39. Some solution in 2 R Fruc 3: the abbot ought not to plead in person, but should entrust legal proceedings to a layman.

129. R Caes V 39. Note, however, certain exceptions, made in favor of pious women and female religious. Moreover, the text well shows that such meals were a serious inconvenience for the abbess, who was thereby distracted from her spiritual obligations.

Chapter 9

FRATERNAL RELATIONS AND CARE FOR THE INNER LIFE (RB 63: 67–72)

OUR INTENTION HERE is to study a group of chapters, which strictly relate to RB. Chapters 64 and 65, and although handled by RB in a highly personal fashion, clearly belong to the plan devised by the Master. Chapter 66, furthermore, corresponds exactly to the position of the 95th and last chapter of RM, the content of which, to a large extent it reproduces. The same is not true of the texts of which we are about to undertake the study: Chapters 67 through 72 constitute a real appendix, in which RB no longer depends upon the sequence of ideas formed by the Master. As for Chapter 63, it links up with the treatise on abbatial succession through the question of 'community ranks', which it treats at the outset (vss 1–9), while its second part (vss 10–19) develops a sort of law on fraternal relationships, exclusive to RB. This second part contains striking similarities with Chapter 72 (*On Good Zeal*), and cannot be studied independently of this chapter. So it seems opportune to assemble Chapter 63 and Chapters 67 through 72 for simultaneous examination. The original character that they share as distinct to RM, and the common tendencies that they affirm prompt us to comment on them together.

However, as we are well aware, the group thus constituted does not form a self-contained whole, which bears no relation to the rest of RB. For, although homogeneous and well defined, it does nevertheless share certain propensities which appear in more than one part of the rule. Therefore our commentary will have everything to gain by retracing the progression of these themes through the whole of RB. By the same token a comparison with the development of these same themes throughout RM will be imposed on us through necessity.

HORIZONTAL RELATIONS

Summarily, and for the sake of providing an initial orientation, it may be said that RB seems to us to be characterized by a certain care for establishing relations among the brethren, which we shall call 'horizontal' (the 'vertical' relations being those which unite each brother to the abbot), and by a more attentive and more subtle consideration of the subjective needs of the brethren. These two tendencies combine in a new insistence on charity, love of God and love of neighbor, an insistence which sets its original impress on the 'vertical' relations themselves, which nevertheless have already been strongly established by the Master. There in a word, lies the relatively new perspective, in which RB in its entirety, but especially in its additional chapters, places the great doctrine on the abbacy inherited from RM and from tradition.

Since our precise purpose is to elucidate this perspective, we need not expatiate upon the beginning of Chapter 63 (vss 1–9). This treatise *De Ordine congregationis* serves at once to conclude the section on recruitment (Chapters 58–62) and to introduce the treatise on abbatial succession (Chapters 64–65). It corresponds to Chapter 92 of RM, but only with regard to the subject treated, for the dispositions adopted do in fact run counter to the Master's. Whereas the latter admits no order of precedence,[1] RB prescribes a rank based on seniority or on merit, the criteria of which it indicates with a certain precision.

By so doing—let us note in passing—RB proves faithful to the cenobitic tradition, in which ranks very early became subject to regulations,[2] whereas the Master gives proof of his originality in excluding them. The two rules present the same contrast on this point that we observed in their legislation for abbatial succession and the 'Second'; RM lets itself be guided by some quite personal views and by the rigorous logic of its educational system, whereas RB returns to the received norms, contenting itself with qualifying them through a few precise definitions.

In the present instance, this manner of renouncing the Master's originalities and aligning with tradition resulted in an effacement of the close relationship which, in RM, united this question of ranks to that of the abbatial succession. The Master deals with ranks only in order to prohibit the designation of a 'Second', as heir apparent of the abbot. In RB the two questions are completely separated: ranks are established, but

Chapter 64 will be careful to specify that no account is to be taken of them in the abbatial election.[3] Only the position of Chapter 63, between the section on recruitment and that on the ordination of the abbot, remains to testify to the original signification of this treatise *De ordine congretationis.*

These summary remarks provide an adequate setting for the first part of the chapter. What is more important than anything else for us here is that the restoration of ranks, in conformity with tradition, was for the RB redactor the occasion for composing the second part of the chapter (vss 10–19), which deals with fraternal relations. The bond between the two parts is so natural and so obvious that it could perhaps conceal for us to the real originality of the second passage. In vain would one seek anything to correspond with it in RM, or even in the tradition anterior to the age of St Benedict.[4] Certainly, the *Vita Fulgentii* clearly shows that identical preoccupations existed in contemporary monasticism,[5] but RB is practically the first legislative text, which had it at heart to give indications of this type on the mutual relations of the brethren.

This second half of Chapter 63 does not correspond to any analogous treatise in the Master, either at this point in his rule or elsewhere, but one does not discover further in RM the detailed regulation enacted here by RB. From the very first sentence (*iuniores igitur priores suos honorent: priores minores suos diligant*), we are faced with a theme which is almost new. This sentence repeats RB 4:70–71 almost word for word (*et seniores uenerare; iuniores diligere*), but when one checks the corresponding passage in the Master, one discovers surprisingly that these two 'instruments of good works' are an RB addition.[6] To begin with, the same conclusion must be drawn, as regards another RB passage, which echoes this sentence: we mean Chapter 72. The two phrases *ut honore inuicem praeueniant* (RB 72:4) and *caritatem fraternitatis caste impendant* (ibid., vs 8) belong properly to RB, like this whole Chapter 72 and the entire 'appendix' of which it forms a part. It is true that *honore inuicem praeueniant* is a quotation of Rom 12:10, as RB itself emphasizes by introducing these words with the formula *ut fiat quod scriptum est* at the end of Chapter 63.[7] It is likewise true that RM cites this same Pauline text (RM 65:8). But this fact does no more than render more striking the original proposition of RB: whereas the Master produces this quotation while speaking of the reception of guests, we here find it applied to the respect that the *brethren* ought to show to one another. Here and now we can note this significant transfer in the re-employment of the same scriptural text. RM deals at length with the marks of charity, which ought to be displayed to visiting monks. On the charity which ought to reign among the members of the community, it shows itself less explicit, and it is precisely this lacuna which RB has wanted to fill, especially in the chapters that we are studying.

But let us proceed with the detailed examination of Chapter 63. Once the general principle has been enunciated, 'hold the elders in high esteem, love the lesser brethren', the text passes to concrete applications. The first of these prescripts concerns the titles of 'brother' or '*nonnus*' which the monks ought to give each other. The ban on addressing each other *puro nomine* has its literal parallel in the *Vita Fulgentii* 53, as we have already pointed out. It is interesting that this witness contemporary with RB made this sign of courtesy as something specially deserved by the abbot, who at that time was Fulgentius. The biographer praises him 'for having shown himself so affable, simple, and accessible to all the brethren that he called no one of them by his simple name (*puro nomine*), and issued his orders without any haughtiness which could smack of worldly authority, humble as his subordinates were'.

This parallel suggests, then, that RB 63 would be especially aimed at the abbot and officers of the monastery when it prescribes, *nulli liceat alium puro appellare nomine* (vs 11). The obligation of giving every monk the title 'brother' would correct the tendency, only too natural in a religious leader who is at the same time a true master of his house, to treat his subjects as is done in the secular *familia*. The warning thus given the abbot would echo the beginning of the chapter (RB 63:2–3): 'The abbot must not trouble the flock, which is entrusted to him; he should *not order anything unjustly, as though he enjoyed unlimited power*; he ought, on the contrary, to bear continually in mind that for all his judgments and actions he will have to give an account to God.' This text in its turn recalls some noteworthy parallels scattered throughout RB: 'The master should always dispose things justly and with due foresight': we have read these words addressed to the abbot in a supplemental note in the treatise on the council of the brethren (RB 3:6). And the same treatise insisted, 'Whatever the situation, the abbot should act in the fear of God and in observance of the rule, knowing that he will have *to give an account to God*, the sovereign and equitable judge, *of all his judgments*' (RB 3:11). This appeal to the tribunal of God, this severe warning directed at the abbot, is repeated in the same terms in the second directory for the abbot (RB 64:7) and in the chapter on the provost (RB 65:22).

Taken as a whole, these texts give out a sound, to which the RM has not accustomed us. The Master is no doubt the first to have developed the theme of 'equity' and 'rendering an account,' whether in his treatise on the abbot or in the short admonition during the abbatial ordination.[8] But apart from those texts specially intended for the abbot, it does not occur to him to insert references to this doctrine in the course of the rule, as if the abbot had particular need of being put on his guard against temptations to tyranny,[9] jealousy,[10], injustice,[11] capriciousness,[12] and imprudence.[13] This fashion of lecturing the abbot is one of RB's characteristic features. It witnesses to a livelier awareness of the superior's weakness and of the difficulties of his office and of a keen concern to remedy his shortcomings. It is therefore at least likely that the obligation of calling all the 'younger' monks 'brother' weighs first of all on this *prior* par excellence who is the abbot.

As for the counterpart of this regulation, 'To call one's elders *nonni*, that is to say, Reverend Fathers' (RB 63:12), strikes us particularly, because it extends to all the more elderly religious the title of father which seemed to be reserved for the abbot. Certainly the appellations *nonnus* and *nonna*, already well attested by Jerome,[14] are nothing but traditional, but the application made of them here in the cenobitic plan to every elder is not otherwise attested in the rules.[15] RM, in particular, knows nothing of this custom; it habitually designates the monk by the term *frater*, and it is sufficient to reread what the Master writes about priests residing in the monastery to perceive with how much reticence he grants the title *pater monasterii*, the traditional equivalent for *abbas*, to personages other than the real superior.[16]

Although less precise and less charged with meaning, *nonnus* does not speak less of fatherhood, as RB stresses when translating it. To give this title to any member of the community indiscriminately is not perhaps 'sloppy talk,' as Péguy might have said, but it surely amounts to using the name of father in a broad and weakened sense, which recalls the generous grant of the title *abbas* by Cassian, to the novice-monk Germanus, who was his companion.[17] This semantic fact brings us nearer to RB 31:2, which demands of the cellarer, *omni congregationi sit sicut pater*. In both cases we are dealing with details, which distinguish RB from RM and which perhaps suggest a certain flexibility in the meaning of the unique fatherhood of the abbot, a flexibility, which could correspond with the facts set out in our commentary on Chapters 3 and 65.

In any case, this regulation 'To call one's elders *nonni*,' just like the preceding one, testifies to the anxiety of which RB redactor has to imposing certain forms, stamped with courtesy and affection, on the mutual relationships of the brethren. On the basis of rank in community, which has been regulated in the first part of this chapter, he establishes rules of good manners, which reinforce the hierarchical structure of the community. This organization of the fraternity, by virtue of which each one receives a precise place and undertakes well-defined duties towards each 'brother' or 'father' introduces a quite new element into the plan of the *coenobium* delineated by the Master. The latter had confined himself to dividing the brethren into decuries, that is to say, to placing them under the surveillance of subordinate officers responsible for extending the educational activity of the abbot to every time and every place. Through the provosts of his *decania*, it was with the abbot that the 'minor' brother found himself in contact. To this 'vertical' structure, RB here joins a supplementary network of bonds, which one would be tempted to call 'horizontal,' did these not also take account of the hierarchical order. To tell the truth, this order is no longer solely a function of the abbot's will and at the service of his educational mission. The abbot, to be sure, may intervene and modify it for good reasons, but seniority is its normal basis, and seniority is not created by the abbot, but by Providence and the inspiration of grace. An older monk will be called 'father', whom no special mandate of the abbot has designated for this honor.

Such is the sense in which one may speak here of 'horizontal relations', meaning thereby certain relations which, by virtue both of origin and intention, are largely independent of the abbatial office. If one prefers to avoid this word because of the hierarchical aspect of such relations, it is at any rate necessary to note that the 'hierarchy' thus devised does not coincide completely with the decanal system, for which provision is made only by RM. In this chapter the RB directions, although imparting added strength to the hierarchical structure of the community, as we said above, do at the same time modify this structure very notably by partially detaching it from the abbot.[18]

Moreover, after endeavoring to characterize these rules of good manners to define the meaning of the new relationships that they indicate, we must particularly notice their appearance in the rule and the fundamental anxieties, which derive from them. The major fact is that the legislator pays attention to the mutual relations of the brethren, and no longer solely to their education by the abbot and his provosts. A new anxiety for uniting the monks to one another appears and it is in light of this that RB now comes to speak to us about the signs of respect to be shown to the abbot.

The directions which follow (RB 63:13–14) present the marks of honor due to the abbot as a particular instance of the principle laid down at the outset: 'Let the younger brethren honor their elders.' This note on the abbatial title is arresting first of all for its obvious allusion to the *uices Christi creditur agere* in RB 2:2, a text deriving from RM. To the title *abbas*, the only one envisaged in the explanation provided by RM 2-RB 2, is here added that of *dominus* which, in fact, refers no less clearly to the person of Christ. There is no originality, furthermore, in this double appellation, of which we possess numerous examples, either in RM or in tradition.[19] As Herwegen has suggested, it is very possible that *dominus* especially was felt to be a mark of honor, and *abbas* to be a sign of affection.[20] Thus would sentiments of respect and love, distinguished at the beginning of the paragraph (v 10), converge upon the representative of Christ.

Furthermore, it seems that the intention of these lines is to give the abbot a new lesson. The warning of Chapter 2 is repeated to him: his name ought to remind him of the Person whom he represents, and prompt him to show himself worthy of him. To this passage, borrowed from the directory for the abbot, the redactor adds an original point: *non sua assumptione, sed honore et amore Christi*, an expression where this fear of the instinct to dominate, which we have mentioned above, particularly breaks through. Again we face here an anxiety to recall to a humble awareness of his dependence on Christ a superior, who is too much tempted to consider himself simply the *dominus* of some secular *familia*.

Before leaving this note on the abbot's titles, it remains for us to point out its affinity with the final directions of Chapter 72 (vss 9–11): *amore Deum timeant; abbatem suum sincera et humili caritate diligant; Christo omnino nihil praeponant.* On the one side and on the other, mention of the abbot and of Christ follow on the reflections on fraternal charity. We follow in a sense an upward path which, beginning from the brethren, rises to the superior and ends with him whom the abbot represents.[21] What is more, the two texts harmonize in associating respect with love: to the expressions already cited in RB 63 there correspond, in Chapter 72, *amore . . . timeant* and *humili caritate diligant*. The affinity between the two passages, then, invites us to comment on them simultaneously, in spite of certain obvious characteristics which distinguish one from the other. Two connected themes come to light, in which we recognize the anxieties peculiar to RB: the love that the brethren bear for their abbot and the emphasis placed on the love of God in the obedience rendered to the superior.

The precept to love the abbot is explicit in RB 72, but is also implicit in RB 63, through the context of fraternal love and of love of Christ, in which the direction on the abbatial title appear. Moreover, we have noted above the reasons, which cause us to think that *abbas* particularly expresses love, and *dominus* respect. Now, this theme of love for the abbot is lacking in RM. It is not that the Master attaches less importance to the relationship between a monk and his abbot, but the linear sketch plan of his relations discloses scarcely anything but the humble respect, with which the brother receives the injunctions of his 'teacher,' as though they were the word of God. The Master's perspective is confined to this basic consideration of the salvific role of the abbot as organ of the divine will. The attitude demanded of the disciple is uniquely one of faith and obedience.

Did the RB redactor feel a need to complete this oversimplified sketch? We are, at all events, indebted to him for these valuable and precise definitions of the love for the abbot. We are perhaps in a position to identify the literary source, from which he derived this idea; we, of course, recall that the second directory for the abbot prescribes for him, *et studeat plus amari quam timeri* (RB 64:15). Now, it is from the rule of Augustine, as we recognized at the right moment, that he borrowed this precept. There we find the coupling of 'love and fear', of which we established the presence, expressed in various ways in RB 63 and 72. Above all we find there that anxiety—so typical of the RB redactor—to enter into bonds of love between the community and its superior. The Master was already asking the abbot to love all his subjects with an equal love.[22] It was the property of RB, under augustinian influence, to arouse the reciprocal love of the subjects for their abbot.[23]

The love which the brethren bear for their abbot takes its place within the stream of love, which has as its object God himself. This connection, only hinted at in RB 72 by bringing the formulas together, is affirmed with the fullest clarity in RB 63: all the signs of honor and affection, which the abbot receives, are in fact addressed to Christ, *dominus et abbas uocetur . . . honore et amore Christi*. Here is a second theme which it is important to point out, since it is scarcely encountered in RM: the subordination to the superior is a matter of love for God. We are told this here in connection with the marks of respect, which the monk pays to his abbot, but it is especially on the subject of obedience that the redactor seized the opportunity to stress this motive of love. The appendix on two occasions insists on it: *ex caritate oboediat* (RB 68:5); *omni caritate oboediant* (RB 71:4).

Does this mean that the Master has avoided presenting obedience as a matter of love? A good number of texts would seem at first sight to prove the contrary. From the beginning of its treatment of the question, RM makes obedience the characteristic of those *qui nihil sibi a Christo carius aliquid existimantes. . .* [24] It is true that this state of soul, in which nothing is preferred to Christ, is according to the Master actually to be found in the small number of perfect souls. It is only in RB that the aim of preferring nothing to Christ is put forward for all who practise obedience, without distinction between the perfect and the imperfect. But at the end of the same chapter, RM seems to have forgotten the distinction drawn at the beginning, and when it speaks again of the *amor ad uitam aeternam ambulandi* (RM 7:47 = RB 5:10), it is in order to ground the obedience of all cenobites on such 'love'. Similarly, when he addresses the postulant, the Master describes obedience as a manifestation of love for Christ: *nunquam nos uel desideria carnis praetulimus amori eius* (RM 90:58; cf. RM 3:23). One might also point out that it is *pro Domino* that one endures the tests of obedience (RM 10:49 = RB 7:38), *propter Christum* that one renounces self (RM 7:52), *propter eum* that one will go so far as to give up one's life, if need be, in this abnegation and obedience (RM 90:59).

Thus the motive of love is not missing from the Master's theories on obedience. We shall notice, however, that these texts do not expressly speak of 'charity'. By employing the word *caritas*, therefore, RB institutes a slight innovation in the two passages of the appendix cited above.

This exactitude in terminology acquires its full meaning, when compared to a most significant addition, which RB introduced into the third rung of humility (RB 7:34). The Master had said: *omni oboedientia se subdat maiori* (RM 10:49). The RB redactor added: *pro Dei amore*, an addition the more noteworthy, as the RB redaction is more concise here, eliminating a good dozen lines of the Master's text. Such an addition is rather surprising for anyone who has understood the plan followed by RM throughout this chapter on humility. Following Cassian, the Master wants to lead us from fear to love by passing through all the manifestations of humility. It is only at the end of the ascent of the 'twelve rungs' that one will arrive at 'charity' as the sublime climax of the work of ascesis undertaken in fear.[25] Until then, no mention must be made of it, as the disciple is considered too imperfect to dare to lay claim to that magnificent crown of all his efforts.

By introducing 'the love of God' at the third rung as the motive for obedience, the RB redactor therefore shows that he did not fully grasp, or make his own, the Master's thought. Unlike his predecessor, he cannot conceive of obedience while failing to take account of the love of God. Mentioning one leads necessarily, under the flow of his pen, to mentioning the other, even though the plan of ascent towards God should have on this account to suffer through its logical consistency.[26] *Pro amore Dei* is, of course, a less compromising expression than *ex caritate*; the redactor by that means avoids a too obvious anticipation of the conclusion of the chapter, where *caritas* must make its triumphant and unexpected entry. However, the Master did not unintentionally abstain from speaking even of *amor* in the course of the chapter, whereas we have seen how he appeals readily to this sentiment to provide the motivation for obedience. In order to remain faithful to the plan traced by Cassian, it was necessary to set love on one side so long as the limit of the indications of humility had not yet been attained. (*Pro Domino*, at the fourth rung, makes only a very subtle allusion to the theme of love, too subtle to upset the plan, which we have just indicated). The addition *pro Dei amore* in RB 7:34 is therefore somewhat out of place, to judge from the standpoint of composition of the chapter, such as the Master had conceived it under the inspiration of Cassian. But this awkwardness shows to what extent love, in the redactor's mind, is inseparable from obedience.

These observations on the third rung of humility throw a certain light on the fact, which we were noting a moment ago: RM does indeed speak of 'love' in connection with obedience, but avoids the word *caritas*. When one examines the Master's texts on the *amor* of the obedient monk, one is struck by the conclusion that the context ordinarily mentions desire for eternal life. Thus, after saying that immediate obedience is actually found in those 'who hold nothing dearer to them than Christ' (RM 7:2), the Master continues: *propter metum gehennae uel diuitias uitae aeternae.* The phrase *amor ambulandi ad uitam aeternam* brings love and the desire for eschatological bliss into still closer association (RM 7:47). Likewise, the *pro Domino* of RM 10:55 ought to be understood 'hope of divine reward' (RM 10:56), and the same is true for analogous formulas. It seems that the Master, when he speaks of the 'love' of the disciple who obeys, is thinking of the desire to be with Christ and to obtain eternal reward. The content of this state of soul, then, includes both hope and charity. Charity is not expressly designated; and even uttering its theme is avoided. It would be rash to affirm that the Master thereby meant to exclude it. However, without drawing any distinction between hope and charity, his thoughts turn more openly to the former.

Possibly the Master is here still dependent upon Cassian and his very lofty idea of the pre-eminence of charity. Whereas hope causes desire for reward, charity consists in disinterested pleasure in the good of virtue for its own sake, without regard for the reward that it merits for us.[27] In such a perspective, it may seem inopportune to speak of *caritas* in connection with the obedience of cenobites. These men who have only begun to tread the path of virtue, these sinners in the process of conversion, have too great a need of stimulation through fear of punishment and desire for eternal life for one to dare to attribute to them so disinterested a motive. Yet *caritas* will play a role in their life, as we shall see further on, but under its aspect of fraternal charity either towards guests and strangers or (more rarely) towards members of the community, and in particular towards sick brothers. Under its aspect of love of God, *caritas* does not arise as a motivation for the life of obedience. Since it is a matter of emerging from sin and taking the first steps on the way leading to salvation, it is still necessary to be content with the inferior motives of fear and hope.[28]

The RB redactor, less conscious no doubt of the theoretical reasons underlying this reticence and also more sensitive perhaps to the universal significance of the commandment of charity and its determinant role from beginning to end of the Christian life, has quite simply appealed to *caritas*, when he had to describe the obedient monk. The word caused him no apprehension. As for its content, he is not worried about defining it by distinguishing it from hope—desire. It is a tender veneration for God, for Christ and for all those, great and small, who represent him. By employing it, RB speaks the simple language of the Scriptures and of the Christian people, without encumbering itself with the formal schemes of spirituality elaborated by the Alexandrians, accepted by Cassian and still recognizable in RM, as well as in those parts of RB which derive from RM.[29]

Love for the abbot, love for Christ in the marks of honor paid to the abbot: such then are the two original contributions in this note on the abbatial title as elucidated by the commentary on it, which is proffered by RB itself in Chapter 72. But let us move on. The next lines (RB 63: 15–17) deal with the marks of deference which the younger brethren should show towards their elders every time that they meet them. The first of these signs of respect is the *Benedic* or *Benedicite*, that is to say, the request for a blessing.[30] This custom is already attested by RM, where it is observed not only when the brethren accost the abbot or greet a stranger, but even among members of the community.[31] The only remarkable thing, therefore, in this RB direction is its imperative character and its definition of the hierarchical order, which must be safeguarded: *iunior priorem petat*. An accepted custom is thus precisely defined in such a way as to make it appropriate to a community organized according to rank.

The following feature betrays the same meticulous attitude of mind, but this time we can discover hardly a single instance of such a custom in the cenobitic tradition prior to St Benedict.[32] Not until the following century, in the rules of Fructuosus (1 R Fruc 12) and Waldebert (Chapter 22) do parallels appear, and perhaps these texts depend on RB. To rise when an elder passes by (*maior*, instead of the usual *prior*, and like it, one of the names for the abbot), to give up one's place to this elder, not to sit down except at his invitation (here *senior*, likewise unique in this chapter)—all these regulations of manners may correspond with a slackening of the upbringing received in secular society and the coarser manners of the population, from which the monastery recruited its members. But it reveals especially a new attention paid by the legislator to relationships among the brethren. No longer are such relationships left to chance or custom. The authority of the rule must provide for them. This canonization raises them to the rank of educational resources, of which the cenobitic school avails itself, along with the relationship with the provosts and the abbot, which almost exclusively held the Master's attention.

By concluding this development with the citation of Rom 12:10, *honore inuicem praeuenientes*, RB returns to the initial theme, *iuniores priores suos honorent* (RB 63:10). Comparison of the two formulas is instructive: the *inuicem* of St Paul, the reciprocal and spontaneous respect, are translated into cenobitic language by a code of etiquette in which the inferior alone bears the cost. Mutual respect is actually, in the RB description, rendered unilaterally by the 'junior,' apart from the title *frater* which his elder accords him. We shall find the same in the chapter *On Mutual Obedience* (RB 71). There also it is laid down in principle that the brethren ought to obey one another (*sibi inuicem*), but who is to obey and who command is swiftly settled: *omnes iuniores prioribus suis oboediant*. It is in this sense of an obedience rendered in conformity with rank in community that we should understand the less precise formula in the subsequent chapter: *oboedientiam sibi certatim inpendant* (RB 72:6).

Thus, whether it is question of 'reciprocal' respect or of 'mutual' obedience, RB presents us with a rigorously hierarchized system. When we discover in it a new care for fraternal relations, insofar as these are distinguished from the relationship with superiors (abbot and provosts), we must guard against imagining these relationships as between equals. Quite the opposite, these newly regulated relations are presented as an extension of the master-disciple relationship.

The first sentence of Chapter 71 clearly testifies to the intention of placing mutual obedience in a prolonged form of obedience to the abbot, *non solum abbati . . . sed etiam sibi inuicem*, just as, in Chapter 63, the title of *nonni* given to the brethren echoes that of *abbas*. Furthermore the redactor is especially careful to indicate the priority due to the orders of the abbot and provost over those which even the most senior might give to their inferiors (*priuata imperia*). One recognizes in such quasi-juridical definitions the same care for clearness and the same dread of encroachments and disorder with which the regulation of the procedure for the council of the brethren is penetrated (RM 3:1–2) and so many other original passages of RB. By taking an interest in fraternal relations, our rule certainly wants to set in motion a current of charity within the community, a 'good zeal' as Chapter 72 defines it. But this spiritual animation is paired with a precise regulation and ends with the constitution of a new hierarchy, that of ranks, which complements the decanal and abbatial organization, while remaining subordinate to it.

Mutual honor and mutual obedience: these two questions, as we have just seen, are allied; RB treats them in the same way. So we shall still be commenting on Chapter 63, when we take note of a text of the Master, which speaks of universal obedience. The penultimate article of the *ars sancta* (RM 3:76) is thus formulated: *omnibus bonis ex toto corde oboedire*. It winds up a series of six precepts relating to a good understanding with one's neighbor: 'Hate no one; do not be over-zealous; do not give yourself up to envy; have no liking for contention; be reconciled with your enemy before sunset. . . .' In both tenor and substance, it is a sufficiently exact equivalent to the maxim previously cited in RB 72:6, *oboedientiam sibi certatim inpendant*. Why, then, has RB not retained it among the 'instruments of good works' in its Chapter 4?

Doubtless we should not insist upon the fact that two lines before this omission RB added several 'instruments', in which we read an allusion to the hierarchical order: *Et seniores uenerare. Iuniores diligere* (RB 4:70– 71). Finally, however, the linking-together of this insertion and this omission has at least symbolic value for us. 'Obey *all those who are good*' became in RB 'obey not only the abbot and the provost, but all one's elders as well'. We have passed from spiritual counsel to the rule, from a spirit of universal submission, for the sake of peace, to obedience due the elders, within the framework of the system of ranks. But RB is not for all that a simple set of statutes, which are indifferent to the values of the soul: 'it is by this way of obedience that the brethren will go to God' (RB 71:2). Obedience is a 'good' (ibid., vs 1), and the rule continues to speak of a reciprocal alacrity in rendering one another mutual obedience (RB 72:6). It is only that in RB general and vague warm-hearted advice has been given concrete expression in a set of laws, which pays close attention to the good ordering of the community.

Here as elsewhere, one can predict that between the Master and his successor there lies a different margin of experience of the common life and its difficulties. The *coenobium* is not fully constructed when only the hierarchical framework of the deans and abbot has been established. The relations of the 'junior' brothers towards the others also need to be regulated and set in the hierarchy. The relations of all with the superior and his officers need to be recalled, emphasized, defined in detail and provided with more strict sanctions. This all results from the weakening of the abbot's prestige, combined with his existence in superior isolation. In RM, he rules the entire existence of the group absolutely and effortlessly. His authority is imposed without protest and his educational activity, whether direct or through the medium of the provosts, is the only thing which retains our attention; the problem of fraternal relations is not even raised. The RB redactor finds himself faced with a more developed situation, in which this ideal scheme requires to be fulfilled.

Honore inuicem praeuenientes (RB 63:17). We recall that the Master applied this text to the signs of respect shown to guests, whereas RB uses it to justify those shown to an elder brother. In both cases, it is to be noted, the 'mutual' honor is in reality one-way only. The hierarchizing interpretation of RB is therefore already that of the Master. Another parallel with RM merits attention: just as the *ars sancta* of the Master involved the precept 'to obey all those who are good,' so RB 'instruments of good works' include the direction, *honorare omnes homines* (RB 4:8), which corrects *honorare patrem et matrem* in RM 3:8, no doubt judged inopportune for monks. 'Honor all men' is more vague and general than 'obey all those who are good.' We must, however, take account of the literary genre of this collection of general counsels, of its scriptural sources and especially in the present case, of the intention to correct an overprecise article in the *ars sancta* of the Master.

These remarks bring us to the end of the commentary on Chapter 63. *Honore inuicem praeuenientes*, included with *iuniores priores suos honorent*, constitutes the real conclusion of this second part of the chapter, dealing with fraternal relations. By reason of their content, the following lines (RB 63:18–19) link up rather to the first part, where rank in community was regulated. The redactor adds as an appendix a note on the place of the children in this community order. Here, no more than in the rest of the chapter, could RB have drawn inspiration from the arrangements previously determined by the Master. RM often mentions the presence of children of less than fifteen years of age, and even of less than twelve, among the brethren. It devotes attention to their dietary régime (quantity of food and meal-times) and to punishments appropriate to their age. For the rest, however, they seem to be treated identically with their adult brethren.

While in principle sustaining this equality, even insisting on it,[33] RB makes a clear distinction between children and grown-ups. Twice in this chapter (vss 9 and 19), and a third time in Chapter 70, it places the *pueri* under everyone's supervision. Consideration of age thus makes an inroad into the principle of seniority, based on time of entrance into the monastery. Every adult can and must, as far as his capacity and intelligence allow, still play a hand in the education of the boy-monks. We shall observe how the educational mission, which the Master had reserved for the abbot and his provosts, is here delegated to many. The hierarchical structure of the monastery, already enriched by the introduction of ranks, is further modified, being varied by the recognition of the role awarded to age.

Our commentary on Chapter 63, which introduces the group of chapters forming the appendix, has already presented us with the principal themes developed in these chapters. As we made our way, we have not failed to point out anything which, in Chapters 67 through 72, repeats or illustrates the subject-matter of *De ordine congregationis.* It now remains to complete this inventory by going though the appendix step by step. Some rapid notes on each chapter will suffice. We shall then be in a position to organize all these notes and collate them with the data supplied by RM.

Although Chapter 66 (*De ostiariis monasterii*) belongs not to the block of texts supplemental to the appendix but to the fund of material transmitted by RM, its place requires a word of comment on it here. Comparison with RM 95 (same title) shows that RB has both curtailed it and added to it. What it suppresses is the rule of life given the porters by the Master (RM 95:4–16): presence at the common reading and at the office, work at their trades, in the service of the hebdomadaries or at the lodge itself, and meals at the abbot's table. The final definitions are also omitted: the door of the monastery always closed; the door knocker (RM 95:22–24).

On the other hand, RB has certain additions which specially claim our attention. First, the qualities required from the man (singular) who is assigned to the door. Already, RM had wanted aged brothers (*aetate decrepitis*), and RB comments on this note, giving it a double meaning: the old man will be 'sagacious, knowing how to give and receive answers', and then too 'his age will not permit him to be running off anywhere'.[34] Care for the reception of strangers, which is already obvious as the first of these requirements, inspires an even more important second additon (RB 66: 3–4). There again a practical note of the Master (*cella intra regias monasterii prope construantur*, RM 95:1) gives the opportunity for a commentary, which lays stress on the material and spiritual perfection with which this service of receiving visitors should be accomplished. The stranger will always find someone who will answer his knock. At the first sound of the knocker or the call of the beggar, one will respond *Deo gratias* or *Benedic*, 'and with all the gentleness resulting from the fear of God, the porter will hasten to give his reply with fervent charity' (RB 66:3–4).

We shall recognize in this addition the note of charity, which has been frequently pointed out in the preceding pages. Even the clumsiness of the style (*cum omni mansuetudine . . . cum feruore*) renders more recognizable the redactor's insistent attitude—the ardor which he seeks to communicate to the reader. Doubtless, he alludes to the temptations to impatience caused by the large number of passers-by, many more, it seems, than RM had foreseen. But this actual circumstance does not by itself fully account for the addition. The style of RB is the same here as it was in the notes on love and obedience. There is the same regard for the individual attitude of the brother, and the same care to arouse devotion in the accomplishment of the duty prescribed by the rule.

Such are the most significant modifications by RB in this chapter on porters.[35] This little treatise loses most of the practical specification, which made the RM text interesting. Almost nothing of the rule of life for porters remains. We do, however, gain some valuable notes on the meaning and spiritual significance of this service. The ideal of charity proposed to the porter gains greater emphasis in proportion to the removal of the detailed, practical hints from the text. The qualities that this brother ought to possess and the manner in which he should fulfill his office, have replaced the list of his functions and his daily program. There is no longer talk of what he might do alongside his work as porter, nor even of the details of what this work consists,[36] but rather of the way in which he ought to deal with the persons that he receives, having in view both the fear and the love of God.[37] This is one of the most notable aspects of the care for the inner life which seems to us characteristic of RB.

The subsequent chapter (RB 67: *De fratribus in uiam directis*), notwithstanding its odd position, is in reality borrowed largely from RM. Its normal place, corresponding to RM 66 and 67, would be between RB 51 and 52. It therefore belongs to the appendix only by virtue of the fact that it follows the chapter on the porter. Insofar as it resumes the liturgical directions of RM on prayers for travellers, it holds no great interest for us. More noteworthy are the additions we read beginning from line 4. The Master had been content to prescribe that monks returning to the monastery after a journey should ask the brethren to pray for them, not without specifying very exactly, as is his manner, the time and place where this rite should be carried out, and the psalm verse to be recited. In RB a more summary description of the rite is given, slightly modified moreover, but an exposition of the motives intended to indicate the sense of this prayer is added. 'It is on account of the faults committed, for fear they may have lapsed while on the journey by seeing or hearing evil things or vain words' (RB 67:4). This remark not only aims at completing what has preceded. It introduces the subsequent addition which forbids relating what was seen or heard outside under pain of punishment (ibid., vss 5–6). The pachomian origin of these lines can hardly be questioned, despite the *quia plurima destructio est*, which seems to echo recent experience and personal assessments. The last addition (vs 7) may also be inspired by the rule of Pachomius.[38] In any case the RM ignores the disadvantages of travellers' tales as much as it does outings from the enclosure without permission. Only the final words of the chapter (*quippiam quamuis paruum sine iussione abbatis facere*) can claim an antecedent in RM.[39]

All told, the RB additions in this little chapter determine the significance of the rite as conceived by the Master who, to judge from the psalm verse that he chose,[40] is not thinking specifically of evil influences met on route. It is probably the pachomian rule and perhaps experience too, which prompted this new consideration. Starting from the pachomian data (not to relate what was seen or heard outside), the RB redactor elaborates the reason for praying for those just returned (evil sights, evil schemings). The threat of 'punishment in accordance with the rule', which in RB punishes the violation of any prohibition almost automatically, could not fail to be brandished here. It was extended to the case of illicit outings, which fits the present context; then later the theme was made more general, without taking account of the subject of outings and without paying attention to the context. Finally it linked up with a precept of RM, at least as regards the tone of its subject matter and probably through a chance encounter.[41]

Insistence on the universal control exercised by the abbot, though not missing from RM, is, of course, a characteristic of RB. We may even say the redactor seems obsessed by the fear that subjects will encroach upon the abbatial domain.[42] As regards the unlimited authority of the 'teacher', RM was no less categorical, but affirmed it with greater calmness. The frequency of the reminders issued by RB, the minuteness of detail to which they are sometimes applied, their general import, without relation to the context in other passages, all seem to indicate a certain uneasiness, as though the abbatial power felt less sure of itself and was seeking self-confirmation.

The temptation could arise also to emphasize in this chapter the addendum *propter excessus* etc. by stressing the new preoccupation for the welfare of souls, which it displays, and the attention devoted to particular needs, of which the Master does not appear to have been clearly aware. But it would not do to exaggerate in stressing so tenuous a factor, all the more as we know its probable literary source. Another much more significant testimony is given us by RB in the next chapter. It will throw full light upon this 'care for the inner life,' the traces of which we are discovering as we go through the appendix.

Chapter 68 (*Si fratri inpossibilia iniungantur*) is indeed one of the most characteristic and most valuable passages in RB. It is no longer necessary, after so many comments, to stimulate admiration for a doctrine so firm and so subtle, so supernatural and so human. If in the preceding chapter, RB was most probably inspired by Pachomius, and we may with equally strong probability designate the *Regula Basilii* (Chapter 69) as the source for this chapter. Relationship between the two texts goes as far as an identical expression for designating the superior: *is qui praeest*, translating *proëstôs*, is the habitual name for superior in Basil-Rufinus. By using it here for the first and last time, RB quite obviously betrays its origin.[43]

As to content, it is indeed the same in both, but RB knew how to arrange it in a sober and lucid presentation which methodically propounds the successive phases through which the obedient monk passes. At each of these stages (reception by the order—avowal of inability made to the superior—final submission), the interior and exterior attitude of the subject is defined in two or three phrases full of meaning: *cum omni mansuetudine et oboedientia . . . patienter et opportune . . . ex caritate confidens de adiutorio Dei*. This description, so admirably done, so dense, so rich in precise and delicate spiritual sayings, constitutes a passage of exceptional literary quality which leaves its basilian sources far behind.

Basil contented himself with establishing that obedience is limitless, and that, after having set out his difficulties, the inferior should resign himself to the superior's decision. Elsewhere, he emphasized the motive of charity which dictates such an attitude (Chapter 82). What we do not find in his rules are indications as to the *manner* of receiving the order, and of setting out one's complaints and ultimately submitting oneself. It is this training which takes the monk by the hand and conducts him from beginning to end of the trial; it is this care for his education which enters into the details of attitudes and sentiments, in order to sanctify everything.

The highly original contribution of this chapter deserves equal appreciation in relation to RM. RM 57:14–16 had possibly served as a long-distance fuse: in that passage, the Master takes measures against brothers who would rail against an order of the abbot to go on an outing. Now our RB 68 follows a short treatise on journeys. The RB 67 through 68 sequence would thus be explicable, because for some monks, outings are a painful form of obedience. Moreover, we must recognize that the chapter on obedience in the case of impossibilities is written in the most general terms and that all allusion to the context of journeys is absent from it.

If, for the rest, a connection between RB 68 and RM 57:14–16 had to be admitted, it could only become clearer that RB is here highly original. For the Master, refusal to obey by a brother is nothing other than a fault liable to punishment. The Master merely confines himself to indicating to the abbot how he should deal with this case: excommunication and appropriate reprimand, based on Lk 10:16 ('Anyone who rejects you rejects me'). In RB the question is handled from a quite different point of view, namely, that of the subject. It maps a line of conduct for the brother who is tempted to evade obedience, which cause him to walk in gentleness and patience, even as far as the heroic execution of the 'impossible' order, out of love for God. The two authors sound an alert against 'pride' and 'resistance',[44] but whereas RM considers the fault as already committed, RB tries to forestall it.

Besides this very remote parallelism, RM 7:11–15, 20–21 must be taken into account. The Master suggests tactfully to the disciple the possibility of only obeying the second summons of the abbot. This concession, which disappeared from RB 5, is justified by an insight, full of human feeling, for the weakness of man's nature. There is a certain analogy between this disposition and the possibility of deferring the execution of an order that has been received, which is granted by RB 68. But the differences greatly outweigh this faint similarity: RM does not speak of 'suggesting the reasons for his inability' to the superior (on the contrary, it is the silence of the inferior, which renders his delay in obeying permissible). Above all, the situation is altogether different: in RB we have a brother who is faced with an 'impossible' requirement of obedience, while here we have an indolent and distracted monk. As on other occasions, the RM standpoint is that of the abbot (how should he behave towards a monk of this sort?) whereas RB takes that of the subject (how should he behave towards authority?).

All we can say is that RB 68, in granting the monk the opportunity to set out his difficulties, indirectly takes up again the idea of RM 7, according to which obedience may brook certain delays. Thus tolerance, recognized by RM 7, but suppressed by RB 5, is reintroduced with a certain bias in RB. Moreover, the difference in quality between the considerations of RM 7 and those of RB 68 is too great to be insisted upon. In RB, it is not a matter of taking into account the slackness of certain temperaments, but of helping souls in temptation to overcome trials, of enlightening them as to their duties, of encouraging them to have confidence and love, and of conducting them step by step to the victory of obedience.[45]

The plan of obedience proposed by the Master is therefore considerably enriched in this little chapter of RB. We already knew that the monk had to go as far as heroism in his obedience, even to martyrdom embraced with joy (fourth rung of humility: RM = RB). In this respect, the present chapter tells us nothing new. But if the limitless demands of obedience had been known to us, no RM text had brought to our notice the picture, at once so exact and so human, of the actual difficulties of the obedient monk, none had attended to our temptations with such foresight and solicitude, and none had endeavored to sanctify every moment of our trial.

Without subtracting anything from the doctrine on obedience, RB has humanized it and brought it within our scope. A new stage—the 'suggestion'—is introduced into the plan of obedience and confers on it a higher value, that of an act accomplished with full understanding, both superior and inferior henceforth acting in full knowledge. A new consideration, that of the personal feelings of the monk and of the 'impossibility' that he experiences, varies and enriches the theme of obedience. It gives place to a deepening of the psychological level, and to an educational effort, which takes intimate repugnance as its point of departure and converts it to the spiritual benefit of the monk. No text illustrates better the original character of RB in relation to RM as regards care for the individual.

The next two chapters (RB 69 and 70) obviously form a unity that we must not divide. The central theme is the affirmation of the abbot's rights in matters of correction: no one may take up the defense of a brother, who has been reprimanded by him; no one may excommunicate or strike another without his authorization. Both these points are missing in RM, but both are abundantly illustrated in monastic tradition. Among the many sources that the *Concordia* assembles, the pachomian texts must probably be given special importance. We have already recognized their influence on the redaction of Chapter 67. Among the parallels cited by the *Concordia* in connection with Chapter 70,[46] the most striking in R Or 13. Now, this text is actually plagiarized from the rule of Pachomius (R Pac 147, Inst 5). It is the sole document which clearly enunciated the principle of control by the superior over all correction, such as we read in RB 70:1–2. Dependence on Pachomius is less certain in RB 69, since many other ancient texts could have furnished the same idea, but the case of RB 67 and RB 70 encourage us to prefer the pachomian rule.[47]

However, one would have an inexact idea of the origin of these chapters, were they looked upon merely as borrowing from the literary tradition of the rules. Chapter 69 first of all strikes us for the liveliness of its expressions, behind which one detects the bitter lesson of experience. *Scandala* (disputes) must have come to the ears of the redactor, and the precision of his remarks on the tie of blood seems to allude to facts that he has observed. We shall note, in the same way, the emphasis of the second clause (*nec quolibet modo* . . .) which only repeats the first. The final sanction bears perhaps the same emotional stamp (*acrius*). Everything therefore indicates that our literary sources have only served to organize the reactions aroused by life itself. We are here dealing with an 'abbot's reaction', such as is so often found in the addenda to RB. A situation, which has been described in RB, has presented itself; and so it has been necessary to insert in the rule a reminder of the old prohibitions carried by Pachomius, Horsiesios, Basil and so many others. This situation—one monk in defense of another, in opposition to their superior—reveals that the authority of the abbot is being questioned, something that the Master never envisaged.[48] It confirms the remarks which Chapter 67 suggested to us.

The same must be said of the complementary chapter on excommunication and on blows inflicted without a mandate from the abbot. This too is a form of 'presumption' (the word recurs six times in these two chapters), that is, encroachment on the rights of the abbot. The citation of 1 Tim 5:20, which follows the first sentence, gives support to the ambiguity. Who the *peccantes* are is not clear: would they be the brethren improperly excommunicated or beaten (they must have committed some fault to be treated thus), or else has the rule in mind the perpetrators of the punishment? In other words, is RB pronouncing a general law valid for every kind of fault, or else does it prefer to punish especially the crime of 'improper punishment,' because of its particular character? I would incline rather toward this latter sense, on account of R Caes V 24, where the same Pauline text refers to the punishment of sisters who have dared to come to blows. It seems that for RB as for Caesarius, 1 Tim 5:20 is aimed against the special fault of those who strike their brothers.[49]

The subsequent sentence (RB 70:4–5) reproduces in essence a passage of RB 63 upon which we have already commented. It will suffice this time to point out that the idea of entrusting the children to the supervision of all the adults hardly agrees with Basil and Isidore, who put them beneath the direction of a single master chosen with great care.[50] On the other hand, RM foresees no specially appointed master for the children,[51] and everything makes one think that they share the lot of their older comrades in all things, as will be the case in RB. They are combined with adults in each 'decade' and therefore come under the supervision of the two 'provosts' of the decade, who care for them in the same way as they do for the adults.

While maintaining this full community life between adults and children, RB accords the former, because of their age and regardless of their rank in community, the right to supervise the latter. To the summons of this rule, previously set out in Chapter 63—and this precision is important— RB adds some hints on the *manner* of correcting the children. It speaks of 'due measure', of 'reason', and of 'discretion'. We have no trouble in imagining how such recommendations could be necessary. The RB redactor is here certainly bearing in mind the facts. The educational mission credited to all the adults demanded a minimum of virtue and common sense, which does not always accompany physical maturity. These monks, whom the cenobitic tradition and RM in particular treat like big children, should not have been well qualified to educate their little brothers. Yet RB entrusts them with this educational task, which associates them with the great mission of the abbot and the deans. The qualities of which they should give proof—'measure, reason, discretion'—are precisely those required of the abbot in the directory of Chapter 64 and in the other supplemental RB texts.

Here we ought to point out once again two characteristic features of RB in comparison with RM. First, the role granted to all the members of the community in the education of their brethren, when RM reserves this function to the abbot and officers expressly designated by him. Secondly, within the framework of this new hierarchical system superimposed on the former, the attention which is paid to fraternal relations, and the insistence on discretion in inflicting punishments on the children.

The last sentence of the chapter (RB 70:6–7) sums up under the same head both of the regulations developed above. The ban on excommunication without a mandate from the abbot and the caution against indiscriminately reprimanding the children are sanctions cut to the same pattern (*disciplinae regulari subiaceat*) and condemned by virtue of the same principle drawn from Scripture, *quod tibi non uis fieri, alio ne feceris* (Mt 7:12). Note the change of viewpoint on excommunication levied without a mandate from the abbot: it was reckoned at the beginning of the chapter as a crime of 'presumption', that is to say, as an abuse of authority. Now, without abandoning this perspective, which the words *qui praesumit . . . sine praecepto abbatis* recall, it is envisaged under a new aspect, that of the injury inflicted upon fraternal charity. Consideration of indiscriminate punishments inflicted on the children, in which the juridical point of view yields to that of virtue and of the manner how to act, has made this change possible.

Thus this chapter, which opens with a claim for the rights of the abbot in matters of correction, closes on a note of charity towards the brethren. The theme of defending the abbatial authority, which stands at the center of the unit formed by RB 69 and 70, is imperceptibly transformed into a theme of fraternal charity, which predominates in the larger group of chapters constituted by RB 63 and the appendix. The quotation of Mt 7:12 at the end of the chapter recalls the final words of RB 61 (on receiving visiting monks), a passage which greatly resembles *Regula Ferrioli* 6. The same scriptural text in this same negative form but in the third person singular, previously figured in RM 3:9 (= RB 4:9). It is not without significance that RB picked this 'golden rule of fraternal relations' out of the theoretical list in the chapter *Quae sunt instrumenta bonorum operum*, in order to fasten it twice over at the end of a chapter regulating practical life. The Master had felt no need to draw on this principle in the course of his rule in real life.

A last observation before leaving this chapter: the prohibition of excommunication or striking another without mandate should be set in relation to the hierarchy of ranks constituted by Chapter 63. It must have been quite a natural temptation for an 'elder' to take over seriously his rights of precedence, his title of 'father', and his marks of respect from the younger monks. All this removed him to some extent from his condition of disciple to confer on him an appearance of participation in the dignity of the abbot. The power to excommunicate and to strike might have seemed in line with these prerogatives. Just as in Chapter 63 the elder is not permitted to call his junior *puro nomine*, but rather is obliged to address him as 'brother', so here the right to correct is withdrawn from his claims. It may also be possible that the same situation underlies the preceding chapter: to defend a brother against a punishment by the abbot might be a spontaneous movement of nature when there existed a bond of blood relationship with that brother,[52] but his awareness of being himself a 'father' in the community could only develop such a tendency.

These two chapters are then an effort to confine within exact limits the sense of responsibility that the brethren feel towards one another. Though RB puts a new accent on fraternal relations and on the hierarchy of rank, it does not mean to diminish the role of the great functional hierarchy, that of the abbot and the deans. The almost nervous insistence with which the redactor never ceases to reserve exclusive rights for the abbot seems to be contradictory, but basically it is proportionate to the new importance that he accords the 'elders'.

It is precisely the following chapter (RB 71: *On Mutual Obedience*), which extends this prerogative of seniority to its maximum. We have already noted how 'mutual obedience' in practice amounts to hierarchical obedience according to rank. What is to be emphasized now is the originality of such a theory compared to the doctrine of obedience propounded by RM. To be sure, RM does counsel 'to obey wholeheartedly all those who are good' (RM 3:76), but this vague and isolated article of the *ars sancta*, which in its context is aimed above all at the good of peace, is of slight importance after the massive, reiterated, and lengthily developed expositions, which the Master devotes to the obedience due to the superior. This obedience is conceived above all as a necessity for salvation: one must submit oneself to a 'teacher' in order that this lieutenant of Christ may make the divine will known and accomplished.

In such a perspective, the objective content of the order given is of primary importance. What is expected from the abbot is the word expressing the will of God. Through him, God himself becomes the agent of the act accomplished by the disciple. The good of obedience consists essentially in this assurance which the disciple has of doing what God wills, its merit rests above all on this persuasion. The personal quality of the one who commands is also a prime condition: the abbot must be an authentic 'spiritual man', a perfect Christian, so that nothing but the divine will may proceed from his mouth. The *coenobium* is thought to be composed of sinners whom a single master conducts to their salvation by teaching them to accomplish the divine law: only he knows it, only he puts it into practice, only he is capable of insuring its observance.

In the face of this plan, the 'mutual' obedience demanded by RB first comes as a surprise, because it supposes that every monk is fit to give orders. It is sufficient to be an 'elder' in order to have the right to be obeyed by a junior. The spiritual qualification of the one commanding, which acts as the indispensable guarantee of conformity between the order received and the will of God, does not seem to be required, as it had been in the Master's theory. The doctrine of 'reciprocal' obedience takes no account of the objective content of the order. It is not concerned with the descent of the divine will into the disciple's existence by means of the command of a qualified 'teacher'. To that objective standpoint which dominated the Master's thought, a wholly subjective standpoint is substituted: obedience (in itself, as a virtuous attitude, regardless of both the personal quality of him who commands and of the salvific value of his orders), obedience is a good; it is a way leading to God.

It would doubtless not be advisable to harden the contrast between the two standpoints into an opposition. Although the Master's doctrine is bound primarily to the objective considerations that we have just recalled, it also suggests, at least by way of allusion, the subjective purport of an unconditional submission to another's will, though he be mediocre or unworthy, in imitation of Christ who submitted himself to men in this world even though he had no need to learn from them what was the will of his Father.[53] Such renunciation of self with a view to God or in the interest of one's neighbor is obviously of meritorious value. Obedience thus conceived cannot fail to appear as a 'good', even if one is more interested, as is the Master, in another aspect of the same virtue, that of the accomplishment of the divine law transmitted by the 'teacher'. If the Master's thought is dominated by the idea of the objective advantages of obedience, by what might be styled the theory of 'obedience for those who are beginning a spiritual life' or 'obedience necessary for sinners', it nevertheless remains open to a higher and more disinterested notion whereby obedience has value in its own right as oblation of self-will and as sacrifice.[54]

Nowhere, however, does the Master express himself in terms as explicit as those used by RB. 'Mutual' obedience is presented in RB 71 as a matter of charity. As such, it is a 'good', a 'way leading to God.' The 'elder' is not asked to give sure direction in the name of God nor to indicate which action is conformable to divine law and to impose its accomplishment on the wavering will of the disciple. The mere fact of obeying, of giving up one's own will to accomplish *ex caritate* that of another, in this we have the benefit expected from obedience. In this perspective, he who commands is not considered as messenger of God and 'teacher' ('Anyone who listens to you listens to me'), but only as God's instrument for accomplishing the sacrifice of him who obeys.

Two important points from this passage therefore deserve to be kept in mind. In the first place, the prestige of seniority here seems to us to attain a loftier degree: the elder has a right to be obeyed. He shares in the abbot's essential function, which is to command. But—and this is the second teaching of the text and the more significant—this authority allowed the elder implies a certain concept of obedience in which the spiritual quality of the one commanding takes a subordinate place. An authentic 'teacher' was needed to inculcate the divine law, but to receive the sacrifice of obedience, it is enough to occupy a situation conferring the right to command. The elder is in this situation: he is obeyed for his seniority. The obedience due to the abbot and his officers is envisaged in the same perspective. The accent is put not on the objective element (content of the order, the 'teacher's' divine mission, authentic sanctity of this man), but on the inward feelings of the monk obeying. Out of love, it is good to obey all one's brethren (in practice: all one's elders), because it is good to make oneself, like Christ, the servant of everyone through renunciation of self-will.

The remainder of the chapter (RB 71:5–9) confirms the elder's prerogative. In addition to the power of commanding granted him, he is given that of correcting, or at least of addressing verbal reprimands (*corripere*).[55] This corollary leads him still further in to the domain of abbatial prerogatives. But it would not be wise to insist on the prestige which redounds to him, for the interest of the redactor is aimed in a different direction. Relations between the young and the old are considered here, as in the first half of the chapter, from the inferior's standpoint. What is meant to be encouraged is the humble alacrity with which the brother receives every reprimand from those above him. This chapter thus pairs off with the preceding one: RB 70 imposes limits on the right of the elder in matters of correction, RB 71 regulates the attitude of the 'junior'. In this sequence we rediscover the alternation in *De ordine congregationis* (RB 63:1I–12): in both places the *prior's* and the *iunior's* behavior are envisaged successively. Chapter 63 regulated mutual relations on the level of precedence and signs of good manners. Chapter 70 and 71 follow suit by regulating them on the level of fraternal correction and obedience.

It is therefore to the inferior here that RB is addressed. It is made his duty to prostrate himself immediately at the feet of any elder who reprimands him. This satisfaction is to be prolonged until the elder gives his blessing. There is no difficulty in recognizing in such terminology the expression utilized in Chapter 44 to describe satisfaction by one who had been excommunicated. The public ceremony, which takes place at the door of the oratory in everyone's presence, is here reduced to an almost private act, which may have no other witness than the abbot or the elder, before whom the younger humbles himself. Note once again that 'any elder whosoever' (*prior quicumque*) is empowered to receive this satisfaction and to give the blessing which terminates the affair. The younger brother behaves before him as he would before the whole community and the abbot.

Severe penalties threaten the one who refuses either to obey his elder (vs 5) or to make satisfaction to him (vs 9). We are accustomed to such rigor. The tendency in RB is to multiply penal sanctions and render them more drastic, as if discipline were less easy to maintain than in the Master's monastery. This not very benign aspect of RB must not be overlooked. While it lays heavier stress on fraternal charity and pays more attention to the inferior's inward feelings as a subject, it simultaneously reinforces the repressive apparatus. It not only hierarchizes mutual relations and regulates them with precision, but also prescribes them under pain of heavy chastisement. This coercive element, incessantly recalled, keeps the reader in the quasi-scholastic perspective which characterizes cenobitic life. Never is it forgotten that it is a matter of training badly converted sinners, humble beginners in the perfect life. Threats of beatings and expulsion frankly corroborate the appeals to charity.

In concluding a word need be said about the traditional documentation of this chapter. As we have said, RM is virtually ignorant of the theme of mutual obedience, and the precise definitions given by RB on this subject are founded on the system of ranks, which we do not find in the Master. Again, RM is ignorant of private satisfaction, whether before 'any superior' or even before the abbot.[56] The only thing which, here at the close of RB 71, slightly reminds one of RM, is the anger of the superior. The Master speaks of it several times as a thing which takes place easily, and which one must try to forestall.[57]

In view of this lacuna in RM, the documentation assembled by the *Concordia* (Chapter 76) is at first sight surprising in its profusion: a group of some twenty texts, half of which are drawn from the *Regula Basilii*. Closer examination reveals that the theme of mutual obedience is in fact illustrated only by a very small percentage of these citations. Once *R Cui* Three is set aside (*Concordia*, n. 14), a text probably dependent on RB, scarcely anything remains except the *R Bas* cited in the first two paragraphs of the *Concordia* (*R Bas* 64 and 13). There again, Basil is not thinking of an obedience organized on a hierarchical basis, according to specific rules. For him, the issue is really one of 'mutual' obedience (*inuicem obaudire*, R Bas 64), a spontaneous propensity to submit oneself to another without regard for rank (cf. R Bas 13). Thus we are led to ascertain that the precise situation which RB describes (obedience of the brother to his elder) is not met in the rules anterior to St Benedict.

Something more need be said, it seems, about the satisfaction made to 'any elder'. Again, solely R Cui 7 (*Concordia*, n. 13) furnishes a somewhat exact parallel. The other rules are concerned only with the regular correction made by authority, or even (such is the case of *R Bas*) with mutual reconciliation after offenses. Truly, then, this RB chapter appears as one of the least documented in tradition, at least as regards regulating 'mutual' obedience and satisfaction on a seniority basis. Although ranks were a well-known institution, it seems no one ever thought of basing rules of good manners (see our commentary on RB 63), of obedience and of satisfaction on the hierarchical order which had been established among the brethren, until quite a late date. It seems that RB is the first document in which directions of this sort appear, and one is justified in thinking that seventh-century rules (R Wal, R Fruc, R Cui) depend on it in this respect.

However, if we consider not the precise regulations which this chapter establishes but the spirit of mutual obedience, which it strives to foster, we certainly must take account of the influence of *R Bas*. Such influence makes itself felt here as in Chapter 68.

Along with Basil, and even more than he, Cassian may have provided inspiration for this text. *Conference 16*, under the title *De amicitia*, in fact deals with obedience. No limitation arising from seniority tempers its demands. The precept is unconditional: one must always give way, even when the other party is of lesser merit. The question is not merely one of prudence and humility, no one ever being absolutely sure that he is in the right, but also of charity. To dwell in concord is so lofty a good that nothing is preferable to it. If God is love, then nothing takes priority over love, nothing is more to be shunned than wrath. To gain possession of that supreme good and repulse that supreme evil, every sacrifice must be made. Self-will especially must be surrendered, the seemingly useful and necessary abandoned, even though one's own spiritual interests are involved. Should a neighbor become irate on our account, even groundlessly, he must be appeased by every means with as much sensitivity as one would use to heal one's own anger. Is not the anger of a brother, in God's eyes and those of a loving heart, as great an evil and as detrimental to ourselves, as our own wrath? Cassian, speaking from experience, never tires of this theme of zeal and sincerity in satisfying the least offenses.

As one can see, Conference 16 is the equivalent of RB 71. Probably the RB redactor was inspired by it both here and in many other passages of the appendix. The only difference separating the two texts is that Cassian has every kind of common life in mind, and not only cenobitic life in the strict sense. For him therefore, there is no question of a hierarchy to be observed in mutual obedience. The only hierarchy he envisages is that based on virtue: 'ordered' charity shows a preference for the more virtuous.

With the next chapter (RB 72: *On Good Zeal*), we reach the end of this whole section inaugurated by *De ordine congregationis*. Mutual relationships among the monks form the theme of this little exhortation to fervor. Here the redactor has avoided all juridical precision as concerns rank. The theme of mutual relations is sublimated in an ideal picture in which all is fervor, spontaneity and love. In this section of brief spiritual counsels, we rediscover the style of the 'instruments of good works'. Plainly, the redactor wanted the rule to end as it had begun, on a very high note, on the level of pure spirituality.[58]

Some have proposed reading into this chapter *On Good Zeal* the development of an element furnished by RM.[59] For the latter speaks of a *zelum boni et honoris desiderium* when it describes the atmosphere of emulation created in the community by the competition to capture the first place (RM 92:51). Without denying the possibility of such a reminiscence, it must be admitted that we are rather far from the context of abbatial succession in which RM mentions the *zelum boni*. If the RB redactor wanted to conserve this element of the rule of the Master, he has greatly refined it. Emulation in good works was sustained, according to the Master, by the desire to succeed to the abbot. Now no other end is proposed than 'God and eternal life'.

In addition, the material for emulation is more explicit. For the Master, it was a question of the observance of the rule, of 'good actions,' of 'holy works' (RM 92:49–50), which embraced all the virtues;[60] among such holy works, humility especially is emphasized (RM 92:2–6) because 'he who desires to be first should make himself the last of all.' In its description of good zeal, RB is more restrained and this restriction centers not on humility but on love. Emulation is developed above all in the domain of fraternal relations: respect, patience, obedience, unselfishness, charity. From there one is raised to relations with God, with the abbot, with Christ, these relations too being envisaged from the standpoint of love. There is no question of the observance of the rule,[61] nor of the complete commandments of God.[62] A number of virtues, which the Master enumerates, are not cited, because they pertain more to the personal behavior of each individual than to fraternal relations.[63] Thus, 'good zeal' in RB acquires a much more explicit acceptation than it had in RM. The issue is very precisely that of an emulation *out of love* in the diverse manifestations of love.

This 'good zeal' has the effect of 'detaching from vices and leading to God and eternal life' (RB 72:2). We have previously been told that 'by the way of (mutual) obedience we shall go to God' (RB 71:2). These attractive formulas deserve emphasis. They attribute to fraternal relations the same effects of purification and of union with God as the finale of Chapter 7 accorded to humility. In other words, monastic ascesis, of which the chapter on humility sketched an outline, is now enriched with a new dimension. The journey of the monk from fear of God to perfect charity via obedience, long-suffering, manifestation of the heart, humility, silence, compunction (to mention only the principal stages)—this whole itinerary taken from Cassian, in which the disciple trod in the footsteps of his master alone, is now expanded and complemented by a new demarcation hitherto poorly indicated. To individual ascesis practised under the direction of a superior is added a new element, fraternal relations. These relations, as we shall make clear further below, were certainly not foreign to the RM field of vision. But it was the special merit of RB to develop the theory, to specify their practice and above all to raise them to the rank of great means of ascesis, which liberate from sin and draw one to God. These 'horizontal' relations, though hierarchized, thus share in the educational power which until now had been recognized almost exclusively in the action of the abbot and his deans. The virtues they develop, all of them facets of charity, stand alongside the great classical virtues described by the first chapters of the rule. Or, if you wish, these are the very same virtues of obedience, humility, abnegation, long-suffering, all receiving a field of supplemental application, fraternal relations and a new coloring, the love of one's neighbor.

No less significantly, 'zeal' in RB ceases to be emulation with a view to winning first place, as was true in RM.[64] Not only do terrestrial expectations and considerations of a personal interest no longer provide the stimulation, but one may even ask whether there is any further question of emulation properly so-called. Would not *zelus bonus* be the equivalent of the *zelus Dei* spoken of in RB 64:6, that is, simply a 'jealousy for God' in the biblical sense of the term[65] or, as we say in English, 'religious zeal', an expression which prescinds from any overtones of emulation with other men and means only ardor in the service of God and commitment to his cause?[66]

Whatever is the exact sense of *zelus bonus* in this chapter, there is no doubt that the idea of competition retires into the background. Since good zeal 'leads to God and to eternal life' (and not to the first place), the monks are urged to fix their gaze far beyond social prominence, on the Ultimate End of the person. Comparison with others here below is much less important than to attain the Transcendent Good.

Christ will lead us *pariter*, 'all together.' The competitive aspect—if competition there is—hardly resembles that of the rivalry instituted by RM. Instead of just one winner and a throng of vanquished, everyone is here called to bear off the prize, each for himself, in a struggle which pits them against no one except themselves.

In *zelus* such as defined by RB, therefore, the accent is placed not on emulation with one's neighbor, but on personal drive, on spontaneity and generosity of effort aroused by the desire for eternal life. We meet again here the 'fervor' already demanded in the directory for the porter.[67] It is the same care for the inner life as is attested in the present appeal, the same recourse to good will, and the same preoccupation to awaken the person's spiritual energies.

RM also speaks of 'fervor', but with marked misgivings. *Feruore nouitio* designates the suspect enthusiasm of the beginner which is opposed to the *probatio diuturna* of the true cenobite.[68] Here, on the contrary, 'fervor' is the outward expression of invisible charity: it is necessary to be fervent because it is necessary to love.

It will be remembered that this appeal for fervor and love, resounded at the end of the little chapter on heroic obedience, *ex caritate*, and in the description of mutual obedience, *omni caritate*. It is a constant note of the appendix and of RB addenda in general. Our redactor exhibits a marked interest in the interior behavior of the subject, and this interest bears especially on charity, which he would have enter into all actions.

Detailed examination of this chapter clearly reveals that it is meant to conclude the appendix and the rule. Most of the short directions which serve to compose it simply repeat what was said in the last chapters. There is no advantage in insisting further on these repetitions, which were studied when we were commenting on *De ordine congregationis* and Chapter 71. Suffice it to direct attention here to those precepts which do not obviously refer to what has preceded.

Note first of all vs 5: *infirmitates suas siue corporum siue morum patientissime tolerent*. These words echo the chapter *On Sick Brethren*, or rather amplify it by extending to the superlative the recommendation read in that chapter, *qui tamen (infirmi) patienter portandi sunt* (RB 36:5). In both chapters, the redactor has in mind not only corporal infirmities but even more those of the mind and soul, which often follow in consequence. The context therefore, is indeed the same, save for the difference that RB 72 can be applied to every non-corporal infirmity, whether accompanied by physical illness or not.

Thus generalized and carried to the superlative, the maxim reflects a characteristic tendency of the redactor to heighten fraternal relations and the virtues they demand. 'Patience' is highly esteemed by the Master,[69] but the only development he devotes to it represents the brother 'patient' in the exercise of obedience.[70] It is towards his superior that the monk ought to show himself patient, but he receives no express encouragement to practise this virtue towards his brethren.[71] On the contrary, RB dwells especially upon the occasions which arise in the daily give-and-take. While assuming the doctrine of the Master on patience in obedience,[72] even insisting on it,[73] RB explicitly teaches another form of patience, that which supports defects in the brethren.[74]

The text continues: *nullus quod sibi utile iudicat sequatur, sed quod magis alio*. This is the only precept devoid of an antecedent in the rule. It brings a real enrichment of the theme of fraternal charity such as has been developed up to now by RB. A reader of RM might be surprised that a brother would find himself in the position of having to choose between 'what he judges useful to himself' and what is useful to another. The pure doctrine of obedience hardly allowed for the possibility of making such choices. The brother is presumed to be accomplishing the will of his superior at every instant: *ambulantes alieno iudicio* (RM 7:48 = RB 5:12). This 'judgment of another' which, according to the Master, rules the entire conduct of the cenobite, is not the will of just anybody, but the will of the abbot to the exclusion of all others: *abbatem sibi praeesse desiderant* (RM 7:50 = RB 5:12).

Here then, RB is envisaging a situation, which scarcely presents itself in the classical perspective of cenobitic obedience. One must, however, reckon with the particular genre of this chapter, which allows for some imprecision. The adjoining precepts on honor and 'mutual' obedience ought to be interpreted, remember, in the light of the precise regulations of *De ordine congregationis* and of Chapter 71, where the 'reciprocity' is tempered by a very strict sense of hierarchy. Here, similarly, we may suppose that the 'interest of another' is no simple matter of individual assessment. This vague formula lends itself all the less to rigorous deductions inasmuch as it alludes to several passages of St Paul,[75] and notable 1 Cor 13:5: *caritas non quaerit quae sua sunt*. What it means to describe is not, therefore, a well defined program of action, but rather a propensity to charity. Let us remember besides that RM itself uses similar formulas when treating of the *ars sancta*: 'Obey wholeheartedly all those who are good' (RM 3:76) is a rather uncompromising maxim, when it stands in a list of spiritual counsels, with neither development nor practical application. Manifestations of 'good zeal' belong to the same scarcely existent genre.

It is none the less remarkable that the RB redactor felt obliged to conclude his work with similar appeals for charity towards the brethren. Care for the interests of others opens up a 'horizontal' dimension in cenobitic life, with which the 'vertical' educative plan will have to be reconciled. This dimension was not unknown in RM, as we shall see, but it was left relatively undeveloped. Here, on the contrary, it receives very special attention.

The final maxims of the chapter, more explicitly than the first ones, are encouragements to love. To love one's brethren, to love the abbot: *De ordine congregationis* gave us the occasion to comment on such precepts. So then, 'Fear God out of love' and 'Prefer nothing to Christ' (vss 9 and 11) alone command our attention here.

Amore Deum timeant seems paradoxical at first sight when one recalls the 'charity which dispels fear' (RM 10:88 = RB 7:67. In reality, far from contradicting one another, the two themes have the same origin and are complementary. The finale of the chapter on humility was inspired by Cassian, *Inst* 4.39. In parallel fashion, Cassian develops the same fear-charity opposition in *Conf* 11.7. Now, in the remainder of *Conference 11*, Cassian goes on to speak of another kind of fear prompted by love which is characteristic of the perfect, just as servile fear was of beginners (*Conf* 11.13).

It is to that theory that RB is alluding here. It thereby proposes to the cenobite the loftiest ideal there is. Charity is no longer presented to the monk solely from afar, as the summit to which his ascesis tends. He is urged to apply himself to it at once. In this we recognize the redactor's distinctive idea which we have already seen appear in more than one original trait of his work, in particular in the addition *pro Dei amore* at the third rung of humility. For him, charity is not so much the peak of the virtues and the crowning of effort, as the present reality, which embraces within itself the whole of Christian life. 'To love God with one's whole heart' is indeed the first commandment in his eyes. Not satisfied to set it (as did the Master) at the head of the 'instruments of good works', he inserts it among the concrete demands of monastic life, presenting it to the cenobite as a program of immediate relevancy.

The last precept: *Christo omnino nihil praeponant* (vs 11) is less original. Besides the patristic sources cited by Butler, we should bear in mind the *ars sancta* of the Master and the 'instruments of good works' in RB, where it has previously figured (RM 3:23 = RB 4:21:*nihil amori Christi* praeponere). Though the recension is slightly different (*amori* omitted, *omnino* added) one may see the reason for this either in the influence of distinct patristic sources,[76] or in a certain intensity of accent proper to this little chapter, which is so full of fervor.[77] In any case, the chapter closes as it opened, on a note of 'very fervent love'.

One can gain further assurance of the personal character of RB 72 by consulting the corresponding section of the *Concordia* (Chapter 77). Benedict of Aniane knew of only three paragraphs of the *Regula Basilii* illustrating 'good zeal'! And of these, the first two paragraphs speak of mutual charity in a general sense, whereas the third (R Bas 78) means *zelus Dei* in the restricted sense of ardor in correcting the faults of one's neighbor. Doubtless, the RB redactor was thinking only of what he himself had previously written as he composed this conclusion, in which he reassembles all the themes dearest to him. The care for horizontal relations, the interest devoted to the inner life, and the accent put on the love of God as the actual motive for one's conduct—all these tendencies distinctive of RB find their clearest expression here.

Yet we ought not to undervalue the reference to Basil furnished by the *Concordia*. Though the parallel between the chapter *On Good Zeal* and the three brief basilian texts selected as illustrations of it is not very close, it was at least as much from Basil as from any other author of a rule that the RB redactor was able to cull the great inspirations of which we have spoken. Who more than Basil insisted on 'fraternity,' who is more outspoken in a 'rule' on the interior and subjective aspect of ascesis, who better indicated, even in the arrangement of his text, the primordial role and universal influence of charity?

But, ultimately, the capital reference is missing from the *Concordia*. It would be necessary to pair off nearly every article of RB 72 with a reference to Cassian, and such references would for the most part be drawn from *Conference* 16. This Conference is truly the source from which he might have derived the chapter *On Good Zeal*, as also the appendix as a whole.

Our effort to expound these final chapters of RB now allows the reader a better knowledge of their content and of the relationship between the themes, whose development throughout the appendix we proposed that he follow. Step by step, we have pointed out what concerned the 'horizontal' relations newly regulated by RB, the increased interest that it lends to certain subjective aspects of the observance of the rule, and lastly the love for God, for the abbot, and for the brethren, which it recommends with fresh emphasis. It is time now to assemble these scattered references. We must methodically list those pieces of evidence, which have been gleaned by our commentary, in so far as the text suggested them, and with no other order apart from the sequence of material in the rule. To this purpose, we shall follow the plan which has guided us from the start: horizontal relations—care for the inner life—theme of charity, not without indicating as often as we can the connections between these three great themes.

HORIZONTAL RELATIONS

The principal axis of cenobitism is that which binds the monk to his abbot, either directly or by means of the deans and other officers designated by the abbot. To this system of 'vertical' relations, which is in the full sense of the word a 'hierarchy,' the *De ordine congregationis* (RB 63) adds another system of relations, that of rank (*ordo*) which is still based, though only in part, on the choice of the abbot (recognizing a particular 'merit'), but of which the normal basis is seniority, a principle of discrimination not depending on the will of the abbot, and similarly the status of the adults in relation to the children is not dependent upon the abbot's choice.

In its final chapters, RB displays a lively interest in these relations determined on the basis of seniority and age. It scrutinizes them, regulates them and indicates their spirit, which may be summarized in a word, charity. It thereby opens a dimension of the cenobitic life which had hardly been indicated in RM, as we shall see.

We call these relations 'horizontal', because they extend to all the community members (and not only between the brethren and their deans and abbot) and because they are organized according to laws, which largely escape the personal intervention of the abbot. The prestige and authority of the abbot are in some measure distributed among all the brethren, insofar as they are 'elders' or adults. The elder is called *nonnus*, which means 'father;' he has a right to certain marks of respect, to obedience, to satisfaction. The adult exerts control over the child on every occasion. Thus every member of the community, by virtue of seniority or age, shares in the educative function which belongs exclusively, in the classical perspective of cenobitism, to the abbot and his officers.

In a still wider sense, the chapter *On Good Zeal* attributes to the life of fraternal relations in charity the purifying and sanctifying effects which had been given by the Master as the characteristic of ascesis pursued under the direction of an abbot. 'Patience' no longer consists solely in bearing with the superior. It ought also to be exercised by accepting the weaknesses of all the brethren. The same holds true for obedience, which becomes 'mutual,' for abnegation, which takes on the aspect of a preference for the good of another (*quod magis alio*. . .), and for humility which makes one submit to the reprimands of 'any elder whomsoever' on one's knees. In the mind of the redactor, this participation by all in the educative task of the abbot does not lead to a diminution of the abbacy. On the contrary, an increasing number of references occur, which tend to reaffirm the authority of the superior. Time and again RB recalls the universal dominion of the abbot over the actions of his subjects. His rights in matters of obedience and correction are reserved to him with special clarity, which the concession of a certain authority in these areas to the elders had rendered necessary.

However, the prestige and power of the abbot seem less assured than they were in RM. Though the redactor cedes none of the traditional positions, the very insistence that he lays on maintaining them seems to testify to a certain uneasiness, behind which one senses that there lie disputes and instances of slackness. Does not the author himself assume a tone of reproof, in order to put the abbot on his guard against the human weaknesses, which the Master seemed to ignore: imprudence, lack of foresight, injustice, jealousy, tyranny? Experience has led the redactor to this more realistic consideration of the psychology of the abbot. By putting his finger on such difficulties of the abbot's office, he gave evidence of that more refined sensitiveness towards the inner life, the indications of which we shall collate a little further below.

Although 'horizontal' in a certain sense, fraternal relations are not on that score any less strictly organized on a hierarchical basis, in imitation of 'vertical' relations. There is talk, to be sure, of 'reciprocal' marks of honor and 'mutual' obedience, but expressions of this sort are immediately qualified by regulations, which establish a one way direction, based on hierarchy of ranks. The younger owes his elder respect, he obeys the elder. Equally to be stressed is the obligatory nature, under pain of punishment, of the different articles of this ruling. Fraternal relations are not simply a matter of counsel left in practice to the good will and spontaneity of each person. On the contrary, they are treated by the legislator with the same seriousness and the same attention to fine points as he devotes to regulating all the details of the observance of the rule. They thus integrate themselves within the framework of a rigorous educational method, in which constraint lends added strength to the voice of conscience, and in which the inspirations of charity are interpreted by definite social obligations.

And yet, the profound meaning of this legislation is to give expression to love. Just as the abbot, according to RM–RB 2, ought to love all his sons, so 'the elders ought to love their juniors'. Reciprocally, the brethren are urged 'to love their abbot', the latter striving, for his part, 'to make himself more loved than feared', and everything suggests to the younger brethren that they put the same sentiments of affection into the signs of respect that they owe their elders. The avowed purpose of such rulings on mutual relations is therefore to foster fraternal charity. Now, this charity in its turn is expressly referred to Christ, to God. Thus the theme of horizontal relations opens on to the great perspective of charity, that is to say, love of God and love of neighbor together, which RB traced with special carefulness, itself a relatively new factor, in relation to RM.

CARE FOR THE INNER LIFE

We noted above the care the redactor has for guarding against certain temptations, which beset the abbacy. He is more clearly aware than the Master of the afflictions, to which the superior is exposed by reason of his weak human nature, and he endeavors to remedy them by means of repeated admonitions. Not content merely to provide the abbot with a complete directory (RM-RB 2), nor even to double it with a second treatise of the same sort (RB 64), which is more attentive to the subjective dispositions, which ought to animate the superior,[78] RB goes so far as to insert in the course of the rule some precise warnings against such and such a fault into which the abbot might fall in such and such a concrete situation. RM presumed that the 'teacher' fully measured up to his definition and that he was an accomplished master setting the example in everything that he taught. With no fear of doing injury to his prestige, RB takes into consideration the subjective difficulties of sinful man.

The psychology of the disciple is likewise studied by RB with more subtlety. The difficulties of the obedient monk have even given the redactor the opportunity to compose the brief Chapter 68, which is perhaps his masterpiece. Nowhere does one better see what RB has added to RM: a more refined sensibility towards the inner life of the monk, and an educational effort more devoted to that life.

On the level of expression, this attention to the inner life usually appears in short adverbial references (*patienter et opportune, patientissime, festinanter, certatim, omnino, caste*), in ablatives with *cum* (*cum omni mansuetudine . . . cum feruore caritatis, cum omni mansuetudine et oboedientia, cum omni mensura et ratione*), and finally in a series of almost stereotyped sayings: *ex caritate, omni caritate et sollicitudine, pro Dei amore, amore, feruentissimo amore, sincera et humili caritate, honore et amore Christi*. A study of RB in its entirety would disclose that such terminology recurs wherever the redactor has set his seal on the Master's résumé. It witnesses at once to an interest in the *how* of the observance and in the qualitative and interior aspect of the actions performed by the monk, and also to an ardent zeal, which seeks to communicate its own fervor.

The care to arouse in the monk a personal movement of generosity, which brings him to love God, his superior, and his confrères is, of course, a conspicuous feature of RB. Further insistence will be laid on the theme of charity, to which we are here and now introduced. What must now be stressed is the intimate and personal character of this drive and this 'zeal'. If RB has been able to find the idea of 'good zeal' in a definite RM text, it has traced an original description of it, in which the personal manner of the redactor appears. No longer is there any question of a 'virtue-contest', with the victor being awarded first place. The social aspect of the competition is effaced, the goal being that all may obtain God and eternal life as the reward for fervent love. The theme of emulation is wholly interiorized. Members of the community are no longer contestants, each of whom gauges his own performance against that of the others, but are rather deeply loved brothers, to whom the common life offers occasion to 'apply the debt of charity'. The interiorization of 'zeal' co-ordinates its very clear orientation towards others: by giving himself to other persons, both divine and human, the personality of the monk is interiorized and deepened.

Comparing RB with RM is equally instructive in the chapter on the porter. Lacking the Master's wealth of concrete details, the RB text does, however, develop the qualities required of the porter, and the meaning of his service as an exercise of patience and charity. Only the spiritual aspect of this charge has retained the redactor's attention. The interest that the Master displayed in practical detail shifts and settles on the religious values which the employment develops. Here again, the RB manner is at once more interior and more orientated towards others.

Finally, we noted an alteration of tone as regards mutual obedience: the 'good of obedience' consists not so much in the assurance, objectively guaranteed by the quality of him who commands, of fulfilling solely the will of God in every action, as in the subjective movement whereby one renounces self-will to accomplish that of one's neighbor, 'in all charity and earnestness'. The interior values of abnegation and of the donation of self appear in higher relief, when obedience is rendered no longer solely to the abbot, who teaches in the name of God, but to any 'elder' whomsoever. From the latter one may not expect the authorized declaration of the divine will, which sets the value of the orders of the abbot. The good of obedience, henceforth, is simply to submit oneself out of love to the will of others.

CHARITY

The evidence supplied above on the spiritual vocabulary of RB have given us the opportunity to reassemble the main references in the appendix relating to the theme of charity. It would be necessary to add to them 'the love that the elders bear for their juniors'(Chapter 63), the encouragement 'not to do to another what one would not want done to oneself' (Chapter 70), and finally nearly all the articles of *On Good Zeal*, in which there is nothing except love for God, for the abbot, and for the brethren.

Already inscribed by the Master at the top of the *ars sancta* list, the first commandment assumes a much increased practical importance in RB. Charity is no longer only the towering summit attained at the end of the ascent of humility. The RB redactor was not able to restrain himself—thereby somewhat confusing the theoretical constructions of Cassian and the Master—from making the love of God intervene even at the third rung of humility, that is, from the point where obedience to the superior enters the picture. This outlook is reflected in the appendix, for charity is twice invoked there as the motive for obedience (RB 68 and 71). It is again 'for love of Christ' that one pays homage to his representative, the abbot. In RB the intention of placing the life of obedience of the monk within a movement of love for God is evident.

Love is therefore, in the eyes of the redactor, the first reality not only in the scale of values and in the order of ends, but also as the principle and motive of action for the cenobite, from this very moment. There is no hesitation in proposing to the monk the 'fear of love' (RB 72) which plays the part of the summit reserved for the perfect in *Conference* 11 of Cassian. Moreover, in all its aspects, 'good zeal' is defined as 'very fervent love.' Not only obedience but the monk's entire behavior ought to be bathed in divine charity.

Love of God is, then, in some fashion brought into the daily life of the cenobite, imperfect as he still is (and we know that RB treats him as such with neither illusion nor forbearance). In like manner, fraternal charity is more closely associated with the concrete life of relationships within the community. This appears more clearly, when we cast an over-all glance at the theme of charity towards neighbor as formulated in RM. Suffice it to mention here that the Pauline precept relative to mutual honor (*honore inuicem praeuenientes*), applied by the Master to the reception of guests, becomes in RB the rule for relationships among the brethren. Likewise, the 'golden rule' (*quod tibi non uis fieri*. . .) is no longer cited as just one among many sayings in the catalogue of spirituality: it intervenes in practical life over two practical details (RB 61 and 70). It is invoked in these two cases to justify by a motive of charity those rulings which concern concrete relations with one's neighbor. Whether it is the attitude of elders towards their younger brethren at issue, or the welcome extended to guests by the porter, or of the whole of fraternal relations, the words 'love' and 'charity' flow immediately from the redactor's pen.

As for charity towards the abbot, what RB has to say is new in relation to RM. It is one consequence of the development which is given to the theme of love of God: if it is necessary to love God, it is necessary to love his representative, the abbot. It is also an extension of fraternal love, the abbot appearing, both in *De ordine congregationis* and in the chapter *On good Zeal*, as a particular case in which the principles of respect and love which rule the relations between brothers come into application to a high degree Thus RB does not institute only 'horizontal' relations of a new type. The 'vertical' relation itself, that which unites the brother to his abbot and which the Master had already defined with a force that cannot be surpassed, is stamped with a new sentiment in RB. The abbot's love for the brethren (RM—RB 2) should find its response in the brethren's love for their abbot (RB 63, 64, and 72). Thus is achieved that setting of the cenobitic life in charity which is so characteristic of RB.

Are the themes that we have just expounded really characteristic of RB? We ought, in conclusion, to put this question. Even though there is no real doubt about the care which the redactor had for regulating 'horizontal' relations, along with a skill in penetrating sensitively into certain subjective aspects of the cenobitic life and a marked preoccupation for charity, the importance of these new discoveries greatly varies, according to whether the themes in question appear more or less new in relation to earlier tradition.

We must interrogate RM in particular, and interrogate it in its entirety. To be sure, the RB appendix is by definition an original section lacking precedent in RM. But might not the themes that it develops have received equivalent treatment from the Master in one passage or another peculiar to RM? We shall begin by considering this last query, trying to specify the links of RB with RM concerning the themes studied. Then we shall say a word about the other sources of RB.

As regards RM, several points may be accepted as certain. There is no need to rehearse the innovations effected by RB on the love of God in obedience, the love due to the abbot, and the precise obligations based on seniority which the brethren owe one another. Yet one may ask whether the Master, although ignorant of the system of ranks and the rules on mutual relations, has not a doctrine on fraternal charity and some care for 'horizontal' relations. What can we glean from his rule on this point?

Taking the word *caritas* as the thread of this investigation, we are impressed immediately by the large number of instances where this word applies to relations with persons from outside: guests and travelling companions.[79] This well conforms to the spirit of early Christianity, in which hospitality appears as the most significant manifestation of charity. In some eighteen cases where *caritas* figures in this context in the Master, it is most often a matter of the very practical signs of fellowship extended to the stranger. One shares one's travel provisions with him, those which he offers are accepted, one dines at his table, and if he comes to the monastery, the fast is broken in his honor and better than ordinary fare is served him. He is escorted wherever he goes, and the kiss of peace is, of course, the sign *par excellence* of this 'charity'.

However, *caritas* also appears, though more rarely, concerning relations between members of the community. Remember that the abbot owes all his sons an 'equal love,' a maternal love (RM 2:22, 30, 31). Remember too the very practical purpose that we believed we were able to recognize in that expression, *aequalis ab omnibus caritas*, is chiefly the equal distribution of all the necessities of life. We re-encounter this very practical meaning, it seems, in RM 27:45, where *caritas laetitae sanctorum dierum* refers to the supplement of wine on feastdays. The abbot displays his affection for the community by his generosity, which is in harmony with the spiritual joy of the solemnity.

Charity naturally figures in the little catalogue of virtues of the new abbot (RM 92:13–15), just as it has its appointed place in the list of 'spiritual works' (RM 4:1). These are very general recommendations from which one may derive no precise rule of life, all the more as charity is there juxtaposed with a large number of other virtues of equal or even superior importance.[80] One article of the *ars sancta* likewise speaks of 'charity' in this very vague sense: *caritatem non derelinquere* (RM 3:31 = RB 4:26).

Directions as general as these may apply as much to relations with strangers as to relations with members of the community. The *ars sancta* does in fact seem to have been composed with no particular regard for the condition of cenobites. The same is not true for the little chapter on the sick (RM 70), in which the Master exhorts all the brethren to 'show themselves full of charity', to 'prove their fraternal charity' by visiting, consoling, and serving their suffering brethren. By acting thus, it is to Christ himself that they devote their care. This text is the more noteworthy as it is almost the only one in which RM preaches charity for the brethren in the community. There is scarcely anything to cite in parallel except the reprimand given by the provosts to any brother who loses his temper with one of his companions while at work: *in mansuetudine et taciturnitate et caritate opera tua perfice* (RM 11:70). And it cites for him, among other scriptural texts, 'To hate your brother is to be a murderer' (1 Jn 3:15). Except for these two instances, the Master did not use *caritas* when speaking of fraternal relations.

But our enquiry cannot be limited to the study of one word, however characteristic it may be. By considering the use of *caritas* in RM, we should be led to think that the Master is more occupied with charity towards strangers than with charity *intra muros*, and that the latter is usually the business of the abbot alone, or else is made the object of recommendations too general to throw very much light on the meaning of common life. Other texts, however, though not employing the term *caritas*, do portray genuine manifestations of love for one's neighbor. Here again, the part devoted to strangers is considerable: alms for the indigent are often mentioned.[81] Sometimes it takes the particularly meritorious form of a curtailment of the daily pittance, to which generous brothers spontaneously consent. There is also care to emphasize the bond linking it to the work of the brethren, which has for its purpose, besides keeping them busy, the obtaining of the wherewithal to be given the poor.

These indications give certain articles of the *ars sancta* their full meaning: *pauperes recreare, nudum uestire*, etc. (RM 3:14–21; cf. RB 4: 14–19). We are sure that for the Master it is not only a matter of vague declarations of 'good works' drawn from Scripture and more or less applicable to the everyday life of cenobites. Noteworthy too, among the marks of charity shown to those outside, are the concessions made to those who purchase objects manufactured by the monks (RM 85:5; cf. RB 57:7–9).

Love for one's neighbor occupies an important place in the *ars sancta*. The second-greatest commandment counts for its real worth (RM 3:2), to be followed shortly by the 'golden rule' (ibid., vs 9). Besides the articles already cited for various reasons, there are two passages on love for enemies which deserve to be pointed out (vss 36 and 75) and which may be understood equally of external enemies and of brothers, with whom one might not be in accord. However, it is certain that *ante solis occasum cum inimico redire in gratiam* refers, in the intention of the Master, to disputes among the brethren, as is revealed by the parallel passage of RM

11:74. In like fashion, the 'malediction' condemned by the *ars sancta* is indeed also a fault perpetrated in the *coenobium*, among the members of the community (cf. RM 11:81–84).

From such cases of parallelism between a general declaration of the *ars sancta* and a concrete situation depicted in the course of the rule, one may conclude that RM 3 is somewhat less theoretical and less detached from real life than appears at first sight. The life of fraternal relationship in community is probably envisaged there in more than one article in which we were tempted to see only vague counsels lacking specific connections with actual cenobitic life.

Note, nevertheless, that these injunctions on fraternal charity are somewhat drowned by the random sequence of strange maxims, which comprises the *ars sancta*. This fact, combined with their very general terms and their abstract formulation, does not contribute to their effectiveness. The mind of the reader is hardly impressed by such concise counsels, which he has met by chance in the medley of lengthy catalog of various recommendations. No doctrine to arrest our attention clearly emerges.

As for the parallel passages that we set in relief in RM 11, they do not manage to attract any greater attention in their context: it is only in connection with the formation of the provosts that the Master makes an incidental mention of anger and cursing. These two offences occur among a number of different failings which the provosts have the mission to correct, and which do not have, for the most part, any direct connection with fraternal charity (an inopportune word, a word in a raised tone of voice, stupid talk, lying, swearing, laughter, a nonchalant attitude). In all this, interest focuses not on fraternal relations in charity but on the individual education that the brother receives from his provosts.

Neither RM 3 nor RM 11 are therefore very significant, where the importance of fraternal relations in the eyes of the Master is concerned. More interesting are the liturgical references, which testify to a concern to have the community pray for certain of its members. Entering upon the duty of reader, entering upon and leaving the duties of the hebdomadary service, the return of brethren from an outing, ordination of a new abbot—all these occurrences are marked by common prayer followed by the kiss of peace. They pray even longer for the newly professed and for the excommunicated brother admitted to pardon (RM 14:25–78).

The case of brothers who have been tempted, is particularly touching: during the prolonged prayer (RM 15–26), the community in an act of compassion adds, if need be, collective penances: a day of fast, abstinence from wine and oil (RM 15:39–44). The significance of this undertaking by the community is plainly indicated by the abbot in his initial discourse: it is a matter of 'offering help to one another out of love' (*subueniamus per dilectionem inuicem nobis*, RM 15:20; cf. Gal 6:2). No less explicit are the texts in which the Master prescribes prayer in the chapter for absent brethren: the sick, the cellarer, those on journeys, and in general all those detained by some service for the community.[82] In his eyes, there is in this an obligation of justice. By failing in it, the community would be deprived of all the merit of its prayers.

A remarkable spirit of solidarity comes into play in these liturgical directions and in the reasons that the Master invokes for their justification. Yet RM remains, in this domain, on the corporate level, without giving directions to individuals. Certainly, it means the brethren to pray for each other, but this ought to be done as a community and in an organized form. Inasmuch as those absent are sacrificing themselves for the sake of the community, so it is that prayer is made in community for them. On the level of personal acts and private initiatives, nothing is prescribed or counseled.

This general assessment of the theme of fraternal charity in RM seems to justify the conclusion that RB has indeed added something to what it took on from the Master.

The chapter *On Good Zeal* has the very same result as would have been expected from the *ars sancta* articles, had they been isolated from the heterogeneous maxims which envelop them and then grouped together and presented in a standard development as so many manifestations of love. Substantially, RB 72 is already in RM. But it was the special merit of the RB redactor to assemble in a separate little treatise centered on love what the Master had said *passim*, and unsystematically, on fraternal charity.

Likewise, RB has introduced innovations by occupying itself with the individual relations which knit brethren together in the bosom of the community. It treats this question in a much broader and more methodical fashion than did RM. The latter has, certainly, some interesting remarks on certain practices animated by fraternal charity: it exhorts the monks to nurse the sick, it prescribes collective prayers and penances for brothers suffering temptation, and it maintains a lively feeling of solidarity for those who sacrifice themselves in the service of the community. Yet on two points RB seems to have surpassed these data.

In the first place, it studies the problem of fraternal relations in its universality, not limiting itself to particular cases such as the sick, the tempted, or the office-holders. It envisages the relationship of any one brother with any other member of the community. In the second place, RB further develops individual manifestations of charity. These, in the Master, were barely indicated except with regard to the sick. The other attestations of charity were directed towards persons from outside (guests, the poor), or else, when it was a question of persons belonging to the community, fraternal love was shown them in collective form.

It should be well understood that we do not claim that the Master and his disciples have never practised forms of charity other than those actually described by RM. But the important thing for our investigation is the textual data and what can be deduced of the author's ideas and preoccupations by means of it. Now the RM text itself, we must repeat, contains few hints concerning the practice of charity on an individual basis. On this point, RB adds important references: mutual respect and affection, marks of honor in words and gestures, obedience, acceptance of reproaches, due measure in correction. This whole code of fraternal relations, which the appendix develops and which is summarized in the chapter *On Good Zeal*, tends precisely to make fraternal charity the soul of common life not only through collective manifestations but also through the personal approach demanded of each brother.

A general review of RM is equally necessary with regard to the care for the inner life.

The Master is far from uninterested in the interior attitude of the monk who obeys. The chapter on obedience terminates with three explicit recommendations on this subject, which have passed into RB (RM 7:67–74 = RB 5:14–17). He is truly obedient, who gives joyously and whose heart remains, in the eyes of God, exempt from murmuring, ill-will and sadness. Note, however, that this interior attitude is simply prescribed, without the Master dwelling upon motives for the opposite sentiments or striving to dissipate such sentiments. The original contribution of RB 68 is precisely to take into consideration the 'impossibility' felt subjectively by the brother, and to trace a line of conduct which both reckons with such repugnance and leads to surmounting it.

The Master also seeks to arouse the fervor of his religious. We are thinking here not only of the 'zeal' roused by the hope of gaining first place—a rather base theory, we must admit, and one which was thoroughly purified by RB—but also of the encouragement given to brethren who spontaneously renounce a portion of food or a period of sleep.[83] A 'spiritual' brother is recognizable by his voluntary sacrifices of this sort. One may thereby see that he 'loves the spirit more than the flesh' and rejoices for the 'good will' God has instilled into his heart.[84] Such generosity no doubt unfolds under the vigilant watch of the abbot and under the shelter of protective rules, which seek to preserve it from contagion by less fervent brothers.[85] However, it would not be well for us to take offense at such a policy, since RB has accustomed us to this very realistic educational system, in which social pressure rarely fails to lend support to impetuous generosity.

More debatable and more disquieting, perhaps, is the insistence with which the Master compares those whose observance of the rule is heroic with their favored confrères. The avowed purpose of this parallel is to stimulate a feeling of shame in the hearts of the less observant.[86] We recognize here the theme of emulation which is vaunted in so unpleasant a fashion, where 'zeal' for the first place is concerned. Thank God, RB in revising the Lenten treatise (Chapter 49), left no trace of competition in the ascetic program. There again, as in the chapter *On Good Zeal*, individual fervor is divorced from all reference to the behavior of others. Thus, in passing from one rule to the other, we progress towards a purer, more personal notion of ascetic effort.

Another noteworthy care of the Master is his preoccupation not to 'lead to despair' the weak by making excessive demands of them.[87] In this we touch upon an element which anticipates RB's solicitude for less vigorous souls, and notably for the brother who is commanded 'impossible' things. While studying the second directory for the abbot (RB 64), we had occasion to contrast the signs of 'discretion' provided by our two authors. RM willingly proffers precision of a casuistic sort; RB, more imprecise and also more flexible, leaves more to the judgment of the abbot, to whom it expressly recommends 'discretion'.[88] But this theme of discretion is propounded in both rules for the sake of the superior. If, in both rules, there is a preoccupation for feelings of discouragement or sadness which might beset the soul of the disciple, the duty of warding off this danger is made the abbot's, the standpoint from which this psychological situation is regarded is the abbot's and that of the abbatial government. The interior attitude of the disciple is taken into consideration, but only from without; and from without also comes the measures meant to help him.

The standpoint adopted in RB 64 is different. This time, the legislator sides with the inferior, in order to consider with the eyes of the subordinate himself the excessive burden imposed by the authority—perhaps poorly enlightened—of the superior. The infirmity is not treated from without, but succoured and tutored from within by a educational effort, this original character of which we have stressed.

An over-all view of RM, therefore, does not weaken what we established above concerning the more refined attitude towards the inner life, of which RB gives proof, especially in the chapters of the appendix.

Since RB adds something to RM, in the sense that we have indicated, we ought to ask whether it does so under the influence of other authors.

The study of Chapters 67, 69 and 70 has made us aware of the influence of the pachomian rule. But that rule takes one direction only: to maintain the prerogatives of the superior. Certain 'abbatial reactions' have made room for those plagiarisms or match-ups with *R Pac*: prohibitions to wander about or to go out without permission, interdiction to take the defense of a punished brother, and right to excommunicate or strike reserved to the abbot and his mandatories.

Broaching the themes of charity and horizontal relations, it is in Augustine and Basil first of all that points of contact must be sought. It is well-known how Basil insisted on 'fraternity' to such an extent that with him this consideration takes precedence in some fashion over that of relations with superiors.[89] Consequently, there is nothing surprising in the fact that *R Bas* furnished us with parallels concerning mutual obedience. It likewise offers rich illustration of the theme of charity towards one's neighbor. Note in particular that 1 Cor 13:5 (*caritas non quaerit quae sua sunt*), a text underlying RB 72:7 (*nullus quod sibi utile iudicat sequatur, sed quod magis alio*), is one of the scriptural proofs which Basil invokes in his famous plea on behalf of life in community.[90]

The same text, however, is also used by Augustine.[91] *R Aug* is no less insistent in its own way that *R Bas* is concerning love of one's neighbor.[92] It pleads in particular for 'mutual honor': *honorate in uobis inuicem Deum cuius templa facti estis* (*R Aug* 11.114–115, cf. RB 64:11). Then again, *R Aug* would have the superior make himself 'more loved than feared' (*R Aug* 15.200), another recommendation which will pass into the second RB directory for the abbot (RB 64:15) and which, in the appendix, is rendered by the counsel given the brethren to 'love their abbot with a sincere and humble charity' (RB 72:10). The honor due to the superior, on account of God whom he represents, is again a point well-affirmed in the augustinian rule.[93]

So many references recalling Basil and Augustine might make one think that the RB appendix depends chiefly on these two Fathers in developing the passages, which it devotes to fraternal charity and horizontal relationships. As a result, one might be tempted to allow that, influenced by the two great doctors of cenobitic charity, RB added a horizontal dimension to the 'vertical' plan inherited from Cassian through the Master. Yet Cassian himself complemented the vertical plan, in accordance with which he ordinarily conceived the *coenobium*. Though the *coenobium* is most often seen in the *Insitutes* as a school in which the master-disciple relationship alone is taken into account, *Conference* 16, as we have seen, makes a magnificent study of the relations which unite the brethren. All the values of cenobitism, poverty, sharing of goods, renunciation of self-will, submission of one's judgment, patience, and silence are there summarized and considered from a new standpoint, that of fraternal charity. What motivates such renunciations here is no longer soley the profit which the inferior reaps from his subjugation to qualified directors but 'the good of peace and charity' among equals. The laws of cenobitism remain the same, but acquire new significance. The school appears as a fraternity; the disciples look at one another and discover that they are brothers. As one can see, in passing from the *Institutes* to *Conference* 16, the reader of Cassian accomplishes almost the same journey as the reader of RB, when he passes from the first chapters to those of the appendix. The inspiration for this appendix can perhaps be sought in Cassian.

The theme of the love for God leads us to the same sources. There also we discover Basil, Cassian, and Augustine. A treatise on the love of God serves to introduce R Bas, of which it is one of the major themes. We have seen in particular how Basil appealed to *agapè* to extend obedience to its heroic limits (R Bas 82). The fear prompted by love may well have been suggested to RB by Cassian. In Augustine's legislation divine charity is both the beginning and the end,[94] *ante omnia diligatur Deus . . . haec omnia obseruetis cum dilectione, tanquam spiritalis pulchritudinus amatores.*

This last expression (*cum dilectione*) recalls similar expressions which we have noted in RB. One could also note the similar abundance of adverbs in the little *Ordo monasterii* of Augustine: *fideliter* (three times), *sollicite* (twice), *pie, omni uirtute.* This stylistic trait probably springs from the same care for the interior quality of the act and the same propensity to recommend fervor which have appeared to us as characteristic notes of the RB redactor. Furthermore, no other literature could have made a greater contribution to the development of sensitivity and care for the inner life than the writings of Augustine. In this respect, though the appendix bears no visible impress of Augustinian influence, it is good to remember that the direction of RB 34 on distributing necessities 'according to the needs of each', is surely inspired by R Aug 5, 17 and 9. It is necessary to reread those developments of Augustine, in order to perceive how far such care to measure renunciation in terms of the real needs and subjective situation of each goes towards the interior realities, and how it could have suggested the preoccupation with the inner life that we have uncovered in the RB appendix.

NOTES TO CHAPTER NINE

1. To be more precise, let us say that the Master refuses to institute any rank of precedence among the provosts, and consequently among the *decaniae*; in so far as the ordering of the brethren within their *decaniae* is concerned, RM furnishes no system of arrangement whatsoever. Does this silence run counter to the explicit rules established by RB? One may think so, for nothing indicates that RM arranges the brethren, in their decania, according to a fixed order. The period of conversion is never mentioned in RM. Even if the brethren were arranged according to a certain rank in their *decania*—which nothing suggests—it is not evident, according to what principle the brethren belonging to different *decaniae* could be ranked in relation to one another. The only concern the Master expresses in this domain is to exclude attributing the 'second' and 'third' places (those which set the holders at the side of the abbot) to appointed office-holders. For the rest, his silence forms too great a contrast with his usual taste for precision for us not to interpret it as really signifying the absence of rank.

2. Let us cite only R Pac Praef 3, and the *Vita Fulgentii* 39.

3. RB 64:2.

4. The two most interesting parallels furnished by *Concordia* 70 are 1 R Fruc 12 (n 5) and R Wal 46 (n 7); these two are seventh-century texts.

5. *Vita Fulgentii* 53: *puro nomine.*

6. RM 3:74–75. Nor does RM have the two 'instruments' which, in RB, immediately precede and follow those we are citing, *elationem fugere* (RB 4:69), *in Christi amore pro inimicis orare* (RB 4:72).

7. Vs 17; note the precise parallel with RB 72:4. Rom 12:10 is already cited by Cassian, *Conf* 16.11.2, under the form *honore alterutrum praeuenientes*. The context in Cassian is different: it is a question of the humility which disposes one to acquiesce to the opinion of one's neighbor. Nevertheless, the entire *Conference* 16, as we shall see, foretells the RB appendix.

8. RM 2:16–22 (equity); RM 2:6, 32–39 (account rendering); RM 93: 19–20 (account rendering).

9. Cf. RB 27:6: *non super sanas tyrannidem*. This 'tyranny' (cf. RB 65:2), is the equivalent of the *libera potestas* of which RB 63:2 speaks.

10. RB 65:22: *inuidiae aut zeli flamma*. RB 64:16: *non zelotipus*. Cf. RB 4:66 (= RM 3:72): *zelum non habere*, and the *zelus amaritudinis malus* of RB 72:1.

11. RB 3:6 and RB 63:2.

12. RB 3:6 (*prouide*) and RB 64:17 (*prouidus et consideratus*).

13. RB 64:12, 14; 61:4. In this last case, not the care to render the abbot attentive to counsels coming from below, in line with RB 3:6 and 65:14–15.

14. Jerome, Lr 117.6 (*sanctum et nonnum*); Lr 22.16 (*castae et nonnae*).

15. The two passages of Arnobius Junior in which *nonnus* figures do not seem to correspond to cenobitic usage. See *In Ps 105* (PL 53:486c) and *In Ps 140* (PL 53:552a).

16. RM 83:4, 8. This title *pater monasterii*, which usually designates the head of the monastery in the *Pachomiana Latina*, is still given to the abbot in RB 33:5. The cellarer is only *sicut pater* for the whole community (RB 31:2).

17. Cassian, *Conf* 1.1.

18. This remark intends only to characterize RB in relation to RM. One will recall that ranks based on seniority are not, in fact, an RB creation, but a traditional institution.

19. VP 3.26.755c (*tanquam patri et domino*); Jerome, Lr 125.15 (*timeas ut dominum diligas ut parentem*), cf. R Mac 7; *Vita Honorati* 19 (*omnes dominum, omnes patrem uocabant*); RM 19:4 (*Iube, domne abbas*) and 61:2 (*Quid iubes, domine pater?*).

20. Herwegen, *Sinn und Geist*, p 372. This interpretation has in its favor the explanation which at once follows: *honore et amore Christi* (RB 63:13). Cf. as well the text of Jerome cited in the previous note. Tertullian opposes to the title *dominus*, which he refuses to give the emperor, that of *pater patriae*, which to him seems preferable. The first is *nomen patriae*, the second *nomen pietatis* (*Apol* 34.2). Eucherius, *De contemptu mundi* (PL 50:724d) recommends: *Dominum quia Dominum uocas, metue; quia patrem, dilige* (cf. Mal 1:6).

21. This ascending order is evident especially in RB 63: the brothers (vss 11–12a); the fathers (12b); the abbot and Christ (13). In RB 72 it is still discernible, but it is upset by the fact that 'honor' comes before 'love' (vss 4,8), as was previously the case in RB 63:10. Besides, the mention of God (vs 9) precedes that of the abbot (vs 10), the latter being followed, nevertheless, by mention of Christ (vs 11; cf. RB 63:13).

22. RM 2:16–22 (= RB 2:16–22) and RM 2:30–31.

23. On non-augustinian parallels to RB 64:15, see above, Chapter 7, n. 75.

24. RM 7:2 = RB 5:2. In RM 3:23 = RB 4:21, the expression *nihil amori Christi praeponere* implies no particular allusion to obedience, to judge from the context. It is rather a question of a universal maxim which envisages monastic life in general (cf. the preceding sentence, *saeculi actibus se facere alienum*, which is, it also, of a very general import).

25. RM 10:87ff = RB 7:67ff.

26. This schema, as we know, was taken by the Master from Cassian (*Inst* 4.39). Cassian makes no allusion to charity in his ten 'indications' of humility. *Caritas* is for him synonymous with *puritas cordis* (*Conf* 1.6). This summit is not attained except at the end of a total purification. Let us observe in passing that RB is here less faithful to Cassian than is RM. From all appearances, the RM redaction must have antedated the RB redaction, since the latter deviates notably from the source.

27. See Cassian, *Conf* 11.8. This opposition between pure charity and the hope of recompense goes back to Clement of Alexandria (*Strom.* 6). It is akin to the stoic conception of virtue.

28. Note that fear (based on faith) makes its appearance at the first rung, hope at the fourth, charity at the peak of the ascent. The Master seems, then, to be following the order proposed by Cassian in *Conf* 11.8: from the fear of punishment prompted by faith, one rises to the hope of recompense, and finally one ends at love of the Good (that is, of virtue for itself, of God for himself). However, it should be observed that the Master recalls the *uita aeterna* from the very first rung (RM 10:11 = RB 7:11), even though this rung, on the whole, appealed much more to fear than to hope. On the other hand, if there is question at the fourth rung of *spes retributionis diuinae* (RM 10:56 = RB 7:39), this mention of hope is no more than a fleeting allusion, the whole rung being concerned with patience. One must therefore cease to look for the tripartite division of Cassian, *Conf* 11.8, in the ladder of Humility. The Master receives his immediate inspiration from another passage (*Inst* 4.39) where Cassian overlooks the intermediate stage of hope, and is satisfied to place fear at the outset and charity at the termination.

29. The transformation of *amore ipsius boni* (Cassian, *Inst* 4.39) into *amore Christi* (RB 7:69) could be interpreted in the same way. The RM 10:90 reading (*amore ipsius consuetudinis bonae*) once again appears here as the intermediate link between RB and Cassian, whose text and thought it reproduces more faithfully (cf. above, n. 25). Both Cassian and the Master define perfect charity on philosophical lines, under the disinterested love of virtue. The RB redactor, here as at the third degree, cannot restrain himself from speaking of the love of Christ. This Christian terminology imposes itself on him without taking into account the considerations of his predecessors. It will be observed, moreover, that for Cassian himself *affectus boni ipsius amorque uirtutum* is equivalent to *amor Christi*, as *Conf* 11.6 shows.

30. *Benedic* in RB 66:3; *benedicite* in RM 19:8; 65:3; 95:20; *benedictio* (understand: the *request* for a blessing) in RM 9:3, 5, 11, 18, 20, 26, 49, 50; 71:2. *Benedictio* has, on the contrary, its normal meaning of 'blessing' in RM 13:46; 19:8 (with *petere*, as in RB 53:24; 63:15). This ordinary meaning ought to be well distinguished from *benedictio* in the sense of 'to say *benedic* or *benedicite*,' 'to ask a blessing.'

31. RM 9:3 (to the abbot); 65:2 (to the guest. Cf. 95:19–20: seculars greeting monks outside of the enclosure); RM 13:46–47 (among brethren). In RM 19:8 it is not clear whether the request for a blessing is addressed to the brother with whom one is working or to God himself.

32. Cf. Cyprian, *Test.* 3.85, citing Lev 19:32.

33. RB 63:5–6.

34. Or 'to be idle' (*vacari*), if one adopts the reading defended by Plenkers, Brechter, and Penco. See this last author *in loco*.

35. We ought to stress, however, the change from the two porters of RM to the single

porter provided for by RB. This evolution parallels that from the two guestmasters (besides hebdomadaries) of RM 79 to the single guestmaster of RB 53. There are likewise in RM two provosts for each *decania*, and two hebdomadaries each week, whereas in RB these numerical precisions are missing. The single RB porter may receive a younger *socius*, thereby raising the number of porters to two once again and justifying the plural of the title. Yet the RB redaction preserves its complete originality. Instead of two equal colleagues, it is now a question of a single incumbent, with a brother under his orders. All the attention is directed upon this incumbent and on the qualities he must deploy. The reduction from two porters to one, like that from the two guestmasters to one only, manifests a greater evaluation of the demands of the office. The personage is depicted more carefully and his spiritual physiognomy and his personal responsibility are accentuated.

36. The Master's dominant preoccupation is that the door be kept closed (95:2, 22).

37. The same contrast between the Master's manner and that of RB can be seen in the chapter on the weekly kitchen helpers. RB is much less rich in practical information than was RM, but the spiritual sense of the service as a work of charity is set in sharper relief.

38. See the *fontes* of Butler.

39. RM 74:1–2, but the context is different (supererogatory fasting). Cf RM 22:4–8.

40. Ps 132:7: *introibimus in tabernaculo eius, adorabimus in loco ubi steterunt pedes eius*, with *Gloria*.

41. The preceding words (*uel quocumque ire*, vs 7) may also be explained as due to the influence of R Pac 84: *neque exeundi in agro neque ambulandi in monasterio*.

42. See in particular RB 44; 49:10; 57:1–3.

43. The expression does appear once, though, in the Master (RM 12:4). It is current in R Pat (PL 102 recension), where it replaces *praepositus,* which figures in the *Par Lat* 12205 recension (see above, Chapter 8, p 000). In RM 12:4, *qui praeest* is omitted by E. But this ms does know the expression which it occasionally substitutes for *abbas* (RM 30:30). Note lastly that in RM 2:1 = RB 2:1 (*abbas qui praeesse dignus est monasterio*), Corbett proposes suppressing *abbas* to recover the primitive *qui praeest* (*The Latin*, p 150).

44. *Repugnare* (RM 57:16). *Resistendo* (RB 68:3).

45. Caesarius of Arles also has depicted the case of the monk who is faced with an 'impossible' order. But his conclusion is totally different: *cum humilitate praebe oboedientiam: si uero non praeuales, impossibilitati tuae cum humilitate postula ueniam* (*Serm* 234, Morin, 884, 1). The final word, then, rests with the inferior: in 'excusing himself,' he avoids the order received.

46. *Concordia*, Chapter 75.

47. *Concordia*, Chapter 74. Note that n 3 (*Lib Ors* 24) appertains to the pachomian milieu, and nos 7–8 to the R Pac itself. N 5 (R Bas 120) is little to the point. Nos 6 and 9 do not expressly speak of 'defense'.

48. RM 13:54–59 envisages only relations with one who is excommunicated, not his overt 'defense'. Cf. Cassian, *Inst* 2.16, and RB 26.

49. In RB 48:20 is already found an allusion to 1 Tim 5:20 (*correptioni regulari subiaceat taliter ut ceteri timeant*). Now, there is question in that place of a clear defined fault, that of garrulity during the time for *lectio*.

50. Only in GR 15.2 does Basil prescribe giving the children *one* master. In R Bas 7, the corresponding passage is still in the plural. Yet even the first edition has demanded of those who are masters the same qualities of patience and competence which will be required of the master in GR 15.2. The *cura infantium* is already reserved to specially designated adults. For Isidore, see R Is 19.

51. RM 50:10–12: during the three hours of 'spiritual work', the boys learn to read and write under the direction of a *litteratus* of their *decania*.

52. Cassian extolled the heroism of a father, who stood by without protest during bad treatment inflicted on his own son, a monk with him in the same monastery (*Inst* 4.27).

53. RM 10:43 cites the example of Christ saying: *non ueni facere uoluntatem meam, sed huius qui me misit* (Jn 6:38). RM 10:49 cites Phil 2:8 *factus est oboediens usque ad mortem*. These two texts, it is true, speak of the obedience of Christ to his Father, not of submission to men. Yet Cassian uses them (*Conf* 19.7) to portray the obedience of Abbot John, an old hermit and accomplished monk, for whom obedience to an abbot is not so much a necessity for salvation (to know and to do the will of God) as a supreme act of abnegation and love, a sign of high perfection. This last conception of obedience comes to mind as soon as one evokes the example of Christ.

54. See above, Chapter 4. Note in particular that the fourth rung of humility, in revealing martyrdom, draws close to this notion of obedience as a sacrifice of love. Yet the word *caritas* is not pronounced until after the twelfth rung.

55. It is not a matter of excommunicating or of striking someone: this sort of punishment was expressly reserved to the abbot in the preceding chapter.

56. The satisfaction before the abbot prescribed by RM 17:8; 23:50; 30:30; etc. is occasioned by public faults, and therefore has a certain public, although minor, character.

57. RM 19:16 (importunate silence); 21:6, 14 (a delay in table service). Cf. RM 92:15 (qualities required of the new abbot).

58. Everything makes one think that this chapter was conceived as a conclusion. The final prayer is particularly significant in this respect (vs 12: *qui nos pariter ad uitam aeternam perducat*, echoing *ducit ad uitam aeternam* of vs 2). RB 73 could have been subjoined later as a second conclusion (it too closes with the evocation of the 'celestial homeland' and of the encounter with God). However, Penco seems to have demonstrated that RB 73 originally followed RB 66, as the epilogue of the rule, before the appendix (RB 67–72) had been annexed. See *Benedictina* 8 (1954), pp 25–42.

59. Thus Jacques Froger.

60. See the enumerations of RM 92:11–25, 79–82.

61. RM 92:8b.

62. RM 92:8a.

63. Thus *taciturnitas, sobrietas, continentia, grauitas, paucis uerbis, patientiae lacrimis, castitas,* in the list of RM 92:79–82.

64. *Zelus bonus*, from the fact that it is opposed to *zelus malus*, does indeed seem to retain a hint of emulation: it is 'jealousy'. but orientated towards the good. In relation to RM, it does in any event import a new element: the absence of any reference to the first place. Emulation in the good no longer has for stimulant the ambition for honors.

65. R Bas 78 (*Conc.* 77, n 3) cites Ps 69:10 (*zelus domus tuae*) and Ps 119:139 (*zelus meus*), both combined in the same sentence. The context of this citation is, in Basil, well defined: it is a matter of 'zeal' for the correction of sinners. We gather from this at least that biblical 'zeal' does not necessarily imply the idea of emulation. Cf. Rom 10:2; Gal 1:4, where the question, unlike the psalm verses indicated above, is purely one of 'zeal for God,' with no thought of competing against others.

66. The *Vita Hilarii* speaks in this sense of *zeli superni aemulatione flagrare* (11), *spiritalis zeli aemulatio* (18), *zelo superno inflammari* 21: in parallel with *studii ardore*). The idea of emulation with other men is missing from the context.

67. Compare RB 72:3: *feruentissimo amore*, and 66:10 *cum feruore caritatis*.

68. RM 1:3 = RB 1:3.

69. RM Ths 46 (= RB Prol 50); RM 92:18 (opposed to *scandalum*) and 80; 90:31.

70. It is question of the fourth rung of humility (RM 10:52–60 = RB 7:35–43.).

71. Concerning the correction of the incensed brother, RM 11:70 speaks only of *mansuetudo, taciturnitas,* and *caritas*. As for *iniurias patienter sufferre* (RM 3:35 = RB 4:30), it could be as much a question of injustices coming from the superior as of those which come from the brethren. Cf. *quibuslibet inrogatis iniuriis* (RM 10:52 = RB 7:35), which deals with unjust proceedings on the part of the superior. Cassian requires that 'injuries'' by the brethren be supported as if they came from superiors (*Inst* 12.33. See below, n. 74).

72. Cf. above, nn. 69–70.

73. RB 58:3, 11 (cf. RM 90:31); RB 68:2.

74. Moeover, the idea and the expression of RB 72:5 are banal. See the citations of Cassian furnished by Butler, to which can be added Cassian, *Inst* 12.33 (Petschenig, 230, 22): *nosmetipsos inferiores omnibus iudicantes, uniuersa quae nobis fuerint inrogata, tametsi iniuriosa sint uel tristia uel damnosa, tamquam a superioribus nostris inlata patientissime toleremus*. Note that here as in RB 72, patience consists in supporting the brethren as well as the superiors. It is the same in *Conf* 16.26–27.

75. 1 Cor 10:24, 33; Phil 2:4. See the notes of Butler who does not indicate 1 Cor 13:5. Cf. Once again RB coincides here with *Conference* 16 of Cassian, citing 1 Cor 13:5. Cf. *Conf* 16.22.4 and 17.19.7.

76. Whereas RM 3:23 depends, like several of the adjoining maxims, on the *Passio sancti Juliani*, n° 46, it is from St Cyprian, *De oratione dominica* 15, that RB 73:4 drew its inspiration, as Butler notes. On the *Passio s. Juliani*, see our note 'Une nouvelle édition de la Règle Bénédictine,' RAM 142 (April-June 1960), pp 217–19.

77. *Omnino* is a word the redactor likes. We would point this out just in the final chapters: RB 63:5; 66:7; 68:2. According to the statistics compiled by Froger, *omnino* occurs seventeen times in RB, whereas it figures only once in RM. In RB 7:10 it replaces *omni hora* as read in RM 10:10.

78. See above, Chapter 7, n. 84 (p 345).

79. RM 60:3; 61:7, 12, 23; 62:3, 7, 8, 11, 12; 63:22 (twice); 71:4; 72:T, 4, 7; 79:14. Same application in RB 53:2; 66:4.

80. In RM 4, two virtues are emphasized by *prae omnibus*: *castitas corporum* and *pietas*.

81. RM 3:14–21; 16:34–37; 27:49–51; 50:7. Cf. also RM 87:39; 91:50.

82. RM 16:45–52 (cellarer); 20:1–14 (all those absent); 55:16; 57:24; 73:15, 19. This 'commemoration of all those absent' is reserved in RB for the last prayer of each canonical hour (RB 67:2).

83. RM 27:47–51 (curtailments of bread and wine; the provisions thus spared go to the poor); 44:12–19 (reading instead of sleeping after Nocturns), 53:6-25 (Lenten abstinence), 38–41 ('superposition', that is, prolongation of the fast, in Lent), 51 (Holy Saturday fast). Similarly RB encourages spontaneous restrictions during Lent (RB 49), but is more categorical with regard to the use of meat from quadrupeds throughout the year (compare RB 39:11 with RM 53:27: the Master's tolerance might be explained by concern to sustain the anti-Manichaean principle of the legitimacy of the use of meat. In the later period of RB, this principle would have lost its relevancy).

84. RM 27:47; 44:8. Cf. RM 53:12, 27.

85. RM 44:19 (the abbot in the middle of the dormitory); 53:16–18 (the 'abstainers' are set apart). Cf 53:32–33.

86. RM 53:7–10, 32–33. Cf. 23:56; 53:52–55 (*erubescant*).

87. On *desperatio* see RM 7:10 (concerning obedience); 22:10 (rank), cf. 92:45; 55:13 (exactitude at the office); cf. the concessions granted to the imperfect over silence (RM 9:46–50), and the concern to avoid causing those traveling the 'bitter sadness' of losing their way on account of an excessively long office (RM 56:14–16).

88. See above, Chapter 7, pp 331–332.

89. See *Le monastère, Eglise du Christ*, pp 36–37, and 'Obéissance et Evangile selon saint Basile,' *Vie Spirituelle, Supp.* 21 (1952) 192–215.

90. R Bas 3. Cf. Greg. of Nyssa, *De Instituto Christiano* 60.5.

91. R Aug 12.135.

92. R Aug 11.101, 111–112, 114–115; 12.140; 14.186–187, and the entire opening (Chapters 5–6); cf. 15.194. The importance of the theme of charity throughout the monastic writings of Augustine, from *De moribus ecclesiae* to *Enarrationes in Psalmos* 99 and 132, not to mention R Aug, is an arresting fact. A. Zumkeller has rightly emphasized it, not without drawing some slightly forced conclusions, however. See above, Chapter One, p 60, n. 14.

93. OM 6.25; R Aug 15.187 (cf. 15.195).

94. Cf. OM 1.1 and R Aug 16.204.

COMPLEMENTARY NOTE

The mutual relations between 'seniors' and 'juniors' studied in RB 63 and 71 are also the object of two chapters of the *Regula Pauli et Stephani*, edited by J. Vilanova, Montserrat 1959 (*Scripta et documenta* 11). These two small chapters spell out the law of mutual charity and unanimity which is proclaimed in the first line of the rule. Chapter 2 describes the elder's attitude, fatherly affection and calm, kind and humble manner of commanding. Chapter 3 demands a sincere and humble obedience from the juniors, with no 'backtalk,' resistance, or negligence. An appeal for concord and unanimity concludes the presentation.

This text reminds one a great deal of RB 63:10–12 in the seniors-juniors pairing. The title *nonni*, expressing fatherhood, also comes to mind, though here it is not an issue of the respect shown by the juniors, but rather of the affection borne by the elders. Lastly, the *Regula Pauli* coincides with RB 71 in treating the obedience due to the elders on the part of the younger brethren. As for the manner of commanding indicated to the elders, RB offers no precise parallel, but it prescribes a similar attitude, composed of goodness, humility, and confidence, both to the abbot (Chapter 64) and to the elders (Chapters 63 and 70). The same care for charity animates both this beginning of the *Regula Pauli* and the appendix to RB.

Probably later than RB (the editor dates it at the second half of the sixth century), the *Regula Pauli* does not appear to depend on it. The coincidence of the two rules is therefore all the more remarkable. We admit, however, that we hesitate over the meaning to be given the word *seniores . . . iunioribus*. Is it really a question, as the editor thinks, of 'seniors' and 'juniors?' It could in fact be a matter of 'superiors' and 'inferiors,' as is suggested both by the meaning of *senior* in the rest of the rule and by the precise context of obedience in the present passage.

CONCLUSION

THE RESULTS OF OUR INVESTIGATION may be resumed under three headings. We shall first assemble the literary evidence regarding the relationship between the two rules. In a second section we shall rehearse the indications which suggest a change of spirit and institutions in RB in relation to RM. Finally, we shall present the conclusions on doctrinal order connected with the nature of cenobitism, of the abbacy, and of obedience, according to RB.

RM AND RB: THE LITERARY PROBLEM

The working hypothesis adopted at the outset was, it will be remembered, that RM is prior to RB. Various observations made in the course of the study seem to have confirmed it.

By the meaning that it ascribes to *praepositus*, understood as 'the Second, the lieutenant of the abbot', RB classes itself among a group of relatively late documents, whereas RM employs the word in its primitive meaning, 'the first, the leader of the group' (Chapter 8). The archaic character of this peculiarity of the Master is emphasized by the fact that E sometimes substitutes *decanus* for *praepositus*, or glosses this last term with its synonym, or completely suppresses it. There are so many indications that this manuscript is dependent on a tradition, in which the original sense of *praepositus* was already causing difficulty. Thus in RM the manuscript tradition itself already bears witness to some extent to the evolution of the meaning of *praepositus* established in RB (Chapter 5)[1].

The homogeneity of texts common to both rules (MB) with texts peculiar to the Master emerges incidentally from the meaning of the word *solacium*. This term signifies 'aid, company' in RM 1:4 = RB 1:4, as nearly everywhere else in RM, whereas RB, in the passages peculiar to it, always understands it in a personal sense: 'an aide, a companion' (Chapter 5, n. 71).

But the most characteristic facts in favor of the earlier date of the Master are those, which our scrupulous examination of the outline and sources of certain chapters has brought to light.

For some time now it has been a generally recognized fact that RM 10 presents a ladder of humility which is more faithful to Cassian and is therefore probably older than that of RB 7. We did not have to insist on this point any more than on the classical argument based upon the RB lacuna at the 'first rung'.[2] But the study of RM—RB 1 uncovered an analogous fact. The presence in RM of a sentence on the economic aspect of the Sarabaites and of a paragraph on the false hermits (vss 11–12) presupposes that the author has *Conference* 18 of Cassian before his eyes. The absence of these passages in RB is better explained as the effect of abridgment, than their presence in RM as the result of an addition following Cassian. Of the two rules, RM proves to be more faithful to the common source and consequently to be in all likelihood, the more ancient.

In Chapter 2, the very regular plan of RM and the small number of themes succeeding one another in a certain order, which is repeated in the two parts of the text, seem to bear witness to a homogeneity of composition, the work of a single mind. This inference receives confirmation from the observations which we made in other chapters. The bipartite structure of the directories for the cellarer and the abbot in RB (Chapters 31 and 64), as well as that of the treatise on the council in RM (2:41–50), derive from the same law of composition which each author seems to obey spontaneously when left to his own unhampered inspiration. Everything leads us to believe, then, that RM 2 is an original redaction. On the other hand, RB 2 from its disordered state, seems to bear signs of revision: its themes are more numerous; they succeed one another without any apparent order; some are repeated in tedious fashion.

An analogous observation can be made on the subject of RB 3. This chapter also, from the standpoint of composition, displays a more complex and less orderly appearance than the parallel treatise on the Master.

Lastly, RB 7 presents at the eighth rung a rather striking anomaly: the scriptural illustration is missing, although one is present at every other 'rung'. RM 10, however, does provide this place with several texts from Scripture, as everywhere else. So the RB redaction shows itself less homogeneous in this respect than the RM redaction. The most obvious explanation for the contrast is that the RB redactor here gave in a little more than was necessary to his purpose of abridgment.

If the composition of RB took its lead from RM, what idea can we form of the redactor's process of composition? The observations that we have made, fragmentary as they may be, do perhaps merit an over-all assessment.

The MS P text, and not that of MS E, seems to underlie RB 1. There is no doubt, of course, that when RB spoke of the *gula* of the *gyrovagues*, it was alluding to the digression on vagabond monks attested by P, and missing in E. Furthermore, the sequence of texts at the end of the RB Prologue implies the state of RM 1 as we know it in P, not as attested by E.

In Chapter 2, RB likewise implies the text of P, since it reproduces RM 2:11–22, which is missing in E, and since it has a treatise on the council of the brethren parallel to RM 2:41–50, a passage also omitted by E. We are therefore justified in thinking that the omissions common to RB and to E can be explained by the same intention to abridge, guided by similar sensibilities. Both presume a reading of the long text as conserved by P, and both of them, swayed by similar preoccupations, enacted suppressions which, moreover, only partially coincide.[3]

In Chapter 5, RB shows no special affinity with either of the RM recensions, so far as the passages which have been reproduced or omitted, are concerned. The digression on the 'two ways' is attested by RB. As for the distinction between the two types of obedience (with or without *mora*), nothing in RB 5 allows us to assert that it was to be read in the Master's text. Yet the allusion in RB 6:3 to the *perfectis discipulis* is an indication that the state of RM, as implied by RB, did include the distinction between 'the perfect and the imperfect' in the matter of silence, and probably, therefore, also in the matter of obedience.

These remarks all tend to suggest that the Master's text which served as the basis for the RB redactor was almost co-extensive with what we read today in P.

The work of the redactor is evidently guided by his anxiety to abridge. However, it has not been possible to obtain this result in Chapter 2, where the extent of the added texts outstrips that of the omissions. This fact is comparable to the insertion in Chapter 64 of a second directory for the abbot, which greatly exceeds the proportions of the parallel admonition in RM 93. *De abbate nunquam satis* . . .

Are there indications of a plurality of redactors? The study of Chapter 2 rather inclines us towards the hypothesis of a single adaptor. For it really seems that the second omission and second addition can be attributed to the same hand, since they overlap exactly. In such an hypothesis, the work of the redactor in the rest of the chapter can quite well be explained: he begins by adding (first and third additions) and then, to compensate, he cuts (first and third omissions).

Attribution to one and the same redactor of the omissions and additions of RB 2 is further suggested by the contrast which the second omission and corresponding addition present from the point of view of content. The suppressed text spoke of the exemplary humility of the abbot and of his equal charity for everyone. The addition urges the same person to take a firm hand and not treat everyone in the same manner. The second text may possibly be meant to amend the first. However, the hypothesis of a plurality of redactors does become attractive when this RB passage is compared with certain sentences of RB 64, which produce an altogether different tone. The same redactor, however, could have been able to go back on himself or to finish his work in his second abbatial directory, in so far as the double tendency towards increased severity and more attentive care for persons can be observed almost everywhere in the parts peculiar to RB.

So far as one can judge from the cases we have studied, the redactor tends to establish little homogeneous units, beginning from the vaster and more complex units that he finds in the Master. Not only does he seek to shorten, but he also strives to reduce to unity. Thus Chapter 1 brings down to almost equal dimensions the notices on the sarabites and the gyrovagues, reducing them to the format of the notice on the hermits. Furthermore, the final exhortation of RM 1:76–92 is suppressed. With it disappears an obviously incongruous element from *De generibus monachorum*, which thus becomes a small treatise, homogeneous and well proportioned, occupying by itself the whole of the chapter.[4]

The same tendency has been able to contribute to the division of the treatise on the abbot and on the council (RB 2 and 3). The treatise on the council was presented in RM as an appendix to that on the abbot. The RB redactor seems to have been conscious of the difference of subject matter and tone between the two passages, and so separated the Master's amalgamation; each treatise becomes a distinct chapter. This division perhaps throws the treatise on the council into somewhat higher relief than the Master would have desired, and it makes it less easy to perceive the arrangement of the whole treatise on spirituality (RM 1 through 10; RB 1 through 7), in which we no longer see with the same clarity the role played by the abbot as the craftsman of the spiritual art. But the redactor, in composing his 'choice pericopes,'[5] cares more about the distinction of subject matter and the homogeneity of the chapters than about the doctrinal cohesion and the general picture so vigorously drawn by the Master.

We have the opportunity in Chapter 5 to establish the competence with which the revision of RM 7 was executed. In this chapter also, we see a complex whole is reduced to a unity of subject and style. The description of prompt obedience is continued smoothly by a sentence borrowed from the eulogy of the cenobites, and closes without any discontinuity by a statement of their interior qualities.

The chapter on the deans offers a fresh example of the tendency which was displayed in the division between RB 2 and 3. Once again the redactor was unable to tolerate the amalgamation of two distinct treatises within a single chapter (RB 21 and 22). However, this new division can be explained for another reason, which did not come into play in the case of RB 2 and 3. this time, of course, the abridgment has not allowed the references relating to the vestiary and the table to remain, which in RM form the setting of the recommendations for the dormitory. Reduced in this way to a treatise on the sleeping arrangements of the monks, the appendix to RM 11 allowed itself to be set up as a separate chapter.

For its part, the directory for the provosts underwent a radical simplification: all it amounts to in RB is a study on the election and eventual replacement of the deans. We are far from the Master's closely packed collection of material, which included a doctrinal prologue on the necessity for having provosts, an ordination ritual, a directory including ten examples of reprimands, a provision dispensing provosts from manual work, and finally a practical appendix on the supervision of the vestiary, the dormitory, and the table!

The directory for the cellarer (RB 31) likewise forms a homogeneous literary unit in place of the composite collection of material in RM 16, which consists of a prologue (in the first person plural) on Providence, and a rule of life for the cellarer.

The series of Chapters 63 through 65 offers an analogous contrast with RM 92 through 94. Both deal with the same questions: ranks, abbatial succession, office of 'Second'. In RM, these three questions are intimately bound together, and one passes imperceptibly from one to the next. Together they form a single treatise, a single discourse. In RB, on the contrary, they are three distinct little treatises, each self-contained. Each chapter exactly coincides with one of these questions. Certain links exit between them, but one would hardly know it except for brief allusions.

We must not however, exaggerate this characteristic of RB. Is not Chapter 64, like the chapter of the Master, a bringing together of unrelated passages: a treatise on the choice of an abbot and the abbatial directory? Then too, we established how the redactor introduced, at the end of Chapter 5, a note on the penal code which sounds incongruous in a chapter on pure spirituality. As much may also be said of the threat of 'regular discipline' which resounds in Chapter 3, and even of the note on the *loca* in the treatise on the abbot (RB 2, first addition).

It remains true, on the whole, that the labor of the redactor tends to isolate the simple elements and to reduce complicated groups to a oneness of subject matter and form. This tendency is naturally connected with the will to abbreviate: an abridgment or a résumé normally obtains the result intended. Yet one cannot fail to appreciate the part played by conscious effort and skill in a work of this kind.

Besides his personal qualities as a writer, which we have studied in RB 31 and 64, the redactor gives proof of a sure taste and a certain deftness, when he simplifies the lengthy, redundant sentences at the end of Chapter 5 and at the end of the third rung of humility.

RM AND RB: INSTITUTIONS AND SPIRIT

Both rules belong to the same spiritual, institutional and literary tradition, that of Christian cenobitism. More precisely, it is to the egyptian tradition, received through Cassian, that RM and RB owe their fundamental structure. As in pachomian cenobitism, the essential framework of the monastery is supplied by the abbot and his provosts.

Traditional as it is, RM is not less stamped by strong originality. To begin with, on the literary level it contrasts strongly with most of the analogous documents through its breadth, organization, and methodical aspect. When the abbatial directory of RM 2 and the treatise on the succession in RM 92 through 94 are placed once more among the other group of texts belonging to the same genre, they play the part of powerful works, through the dimensions, richness of content and vigor of their arrangement.

On the level of doctrine and institutions, the Master's originality is doubtless to be sought in the inexorable logic with which he pursues the application of some traditional principles of cenobitism. He pushes the method of monastic education invented by Pachomius to the extremity of its consequences and even to the absurd. This logical instinct gains for us valuable theoretical insights into the nature of the abbacy. In this respect, the Master does not innovate; his doctrine is fully traditional. But it represents an effort of exposition and systematization found nowhere else. Not less to be valued is the work that the Master has done to arrange the elements of cenobitic life according to a methodical plan. The architectural structure of RM by itself teaches what this life is. We have only to look at the place assigned to the treatise on the abbot or to the directory for provosts, in order to understand what part these officers play. We are indebted to the Master for the most remarkable effort made in antiquity to create a mental picture of cenobitic life.

This effort encompasses the doctrinal and institutional aspects of cenobitism in their entirety. It begins from the loftiest principles and descends to the most practical details of monastic observance. On this level of practical definitions, dominated by the relentless logic of the system, we again encounter the originality of the Master, but this time in a more debatable form.

It is a personal idea of the Master to set two provosts over each *decania*. He was careful to give us the key himself to these numbers. The pachomian system of the 'Second' does not prompt it, nor the biblical model of groups of ten, but the logic of his own educational method. He hopes by this means to guarantee the continuous supervision of the brethren. Traditional forms of organization thus receive from him an original interpretation, as a duty connected with the preoccupations of a teacher, which are personal to him.

He feels the need to provide for and regulate everything. In him the classical doctrine of discretion hardens into a classification of two forms of obedience and two forms of silence, adapted to the two categories of disciples. The same tendency to casuistry is displayed over the question of meals taken outside the monastery (RM 61).

He found in tradition the principle of absolute submission to an elder. He has derived his extravagant hypothesis of transfer of responsibility: the master alone will have to answer for what his disciples have done at his orders. As long as they obey, their security is complete; they need worry no more for their soul than for their body. In developing these views, the Master is paving the way for Columban more than he is following Cassian.

But the triumphant climax of the system is reached in the last chapters of RM, in the treatise on the abbatial succession. Here our author's passion for education and imprudent logic find full play. Two preoccupations wholly dominate his thoughts: to guarantee to the monastic school a master, who is 'the best' among the brethren, and to exploit the issue of the succession for the benefit of the education of the community. From these laudable but too narrow premises, he derives the indefensible competition in virtue, about which we know. His scheme takes no account of any given fact, custom, or juridical standard. It develops solely according to the logic of the educational method instituted by the rule.

In this method, the role of the abbot is preponderant and even, in a sense, exclusive. It is only in their function of tutor-supervisors, prolonging the educational activities of the abbot, that the provosts hold a place in it. Their mission is much more restricted in RM than in Cassian. The Master wanted the abbot to be the sole practitioner of the *ars sancta* in the monastery, which was no doubt quite possible in the small community for which he was legislating.[6]

This desire to emphasize the abbatial function clearly penetrates Chapter 10. Rungs 3, 8, and 9 define the spiritual counsels given by Cassian in his corresponding 'indications', by relating them expressly to the obedience that a brother owes to his abbot and the rule of the monastery (rungs 3 and 8), or to the silence that he is bound to observe—*usque ad interrogationem*—until the abbot puts a question to him (rung 9). Furthermore, the first four rungs are refashioned in such a way as to offer a more complete and more reasoned justification for obedience, and to confirm the necessity of submission to the abbot.

The Master is occupied above all with propping up the authority of the abbot in his capacity of commanding officer. Execution of the orders received, in preference to his own will, is what he requires of the disciple. On the other hand, he exhibits hardly any interest in the relationship of the monk with his superior on the level of spiritual direction. He has not retained the description of such relations as drawn by Cassian in 'indications' 2 and 3: a trustful confession of thoughts on the disciple's part, judgment and discretion on the director's part, which in turn is received with joy by the disciple. The opening of conscience, as portrayed by the second indication became, in the fifth rung, a confession of evil thoughts considered as a special exercise of humility, and no longer eliciting a word of direction from the elder in response.

Abbatial authority is jealously safeguarded in the treatise on the council where, however, the brethren are granted a certain right to be consulted on the subject of the *res monasterii*. The Master's position remains basically that of primitive cenobitism, which does not subject the administration of the abbot to any control, whereas the more recent rules deny him such complete autonomy.

The abbot's predominance or better, his omnipotence, appears no less clearly when one compares certain characteristics of RM with what we learn from other late rules, those of Fructuosus in particular. We know from such documents that the burden of the abbatial task and the weakness of the abbots have led to assigning an ever-expanding role to his lieutenant, the 'Second' or *praepositus*. Nothing of this sort appears in RM. The community is small, and the abbot, whose prestige is complete, suffices for everything. At table, at the distribution of work and in the dormitory, it is he who presides and supervises, in actual fact directing the community. The Master could see no reason for a 'Second', and this personage, if a chance accident in the abbatial succession obliges him to be instituted, will have no other role than to substitute for the abbot when absent.

The abbatial function is thus from all appearances at its zenith in RM. It benefits from the small size of the community, thanks to which it can do without a 'Second', and can best take on the functions of the *prae-*

positi. It benefits, too, from the unlimited authority which primitive cenobitism recognized in abbots and also from the effort of reflection attempted by the Master to furnish it with a more explicit theological justification and finally, no doubt, from the privileged situation enjoyed by the legislator-abbot, to whom we are indebted for the rule. One imagines him as sole master of his ship, hands unfettered by any local tradition or external influence, wholly free to devlop his educational ideas and extend their application to the practical sphere. This situation seems to imply a period very close to the foundation. The naive schematization, and the simplistic logic, inadequately based on experience, of this forceful and extraordinary document could thus be explained.

Among the lacunae in the RM, the lack of interest in fraternal relations can particularly be observed. It can be perceived not only in the paucity of references in this area (the theme of charity is not developed except as regards the illnesses of guests), but also in the block of material consisting of 'indications' 4 and 5 of Cassian, which causes to be included under the rubric of 'obedience' (fourth rung on humility) the development of a theme, which originally concerned relations among the brethren. To tell the truth, the Master's field of vision is entirely absorbed by the relationship of the brethren to the abbot.

The absence of allusions to the failings of the abbot or provost is equally striking. The prestige of these educators scarcely permitted faults on their part to be contemplated. Here again one does not know whether we must hold the set purpose of schematization or the lack of experience with men responsible.

In what sense has the RB redactor modified the work he revised? This is not easily expressed in a single sentence.

Jacques Froger saw very well that RB was both shorter and more complete than RM. Less profuse in details, it makes significant additions to the essence of the *Institutions*. We have seen this law enter into play in the treatise on the council, where, besides the plenary council common to all rules, a council of elders appears which is peculiar to RB. These elders, that is, the deans probably, fulfill several roles, which were not yet foreseen by RM: *senpectas*, spiritual seniors, roundsmen, master of novices. Although reluctantly, RB also envisages the creation of a genuine office of 'provost' or abbot's lieutenant and prescribes the establishment of several permanent officers, whose function was not yet assured in RM by any determined title, or which were fulfilled in rotation on a weekly basis: infirmarian, guestmaster, guests' cook, bell-ringer.

Cenobitic institutions therefore have passed in RB into a more complex and more developed state. An analogous process tends to define certain regulations. Thus, the procedure for summoning and conducting the council is more carefully indicated than it was in RM, in the very first sentence of RB 3. The same note of juridical exactitude is more carefully indicated in the sentence of RB 71, which gives priority to the orders of the abbot and provost over all the *priuata imperia*. The very notion of orders coming from persons not belonging to the hierarchy is, moreover, an RB innovation. As much should be said of the whole regulation of ranks and of the relations springing from them: titles, respect, 'mutual' obedience, correction. This rule on fraternal relations is entirely new, and evidences care to promote the spiritual counsels given by the Master in the *ars sancta* to the rank of precise and obligatory precepts.

On the other hand, the general characteristic of RB in comparison with RM is its lack of precise details of monastic observance. Froger rightly attributes this vagueness to the process of abridgment. The editor's anxiety to abridge obliges many details to be sacrificed. But this characteristic of RB does not result automatically from abbreviating. The redactor would have been able, had such been his preoccupation, to condense into a few words a great number of his practical hints. Now it is not in this direction that he orientates his work of summarizing. He replaces the rule of life for the cellarer (RM 16) with a directory analogous to that for the abbot, a spiritual admonition devoid of practical influence. The chapter on the deans does not try to tell us anything about the activity of these personages, but lingers over a question, upon which the Master only lightly touched, that of choosing them well. We no longer have any precise knowledge of the porter and his occupations, which were completely regulated by the Master, but RB stresses the qualities of the man and the charity of his welcome. The service of the weekly kitchen helpers is scarcely outlined, whereas the spiritual sense of the function, understood as a meritorious work of charity, is stressed.

In all these cases we can recognize the same interest in the spiritual and subjective aspect of the tasks and the same indifference towards practical regulations and objective definitions. Not content merely to abridge, RB modifies the perspective in which the realities of cenobitic life are studied. If it shows itself singularly vague, the reason is not only because it summarizes, but also and chiefly because the interest of the redactor upon the qualitative elements, the emphasis on which leaves only a little space for describing the actual observances.

In the chapter on the ordination of the abbot, RB purely and simply omits the long ritual of the Master. It seizes upon the brief monition addressed by the former abbot to his successor and transforms it into a genuine abbatial directory, developing the themes, dear to the redactor, of mercy, moderation and discretion. Here again, the suppression of practical detail cannot be imputed solely to the intention to abridge, since spiritual developments which are copiously described, come to be inserted in the vacated places.

The same tendency to pass from the exact to the indefinite is observable particularly in the numerical indications. One word would have sufficed to tell us whether there are one or two deans per *decania*, but that word is not uttered. We remain in the same uncertainty as regards the weekly kitchen helpers. Perhaps their number is thought to be known to the readers, for the redactor takes the trouble to specify that there will be *two* brothers in the guests' kitchen, a new service unknown to RM (53: 17). We meet again the redactor's customary lack of precision on the question of roundsmen ('one or two'), of those who preside at table ('one or two'), of the number of brethren in the dormitory ('ten or twenty').

Similarly the RB redactor seems uninterested in the Master's casuistry. He radically simplifies it as regards meals taken outside: *etiamsi omnino rogetur a quouis* (Chapter 5). He suppresses it in the treatise on obedience and silence. One sole ideal is proposed for everyone. The legislator does not condescend to specify how often the imperfect may leave an order unanswered, and in what cases they will be excused for having broken the rule of silence.

Instead of such casuistic definition, the redactor suggests that the abbot cultivate discretion. The duty of looking after the weak, which dictated to the Master his ruling on the 'two obediences', is represented in RB under the form of counsels of prudence and merciful charity.

In this we have a striking example of the transition from a particular rule to a general theory, which is carried out on several occasions in RB. Thus the redactor, beginning from the two regulatory articles which he read separately in RM, formulated the general law which we read in RB 53: 19–21.[7] One may compare with those facts the over-all study, which RB devotes to fraternal relations. RM envisaged solely certain particular instances of charity: for brothers in temptation, the sick, and the absent. RB studies the problem of fraternal charity in all its fullness: any brother whosoever will know how he should behave towards any other member of the community whomsoever.

Notwithstanding this aptitude for generalizing, the redactor does not appear interested in the Master's 'abbatial theory'. He has sacrificed the important passages of RM 1 and 11 on 'teachers', and we may marvel that RB 5 has preserved the single allusion to that doctrine that our rule makes.

However, the abbot's position in RB well remains what it was in the eyes of the Master. It is at least the intention of the legislator to maintain the abbot's rights. He even defines them more precisely in the treatise on the council, probably to cut short disorders. He reverts to such rights time and again: three times in the directory for the cellarer, in each line of Chapter 44 and in the generalizing notes at the end of Chapters 49 and 67. He reacts not only against insubordination of the 'second', as did the Master. The same struggle to safeguard the abbot's rights is conducted against deans 'inflated with pride', and against the priests of the monastery who are guilty of 'rebellion'. In this case, as in that of the provosts, even expulsion is foreseen (the Master envisaged only the deposition of the 'Second').[8]

Recall to the abbatial authority was especially necessary in the chapters of the appendix, since they institute a new hierarchy, that of seniority and of age, to which are accorded certain of the abbot's privileges. And then too, Chapter 69 forbids 'defending' a brother against the abbot; Chapter 70 prohibits striking or excommunicating another without the abbot's permission, and Chapter 71 forbids giving priority to 'private' orders over those of the abbot.

That the abbacy has lost none of its importance in RB is again shown by the space reserved for the treatise on the abbot. In a rule which is two or three times shorter than RM, the abbatial directory of Chapter 2 is notably longer, and a second directory peculiar to RB is added in Chapter 64.

We shall lastly notice the propensity to an increased severity. The redactor would like the abbot to take immediate measures against faults, and he exhorts him to use the rod if it is a question of 'hard' subjects. This 'second addition' of RB 2 replaces a text in which the Master encouraged the abbot to show himself humble as a child and loving as a father and mother. In the chapter on the council, the redactor inserted, somewhat in contrast to the 'spiritual' genre of the first chapters of the rule, a threat of ''regular discipline' directed precisely against anyone who would dare to dispute with the abbot. Even more unexpectedly, a penal note comes to close the chapter on obedience, demanding 'satisfaction' and 'amendment' on the part of the grumblers. Through the whole length of the rule, this tendency to multiply sanctions or render them more severe is disclosed. This display of intensified repression is evidence of the desire not to let the power of the abbot be impaired.

But at the same time, it is evidence for a more difficult actual situation than in RM. A certain anxiety betrays itself in these severe remarks. The redactor himself does not assume the attitude of boundless confidence in the abbot and his provosts, as does the Master. He believes that he ought to rebuke the abbot and put him on his guard against tyranny, jealousy, injustice, want of foresight, and imprudence. Perhaps he is aiming at the abbot in Chapter 63, when he demands that the lowest members of the community be entitled 'brother'. In any event, the same chapter reminds him that it is not due to himself personally that he has a right to the title '*dominus*' and '*abbas*'. On several occasions the abbot is invited to listen to views coming from his inferiors, such as criticisms of the visiting monk, request of the community to have a provost, or opinions offered in council. Consciously or not, but in any case significantly, the redactor transforms the standard maxim in RB 6:6 (RM 8:37) into a lesson meant for the abbot, a maxim which originally aimed at his subordinates (RB 3:6). This tendency to recognize the abbot's limitations as a fact and to make an issue of them in front of his disciples receives its most striking expression in an addendum in RB 4:61: 'obey the abbot in everything, *even if he himself—God forbid!—acts otherwise*. . .'

This realistic outlook, which the redactor has for the weaknesses of the abbot, corresponds to a certain relaxation of the abbatial power. If the redactor has a tendency to consolidate the authority of the superior, as we have seen, he nevertheless registers several norms which mark a regression, compared to the omnipotence that the abbot enjoyed in RM. It is no longer the abbot who designates his successor, but rather the community, with the approbation of the bishop. In spite of its undisguised aversion, the rule ratifies the change of 'Second'. This *praepositus* will be designated by the abbot 'with the counsel of the brethren who fear God', and not by surprise, as in RM. Difficulties between abbot and provost are envisaged, which necessitate the expulsion of the latter, an extremity, for which the Master does not provide. Finally, the deposed provost is replaced in such a manner that the office does not remain vacant, as in RM.

Even the norms that the redactor rejects are indications of a situation, where there is conflict.If he opposes with so much indignation the ordination of the provost by the bishop, *ex aequo* with the abbot it is because such an abuse is rampant around him, whereas there was no question of it in RM. The same should be said of the partisan struggles which, according to the testimony of RB, divide the 'clientele' of the abbot and that of the provost. Temptations to jealousy, against which the abbot is put on his guard, likewise indicate the importance assumed by his officer alongside the principal superior.

If the provost is forced upon the RB redactor, it is because the abbot cannot alone suffice for the task. The increased number of brethren makes division of the work a necessity. In fact, the abbot is surrounded by several new collaborators, whom RM did not know. Assistants are provided for the cellarer and the custodians of the tools are increased in number. The temporalities of the monastery also seem to be heavier: the 'third addition' of RB 2 cautions the abbot against becoming excessively absorbed by material cares.

The situation might be summarized by saying that the abbot has to face a heavier task with a more disputed prestige. The RB redactor seems more conscious than the Master of the weakness of superiors and the weight of their charge. The two very similar directories of RB 31 and 64 show concern to help the abbot and his cellarer to carry their burden. The manner in which they ought to assume it and the virtues to be specially cultivated, are indicated to them, the intention being to preserve their peace of soul. Perhaps it was the same awareness of the human limits of the abbacy which inclined the redactor to complement it by organizing the fraternal relations.

The scheme of fraternal relations contained in the final chapters of RB is, of course, the newest element of this rule in comparison with RM. The brethren are no longer bound only to the abbot either through the leaders of their *decaniae* or directly, but are involved in a supplementary network of 'horizontal' bonds. The basis of this system is rank. Although the abbot can intervene in it, by promoting or degrading someone, seniority in the monastery is its normal basis. An order partially independent of the abbatial will is therefore created among the brethren. In the case of the children, age confers on the older brethren a right of supervision which will be exercised, to be sure, under the abbot's control but which does not spring from the abbot's appointment and mandate, as does that of the deans.

Rank serves to define the respective duties of 'juniors' and 'seniors'. There are precise rules concerning titles of address, speech, respect, obedience and the acceptance of reproaches. On these last two points, transgressors are threatened with punishments. Abuses of authority—'to defend' a brother, to hit or excommunicate someone without a mandate—are likewise denounced and punished. All this regimentation has an undeniably juridical aspect even though it is ultimately meant to sustain fraternal charity and promote the 'good of obedience, by which we go to God'. The two aspects—spiritual fervor and legalistic rigor—can equally be discerned.

The redactor, then, has the intention of further structuring his community by regulating the relations of the 'minor' brethren, which had been practically left unstudied by the Master. Though he speaks, according to the scriptural expressions, of 'mutual' honor and obedience, he organizes these relations in a hierarchical sense. One respects and obeys *one's elders*. In certain ways, this new hierarchy of rank can be considered as an extension of the hierarchy constituted by the abbot and provosts. The 'elder' enters into the participation of certain prerogatives of those who traditionally enjoy the role of educators in the *coenobium*. The hierarchical structure of the monastery becomes more complex and is at the same time reinforced.

But the redactor's overriding concern is perhaps that of charity. This can be seen from a certain number of references scattered throughout these chapters, and above all in the chapter *On Good Zeal*, which gives, in conclusion, the spirit of this legislation. Fraternal love is there placed on the same level as the great virtues of the first chapters of the rule: by it one goes to God. It appears as the fundamental element of cenobitic asceticism.

So it is ultimately through charity that the redactor wants to unite the members of the community to one another. In the appendix, he stresses the love that the brethren bear for one another and on their love for the abbot. In Chapter 64 he urges the abbot to love the brethren and to make himself loved by them. The same concern for promoting reciprocal charity is affirmed at the end of the directory for the cellarer: neither he nor his assistants ought, through rough behavior, to be cause for 'scandal,' distress, or sadness. 'Serve out of charity' becomes the leitmotiv of the chapter on the weekly kitchen helpers. The 'fervor of charity' is given as the characteristic of a good porter.

Concern for the peace of souls goes hand in hand with this insistence on charity. We have just noted it in connection with the cellarer. If the redactor shows such predilection for this office, in contrast to the summary treatment of the decanal function, the reason is no doubt because he is aware of the importance of the relation between the cellarer and the brethren regarding their 'equanimity'. He stresses, too, the cellarer's solicitude for persons, where the Master had positively recommended only taking care of things.

The abbot, also, must be no more 'turbulent' than the cellarer. The entire RB 64 directory seeks to inculcate in him a concern for weak souls: *ne quid nimis*! The theme of discretion is developed in this unilateral sense: avoid an excess of rigor. The same note is struck in the addendum at the end of the prologue, which exhorts the apprehensive beginner 'not to run away.' The kitchen servants should not be made to feel discouraged or overwhelmed, or the infirmarians overtaxed by the demands of the sick, and the brethren should not have 'just' motives for grumbling about excessive fasts.[9] Even the 'excommunicated' brother is consoled in his isolation by the visit of the *senpectae*, 'from fear lest excessive sadness beset him'. Notions of this sort are frequent in RB, but rarer in RM. The redactor thereby shows a keener sense of the personal and interior difficulties encountered by weak souls.

Such care for the inner life appears also in the frequent appeals for fervor, which punctuate RB, notably in the form of adverbial locutions. We note, in the same sense, the interiorization of the theme of emulation in the chapter *On Good Zeal*. But it is above all the admirable Chapter 68, which shows the degree of progress realized by the redactor in comparison with his source, in the sense of more attentive consideration for interior dispositions.

This little chapter on 'impossible commands' offers not only a psychological, moral, and even literary interest of the first order, but shows besides how the redactor has been led, by reading Basil and by his own personal experience, to reintroduce in much perfected form the 'delay' in obeying conceded by the Master, which RB 5 had suppressed. Moreover, it permits us to be present at a scene of spiritual direction, in which the monk exposes his difficulties to his superior and accepts his decision unconditionally. Have we not here, in part, a renewal of the situation described by Cassian in 'indications' 2 and 3, which the Master had separated and transformed, in order to make them his rungs 5 and 3? Experience of the difficulties of the obedient monk in this way led the redactor to resume contact on an important point with the great tradition represented by Cassian, over and above the modifications, which the Master had caused the letter's text to undergo.

Experience and tradition. We have just discovered how these two treasures come together to enrich RB with its jewels. The same observation holds good for all the developments, which the redactor has erected on the foundation, which RM would offer to him.

Only experience of certain encroachments, it seems, could have prompted the redactor to define the council procedure more precisely, just as is indicated at the beginning of RB 3. Experience must also have led him to create the council of 'elders' which was unknown to the Master. In this 'innovation', however, he agrees with the greek basilian rule, which he probably did not know, and the pachomian tradition, whose direct influence on this precise point is uncertain. Whether dependent on those 'sources' or not, it is in fact a traditional institution, which he adds to what he received from the Master.

The same two aspects come to light in RB 67. What the redactor annexes to the Master in this chapter comes both from the rule of Pachomius and from personal observation. It is still the pachomian legislation, combined with the poignant lessons of experience, which inspires RB 69. Generally speaking, the whole appendix assumes the boundary of an experience of the common life and its difficulties between the redactor and his source. If RB tries to structure the community further by specifying 'horizontal' relations, it is because its community life raised problems, which had been little studied by the Master. But at the same time RB links up, at least as regards the institution of ranks, with a well-established cenobitic tradition, which RM had undervalued. The theme of charity, which inspires all the legislation of the appendix, may also hark back to Cassian, Basil and Augustine, and it is certainly to this last that he owes some of his most arresting expressions.

Experience must also have induced the redactor to abandon the Master's somewhat simplistic attitude in respect of members of the hierarchy. If he rebukes the abbot instead of supposing him to be impeccable, the reason is because he has experienced his weaknesses both in himself and in others. If he envisages the deposition of the deans, it is because he has previously encountered pride in them. The voice of experience resounds with full clarity in the first sentence of the chapter on the provost: *saepius contigit* . . . or in the *quod experimento didicimus* of RB 59:6, or again in the disillusioned observations on the 'monks of our times' and their attachment to wine. The same sort of conclusions no doubt explain the redactor's insistence on the selection of persons truly 'worthy' and capable, whenever there is question of an office to be filled. He delights in speaking of the qualities required for each employment and of the virtues to be exercised in it. He seems to take better account than the Master, of the importance of the questions of personality for the good functioning of this educational system, the *coenobium*.

It must again have been experience which counseled increasing the number of the abbot's colleagues. But collective experience weighs more than that of the individual, who wrote RB. In the field of institutions, important transformations are rarely the sudden achievement of a single person. One remembers, moreover, that the increased number of brethren chiefly explains the contrast between RB and RM on this point. The redactor once again rejoins the tradition prior to the Master. As we have seen, the Master had placed in the abbot's hands certain duties, which in Cassian belonged to the provosts. By granting the deans more liberty of action and by creating new offices, RB returns to a less centralized regime.

The tendency to prefer traditional themes and institutions is one of the most interesting characteristics of the work of the redactor. This is noticeable from the very first chapter: the passages, which RB selected from the composite ensemble of the Master, are precisely those which derive from Cassian, whereas the passages which originate with the Master (satire on gyrovagues, final exhortation) are summarized or sacrificed. The redactor seems to have been guided in his choice by an instinct for tradition. An expression that he uses casually may even constitute a reminiscence of Jerome, the distant source of *De generibus*.[10] What is more personal in RM is what he finds less interesting, whether the issue concerns 'abbatial theology' as here, or, in the subsequent treatises, the casuistry in favor of the 'imperfect' and the theory of the transfer of responsibility, or even, in the abbatial directory, the 'childlike' humility of the abbot.[11]

This tendency has important consequences in the legislative field. It really seems that one ought to attribute to it a decisive role in the transformation of the treatise on succession. Ranks, election of the abbot, office of second: on these three related matters RB takes a stand opposed to the Master's views. Carried away by the logic of his educational preoccupations, the Master had legislated in a highly personal fashion, without apparently taking account of the traditional customs which had previously. The redactor has not retained their original features. He has brought the personal work of the Master into line with the traditional positions, yet not without retaining certain aspects. His situation—less secure when compared to the Masters—and the lesser independence that he enjoyed as legislator could have inclined him to take this backward step. But nothing proves that he regretted sacrificing the Master's original features, apart from the exclusion of the provost, for which he does not conceal the preference that he is powerless to adopt. The indifference that we have seen him exhibit towards the more personal parts of the rule of the Master, and the instinct for tradition, which habitually guides him are the motivations that must have entered into play elsewhere.

In the chapter on the deans, the redactor left on one side the Master's prologue, which developed a new aspect of the ''abbatial theology'. He displays no more interest here for that doctrine than in Chapter 1. He displays equally little interest in the function of deans as tutor-supervisors in the service of the abbot, described with such complacency by RM. He has not a word for the parallel between deans and priests, an original theory of the Master, but he reintroduces Old Testament typology (Moses and his 'deans' in the desert) which, though neglected by RM, was no less prevalent in tradition. Although he abandons the superannuated terminology of the Master (*praepositus* to designate the dean), he substitutes terms no less traditional (*decanus, senior*).

It is again from tradition that were derived certain touches of Chapter 31, which are missing in the Master. The 1 Tim 3:13 citation probably comes from R 4 Pat. The theme of 'divine things', grounded in RM on Mt 6:33, becomes in RB that of the 'sacred vessels', which seems more traditional, being attested by Basil, Cassian and R 4 Pat.

In brief, the redactor has particularly retained from RM material which it offered, and which was less original and more conformable with tradition, and in its turn, has completed it by adding traditional elements. The work of the Master lost in it much of its boldness and power. Even from the literary point of view, RB is more like the general run of cenobitic rules than RM. Its greater conciseness and its less clear arrangement, which is often even problematic to interpret for lack of explicit linking passages, reinstate it in the usual genre of such writings. Although the redactor has borrowed from the Master's overall plan, which shows a personal effort in picturing the cenobitic life, he has no scruple in breaking off here and there and especially in blurring the outlines by making the links disappear.

Hence RB tends to reduce to the ordinary standard of cenobitic literature a work which had distinguished itself for its uncommonly wide scope. But even so, it retains a certain breadth of treatment, an arrangement and a richness of content, which set it apart. The major idea of RM remain, though deprived in one respect of their expressive force, but also of their narrowness and over-rigorous logic.

From RM RB derives a particularly clear presentation of which might be called the 'vertical' axis of the *coenobium*: abbot and deans. By that means it is allied to egyptian cenobitism. The hierarchical framework of the monastery is indeed that which Pachomius had conceived and Cassian had described; but to that vertical structure, brought into the foreground by the Master's methodical genius, RB has joined 'horizontal' relationships which complete it. This new, painstaking attitude—at least as regards the charitable inspiration which stimulates it—relates RB to Cassian, Augustine and Basil. Again, it is of Augustine and Basil that the redactor's attention to interior values causes us to think. These elements enrich and render subtle the powerful but simplistic schema bequeathed by the Master. In RB, two traditional currents converge and, so to speak, marry. To speak of 'marriage' is not too strong, but these 'horizontal' relations themselves are regulated with precision on the pattern of hierarchical relations. The horizontal relations are fully integrated into the educational system defined by hierarchical relations. Then too, though 'vertical' relations are enforced vigorously by means of sanctions, they acquire more human flexibility and spiritual depth.

The ultimate success of RB is no doubt attributable in large measure to these qualities. It won acceptance no doubt because it constituted the most complete breviary of tradition. Its deficiencies themselves proved advantageous in the long run. A summary in general terms lends itself better to interpretation and adaptations, which are the condition of all survival, than do the minutiae of a text such as RM.

CENOBITISM, ABBACY, OBEDIENCE

The *coenobium* is a reality *sui generis*. If a parallel is to be sought for it, we must think of the Church before anything else. One of the merits of the Master is to have rendered explicit this comparison which usually remained implicit and latent in cenobitic literature.

The Church is its prototype and not one or another kind of secular society. The benedictine monastery, like the pachomian *coenobium*, does not deliberately imitate any other model, except the religious community described in Scripture. The Old Testament inspired the decanal organization. The abbot and his 'deans' or 'heads of houses' play the roles of Moses-Joshua and the elders of Israel. This reference to Exodus, a *locus classicus* in cenobitism, was replaced in RM by the more precise parallel with the Church of Christ: abbot and provosts reproduce in the monastery the ecclesiastical hierarchy of bishop, priests, deacons and clerics. It is only by means of this ecclesial parallel that comparisons with certain secular institutions can be made. Thus RM 11 recalls the Roman *familia*, and the cenobitic *decani* may be compared to their military namesakes.

The sources of cenobitism are therefore almost exclusively biblical and ecclesial. Hence the profound homogeneity of this tradition. We have seen it when we were reviewing the directories for superiors. Highly varied with regard to their presentation and the degree of reflection that this entails, they differ little from one another when we consider their themes, inspiration, and even scriptural illustrations.[12] Beginning from identical biblical data and understood in an identical ecclesial context, they result in an identical type of abbot: pastor, teacher and educator of his disciples in the name of God and in view of eternal life. It seems rather futile to try to set in opposition different conceptions depending more or less on regional temperamental characteristics: Benedict the Roman, Pachomius the Egyptian, and so on.

There are nevertheless points where one discerns some notable divergences in this otherwise unified tradition. The decanal organization, for example, is missing in an entire branch of cenobitism, beginning with Basil. In this respect, RM and RB obviously link up with the egyptian tradition through Cassian. The same must be said of the attitude adopted towards eremitism. Here too, Basil is in a class apart, together with certain pachomian texts, whereas the body of tradition sees in the solitary life the peak of asceticism and the crowning of cenobitic education. Our two rules are no exception in this field.

The *De generibus monachorum* of RM—RB 1 gives no preference to cenobites from the fact that it lists them 'in the first class' and calls them *magnum genus* (RM) or *fortissimum genus* (RB). One cannot even speak of a choice between eremitism and cenobitism. Hypothetically addressing himself to cenobites, the Master categorizes their kind of life in comparison to the higher degree of asceticism, the solitary life. The gist of the text is to insist on the preliminary necessity of the *coenobium*. But its praise of the life of the anchorite is boundless. This form of life appears as the glorious and desirable life beyond cenobitism.

Such an outlook accords well with the manner in which the Master generally envisages the life of the community. The community of brethren in charity is not what holds his attention. If he compares the monastery to a church, it is solely to the extent that this 'school' possesses, in the person of the abbot and his deans, a genuine hierarchy of 'teachers' instituted by God, like the bishop and his clergy. The master-disciple relationship is in his eyes the definition of the *coenobium*. Once the Master's teaching has come to produce its fruit, the perfect disciple will have nothing, in principle, to keep him in the life of the community.

At least, he will not be kept by the community when it is considered as an end in itself, after the fashion of Basil and certain modern commentators. It would, of course, be necessary to take account of the attraction of a concept of obedience, which is already making its way in Cassian. This virtue is regarded as an absolute value on account of the example of Christ and of the humility to which he is the token. Thus envisaged, it appears valuable enough to justify perseverence *usque ad mortem* in the *coenobium*, even in the case of the 'perfect'. Moreover, RM does not in fact give any practical indication of this matter: the passage to eremitism is neither countenanced nor discountenanced; the legislator is not concerned with it.

There is nothing to indicate that RB holds a different position in this respect. It reproduces the paragraph on hermits just as it is and in its entirety, unlike those which follow.[13] The doctrine, then, remains the same. Yet the interest that the redactor devotes to 'horizontal' relations and fraternal charity indicates a livelier sensitivity on his part for the values of the life of the community. The *coenobium* figures less as a school in which the abbot and deans are everything, and more as a society of brethren in which each has a role to play in the sanctification of his neighbor. Mutual love is set in the first rank of virtues which bring us near to God. It offers the great monastic virtues a new field for their application and new motives. To be sure, this animation of the cenobitic life does not cancel its orientation towards eremitism, which is affirmed in Chapter 1, but it perhaps accentuates the cost attached to cenobitism itself. Like obedience, fraternal charity tends to figure as a primary value, giving the *coenobium* a significance independent of its preparatory role for the solitary life.

The abbot is constantly compared, in cenobitic tradition, to a pastor of the people of God, the Old or the New Testament. The Master's favorite term to characterize his function is that of *doctor*. This word in RM designates all those who, following in the footsteps of the prophets of the Old Covenant and the apostles of Christ, now rule communities of the faithful. It therefore applies both to the hierarchy of the churches and to that of the monasteries. There is no tendency to exalt the latter as opposed to the former by claiming for the monastic hierarchy an independent authority, which would derive its origin from investiture by the Spirit alone. No relationship seems to exist between the 'abbatial theory' of the Master and the doctrine of private inspiration developed by the Priscillianists. Monastic tradition is what furnishes the Master with the term *doctor* to designate the abbot, along with the citation of Lk 10:16, as a basis for his authority. RM was content to deepen and systematize these elements.

Although the thesis of the abbot-teacher had no other purpose than to give a better foundation for the obedience of the monks in the line of the cenobitic tradition, it indirectly raises the problem of the relationship of the abbacy with the hierarchy of the Church. It is a fact—paradoxical but linked to the essence of cenobitism—that its own hierarchy is by right non-clerical. Certainly documents contemporaneous with RM and RB bear witness to the existence of priest-abbots. But this fusion, of which RM and RB seem unaware, leaves the distinction between the two sorts of authority intact. The office of abbot is, by its nature, one which does not entail any sacramental ordination.

In this respect, the title *doctor*, which the Master gives to the abbot, suggests rather felicitously what he is: a 'spiritual' man, who owes his authority to charisma and not to a Holy Order, in the line of the pneumatic hierarchy, which had its recognized place in the earliest days of the Church.[14] Like the teachers of the apostolic age, the heads of the *coenobia* are recruited by a non-sacramental method, which is that of designation by the Spirit. Like them, they belong to the unique hierarchy of the Church, although to a different category from ministers sacramentally ordained. And just as the early *didaskaloi* lived under the authority of the apostles, so the cenobitic 'teachers' are subject to the successors of the apostles

This linking up of abbots and New Testament 'teachers' has not been carried out methodically by RM. It is even partly contrary to the Master's intention, which is to merge abbots and bishops under their title and not distinguish the former from the latter, as we have just done. But by emphasizing in this way the continuity which unites the abbacy back through the centuries to the *didaskalia* of earliest times, [15] one of the characteristics, which the ancient cenobitism guarded most jealously is brought to the forefront: the original character of its own hierarchy in relation to the clergy of the churches.

This characteristic, as we were saying belongs to the very nature of cenobitism. The *coenobium* is, of course, fundamentally an attempt to organize on a community scale the spiritual fatherhood of the desert. Everything depends on the grace of the 'father,' that is to say, of a perfect monk, whom the Holy Spirit has made capable of leading disciples to perfection. It essentially means that the abbot is in truth an accomplished monk, radiant with the Spirit and owing his authority solely to the successful outcome of his search for God and to the Holy Spirit's presence in him. It is his conformity with Christ, and that alone, which must be the foundation of power, and not hierarchical investiture conferred in a sacramental manner.

The abbot is therefore in every respect similar to a bishop, and yet in principle he is in no way invested with a holy order. If he governs a community of the faithful in the name of Christ, that community is a *schola Christi*, similar in every respect to the Church, but only analogous with it.[16] This paradox becomes clear only by going back to the origin of the cenobitic abbacy, which is the relationship of master to disciple in the desert. For it is in so far as he is a monk and a master of the monastic life that the abbot fulfills a pastoral mission analogous to that of a bishop. This mission flows from a solitary encounter with God, and its only purpose is to lead souls to the same authentic encounter in an authentic solitude.[17]

Accomplished as a monk and pastor, analogous to a bishop, the abbot is lastly father of a family. This paternal aspect, hardly suggested by the texts, does not result from an outward imitation of the Roman *familia*, but from the exigencies of the abbot's pastoral task *sui generis*. It is not the ancient writers who compare the abbot to a *paterfamilias*, but we ourselves, who are led to this parallel, when we reflect on the particularities which distinguish the abbot from the bishop. It is a fact that the abbot exercises a more complete power over his flock, since he rules not only their consciences but also the practical detail of their daily actions; he governs not only the assembly for prayer but also the monastic society in all its aspects. This full authority over the whole community and over each of its members makes him more than a Christian pastor of the ordinary type, and more than a simple church leader.[18] By the temporal power that he exercises in his lifetime over his subjects, whose vow of stability binds them to the monastery, he resembles the father of a family in ancient times.

How does this temporal authority emanate from the pastoral mission of the abbot? It is because his educational task has as its precise aim to teach perfection. The disciples are seeking renunciation: as a result, it is the duty of their master to take their entire existence into his hands. Their goods, their activity and their will itself are handed over to him, in order that he may make of them what God ordains. There remains between them and him not the least depth of layer of goods and worldly responsibilities which are outside the control of his authority as Christian pastor. He can and must be 'master' of the Christian life in its fullness, that is to say, down to the practical details of a life entirely applied to renunciation and search for God.

Monk, pastor, father of a family: there is, then, an organic bond between these diverse elements of the abbatial function. Before all else the abbot is a monk, and a perfect monk, a master of the monastic life. Since this *magisterium* is extended to a community, the monk assumes the aspect of a chief officer of the Church; his situation is analogous to that of a bishop. And because this community is composed of men who have renounced everything to seek perfection, the authority of its pastor embraces even the temporalities, without excepting anything of that which goes to make up the life of the individuals and of the collective whole.

This theoretical scheme aims at separating the essential components of the abbacy, in the logical order in which they were joined together. It cannot be observed with the same clarity on the level of historical evolution. To be sure, the transition from the 'spiritual father' to the cenobitic abbot was a reality, which had been lived through, in the case of Pachomius and the majority of the founders. But this process, according to which the abbot comes first and begets the community, is not to be observed everywhere, even at the beginnings. In the basilian fraternities it is rather the pre-existing community, which gives itself, in the person of the *proestos*, the head which is indispensable for its functioning. The superior appears as one of the organs of the body—the eye, as Basil says—rather than the man who constitutes the *raison d'être* of the assemblage of disciples in the pachomian fashion.

Besides, even in the case where the grace of the 'father' has begotten the community, in the generations to come, it is already in existence in the persons of its newly appointed abbots, because they are most often recruited from its own body. As a result, the abbacy sooner or later ceases to be the sole axis of the common life; the community tends to assume a consistent character and a value partially independent of its head. This is the kind of development at which one is present, when one passes from RM to RB. One of the most significant facts in this respect is the method of appointing the abbot. At the very beginning it seems natural for the 'master' of the cenobitic school to choose as his successor the man, whom he judges to be the best of his disciples. Later on, as the abbot's role as 'teacher' becomes blurred, the duty of electing its head is restored to the community.

In pursuing this line, one easily comes to consider the abbacy as a solution to the problem of government, which arises for the monastic community in the same way as for any other society. This problematical situation, in which the community is the first reality, is justified from an empirical point of view, when one considers the lasting character of the *coenobium*, which outlives its successive superiors. However, we must not let ourselves forget the primitive ideal of the cenobitic institution, which is to extend and to organize on a community scale the spiritual fatherhood of an exemplary monk. In such a perspective, the abbacy has no need of external justification, through considerations of expediency, which are more or less bound up with the historical predicament. It imposes itself directly and by internal necessity, since it is above all to benefit from the conduct of such a master that the monks are united round the abbot.

For the rest, whether one envisages the abbacy as the *raison d'être* of the *coenobium* or, on the contrary, as a simple organ of it, it will always be necessary for the abbot to be an authentic master of the perfect life. The charisma of the 'teacher' is in any case indispensable for him. Nothing can take the place of personal grace, in as much as the abbot, in contrast to the priest, is not invested by a sacrament. We are here touching a crucial problem of the abbacy. The *coenobium*, like any society, wants to continue its existence beyond that of its transitory superiors. As a result, the abbacy necessarily becomes an institution. In the place where there is a permanent society, there is also a permanent office of head. The place of the abbot *must* in any event be filled; the institution demands an incumbent who may do no more than guarantee the administrative part of his task, without which the collective entity could not survive. The charisma, however, does not depend on the will of men. It is the Spirit who bestows it on whom he wills. Institution and charisma, men's desire and God's liberty—who could make himself guarantor of such a convergence? On it, however, depends the fate of the abbacy and of the *coenobium*.

The monastery is a school, the abbot is a master, and the monks are disciples assembled to hear him. Obedience in this perspective in no way appears as a requirement of life in the community and as a service for the common good. The superior is obeyed not because he is the representative and interpreter of the collective interest, but because, by obeying him, one hopes to fulfill the whole law of God and to imitate Christ. The personal quest for salvation is the motive, which causes the adoption of obedience. If there is a point at which the individual relationship of the monk with his abbot appears clearly as the principle that constitutes cenobitism and precedes and begets the community of brethren, it is indeed the theory of obedience, such as the Master professes, followed by RB.

However, the doctrine of obedience causes two distinct aspects of the abbatial function to appear. First the abbot can be considered as the vicar of Christ: ' Whoever listens to you, listens to me.' In this case his role will be in some way prophetic: he transmits the word of God, reveals his will and speaks in his name. The superior, in imitation of Christ, can also be regarded as the agent of the crucifying will of the Father: 'I have come not to do my will, but the will of him who sent me.' 'He was made obedient unto death.' In this second case, the authority of the abbot as a 'teacher' commissioned by God and the value of his orders as the expression of the divine law will no longer be the direct motives for obedience. The prophetic role of the abbot will be less in evidence and his role as the agent of Providence in the consummation of the sacrifice will be more apparent.

To render obedience to the abbot *as to Christ* and *after the example of Christ* are two ways of viewing obedience in relation to Christ: they therefore entail two conceptions of the abbot's role, which are not opposed to one another, but complementary. On the one hand, he transmits to his disciples the law of God, on the other he counters self-will and mortifies their desire. In both instances, it is the same cross of Christ which the abbot presents to the monk, but sometimes he proposes it by shedding light on it, while at others he imposes it by painful commands, when it is not simply by his own deficiencies.

Of these two roles, it is only the first which properly belongs to the abbot. For, of course, it is a matter of objective mediation between the Lord and men. One must be an authentic representative of Christ in order to transmit his word without alteration. In the second role, on the contrary, the abbot may be replaced by other less qualified workers. What really predominates in this second perspective is the inward benefit, which the obedient monk gains by his sacrifice. To impose the cross, there is no need of a 'teacher' specially accredited by Christ: the most ordinary neighbor suffices. It is in the logic of this second aspect to obey not only the abbot but all the brethren. This is what the RB redactor grasped so well.[19]

But if this second role of the abbot is not strictly reserved to him, it does nonetheless fall within the extension of his incommunicable mission of *uices Christi*. To instruct does not suffice, it is equally necessary to train and to test. The word of Christ teaches abnegation, and it would indeed be poorly dispensed were there not joined to it, by way of practical application, the rule which mortifies and the precept which puts to the proof! The abbot is simply carrying out his educational task, accomplished in the name of Christ, when he opposes self-will and furnishes the obedient monk with material for his sacrifice.

And so, at the conclusion of this study, we may come to rest upon the simple and profound dictum in which the Master has summarized the conviction of all ancient monasticism, and which today RB still offers to our faith: in the monastery, the abbot stands in the place of Christ.

NOTES TO THE CONCLUSION

1. Our conclusions on the archaic character of the meaning of *praepositus* in RM can serve not only to place this rule in relation to RB, but also to some extent, to date it. Without wanting to go back as far as the generation of Jerome, Augustine and and Cassian, it seems prudent not to go much earlier than 500. This chronological indication is to be compared with suggestions furnished by our study on the council: in that field, RM anticipates the age of Justinian. One would willingly place it in the first years of the sixth century.

2. However, we have observed that the last two paragraphs of the first rung (self-will and desires of the flesh) were probably an addition to the primitive RM text. RB would therefore be dependent here also on a text of the Master 'already interpolated,' to use the expression of Hubert Vanderhoven, or at least completed by the author himself, as we are inclined to believe.

3. Note besides that the two developments which make up the treatise on the council in RM 2:41–50 are both attested by RB 3 (see Chapter 3, Vol. 1, p 177, n. 28).

4. The homogeneity of RB 1 is of a different character from that which we have recognized above in RM 2: homogeneity in poverty or simplicity in one case, homogeneity of order in the other.

5. The expression is Froger's.

6. At the third rung, the ***maior*** (that is, the abbot) replaces the ***senior*** of Cassian (that is, the ***praepositus*** or 'head of ten'); at the fifth degree the substitution is still more explicit: ***abbatem*** for ***seniorem***. Thus, it is the abbot, and no longer the provost as in Cassian, whom the monk obeys and to whom he confesses his thoughts. See Chapter 4, Vol. 1, p 248, n. 101, and Chapter 5, p 261.

7. Chapter 5, n. 74.

8. The expulsion prescribed in RM 83 has in mind a different case: that of the *sacerdos* admitted to the monastery in the capacity of a guest (cf. Chapter 6).

9. RB 41:5. See also RB 34 (do not become downcast on the subject of material things; concerning this 'may all the members be at peace'); RB 38 (the fast must not be too hard for the reader); RB 48 (do not become downcast, should it be necessary to do the harvesting; do everything with moderation, however, on account of the weak; they ought not to be overwhelmed or driven to flight).

10. Compare RB 1:13 with Jerome, Lr 22.35. That this letter was familiar to the redactor is suggested by RB Prol 3, which reproduces another expression from the same letter (Lr 22.15).

11. The image of the child is based on the Gospel, as goes without saying, but is attested nowhere else in the tradition of the directories for abbots.

12. On several occasions (Chapters 2, 3 and 64) we have found RB curiously close to the Greek text of Basil, a text probably unknown to Latin-speakers.

13. We do not see how Penco (pp lvi–lvii) could write that 'St Benedict has abandoned eremitism in his rule as in his own life'. In this respect, the only difference between RM and RB which Penco can find to point out is the fact that the Master foresees the encounter of the brethren with the hermits in the course of their outings. The presence of this detail in RM and its absence in RB do not seem to us at all conclusive. For his part, Owen Chadwick affirms (*John Cassian. A Study in Primitive Monasticism* [Cambridge University Press, 1950] pp 175–76 that Benedict broke with Cassian by abandoning eremitism. The element of truth which this statement harbors may be reduced to this: RB is a rule for cenobites, and nothing more.

14. See H. Chirat, *L'assemblée chrétienne à l'âge apostolique* (Paris: Cerf, 1949), pp 55–57, for a glimpse of light on this question.

15. The Master was no doubt no more conscious of this continuity than were his contemporaries. People in the fourth and fifth centuries, no longer knew exactly who were those 'teachers', mention of whom they read in the apostolic writings. The varied explanations of commentators bear witness to this difficulty (cf. '*Le monastère, Église du Christ*,' p 39, n 62). The ***Didaskalia***, at least as an officially recognized charismatic document enabling one to govern the Christian community and to perform liturgical functions, had completely disappeared at a very early date. It was, as Chirat notes, one of those *provisional* arrangements, which abound in the apostolic age. One may nevertheless ask whether the abbacy might not have been, in certain respects, a resurgence of that vanished institution.

16. See '*Le monastère, Église du Christ*,' pp 25–42. Jean Gribomont has several times thrown light on the basilian idea of the fraternity-body of Christ, notably in *Studia Patristica*, vol 2, p 410, and n 1. The community is conceived as a local church. It is in fact, a matter of a 'religious house' distinct from the secular parish. But Basil seeks rather to cause it to be forgotten, either in order to bring a peaceful end to conflicts or, above all, because of personal conviction. In his eyes, the gift of oneself in charity is superior to any ascetic practice. The ecclesial theme in Basil is therefore closely connected with the law of fraternal charity, which is insistently proclaimed at the beginning of the rules. On the other hand, in the Master's writings the comparison of a monastery to a church is instituted not on the level

of fraternal relations, but around the vertical axis which binds brethren to abbot: the monastery is a church because it has a true 'teacher' for its head. RB, which exhibits very little interest *ex professo* in this ecclesial theme, has in fact harmonized these two structures.

17. This holds true only in the 'egyptian perspective', which remains that of our two rules. With Basil, on the contrary, the community is an end in itself, having no eremitical *hereafter*. But whatever perspective is adopted, it remains true in any case that the monastic superior leads his subjects to renunciation and to evangelical perfection, which implies on his part the practice of renunciation and the perfect life. Now, the practice of the evangelical counsels is a matter of personal grace and ascesis. Ordination cannot dispense one from such experience, and the grace of the sacrament of Holy Orders does not directly tend to promote it.

18. The originality of the cenobitic hierarchy in relation to the ecclesiastical hierarchy is to be compared with the fact that we pointed out while studying the Old Testament type common to both of them. Although both refer to Moses and his assistants, it is not following the same line: the 'deans' of the *coenobium* are a continuation of the 'captains of ten' (*Exodus, Deuteronomy*), whereas the 'priests' of the church follow on after the seventy 'elders' of the *Book of Numbers* (see above, Chapter 5, pp 268–269).

19. Cf. Cassian already at an earlier date, *Conf* 16.6.

ABBREVIATIONS

This table does not furnish a complete bibliography. It does not even contain all the texts cited in this work. Only those documents are indicated whose frequent use has necessitated the establishment of an abbreviation, or whose reference requires specific information.

As often as possible we have depended on the *Clavis Patrum Latinorum C1, Sacris Erudiri,* 3 (Steenbrugge: In abbatia S. Petri, 1951), where the full reference may be found. Otherwise, we have specified the edition used.

1. Monastic Rules

RB — *La Règle de saint Benoît. Introduction, texte, traduction et notes* by Adalbert de Vogüé, Sources Chrétiennes 181–82. Paris, 1972.
Benedicti Regula, CSEL 75, ed. Rudolf Hanslik. Vienna, 1960.
The Rule of St Benedict: A Commentary, trans. by Urban Schnitzhofer (Canyon City: Holy Cross Abbey, 1967). (Originally published as *Die Regel St Benedikts*, ed. Basil Steidle. Beuroner Kunstverlag, 1957).

RM — *La Règle du Maître. Introduction, texte, traduction et notes* by Adalbert de Vogüé, Sources Chrétiennes 105–6. Paris: Cerf, 1964.
The Rule of the Master, trans by Luke Eberle. Kalamazoo: Cistercian Publications, 1972.
In the present study, all references to RB and RM cite chapter and verse as follows:
12:4 = Chapter 12, verse 4
The same is true for the Prologues (Pr), and the additional introductory piece to RM called the *Thema*. But the length of this last mentioned

piece requires subdivision. Hence its three parts are reckoned separately and entitled *Thema* (Th), *Thema Pater* (Thp), and *Thematis sequentia* (Ths). The abbreviation T designates chapter titles in the body of the two rules.

The RM manuscripts are designated:

A = *Monacensis latinus* 28118.

E = *Parisinus latinus* 12634.

P = *Parisinus latinus* 12205.

R Aug — *Regula Augustini*. 1839. (Ed. by Donatien de Bruyne, 'La première règle de saint Benoît', *Revue Bénédictine* 30 [1930], pp 320–26.) Several English translations.

The *Ordo monasterii* (ibid., pp. 318–19) is designated by the special abbreviation OM.

R Aur M — *Regula Aureliani ad monachos*. 1844. PL 68:385–398.

R Aur V — *Regula Aureliani ad uirgines. Cl.* 1845. PL 68:399–406.

R Bas — *Regula Basilii*. PL 103:487–554. The *Long* or
LR — *Detailed Rules* of Basil (PG 31:889–1052) have the
SR — abbreviation LR; SR = the *Short Rules* (*ibid.*, 1051–1306). English trans: *The Ascetic Works of St Basil*, tr by W.K.L. Clarke, London: (Society for Promoting Christian Knowledge) 1925, and M.M. Wagner in The Fathers of the Church series, ed. by R.J. Deferrari. New York, 1947ff.

R Caes M — *Regula Caesarii ad monachos. Cl.* 1012. PL 67: 1099–1103.

R Caes V — *Regula Caesarii ad uirgines. Cl.* 1009 (ed. by Morin).

R Col C — *Regula Columbani coenobialis. Cl.* 1109. (*Sancti Columbani Opera*, ed., by G.S.M. Walker. Dublin: Institute for Advanced Studies, 1957, pp. 142–68.)

R Col M — *Regula Columbani monachorum. Cl.* 1108. (Walker, pp. 122–42).

R Cui — *Regula cuiusdam. Cl.* 1862. PL 66:987–94.

R Fer — *Regula Ferioli. Cl.* 1849. PL 66:959–76.

1 R Fruc — *Regula Fructuosi Complutensis. Cl.* 1869. PL 87: 1099–1110.

2 R Fruc — *Regula Fructuosi communis. Cl.* 1870. PL 87: 1111–27.

R Is — *Regula Isidori. Cl.* 1868. PL 83:867–94.

1 R Mac — *Regula Macarii. Cl.* 1842. [1]PL 103:447–52.

2 R Or — *Regula Orientalis. Cl.* 1840. [2]PL 103:477–84.

2 R Pat — *Regula Patrum.* PL 103:441–44.

3 R Pat — *Regula Patrum.* PL 103:443–46.

R 4 Pat — *Regula Serapionis, Macarii, Paphnutii, et alterius Macarii. Cl.* 1859.[3]

R Pac — *Regula Pachomii.* Armand Boon, *Pachomiana Latina*. Bibliothèque de la Revue d'Histoire Ecclésiastique, fasc. 7. Louvain: University Press, 1932:

- Pr = *Praecepta.*
- Inst = *Praecepta et Instituta.*
- Iud = *Praecepta atque Iudicia.*
- Leg = *Praecepta ac Leges.*

English translation by Armand Veilleux, *Pachomian Koinonia*, II. Cistercian Publications, 1981.

R Tar — *Regula Tarnatensis. Cl.* 1851. PL 66:977–86.

R Wal — *Regula Waldeberti. Cl.* 1863. PL 83:1053–70.

We cite the *Concordia Regularum Patrum* of Benedict of Aniane (PL 103:713–1380) by the siglum *Conc.*

2. Lives

Life of Anthony — (Athanasius). Tr. by Robert Meyer, Ancient Christian Writers, no. 10. Westminster, Md.: Newman, 1950.

Vita Caesarii — (Caesarius of Arles). *Cl.* 1018. PL 67:1001–42.

Vita Fulgentii — (Fulgentius of Ruspe). *Cl.* 847. PL 65:117–50.

Vita Honorati — (Honoratus, founder of Lérins). *Cl.* 501. PL 50: 1249–72.

Vita Hilarii	(Hilary of Arles). *Cl.* 506. PL 50:1219–46.
Vita Martini	(Martin of Tours). *Cl.* 475. PL 20:159–76.
Vies Coptes	*Les Vies Coptes de saint Pachôme et de ses premiers successeurs,* tr into French by L. Th. Lefort. Louvain: Bureaux du Muséon, 1943. English translation by Armand Veilleux, *Pachomian Koinonia,* I. Cistercian Publications, 1980.
VP	*Vitae Patrum*, PL 73–74.
Greg. Tur. VP	Gregory of Tours, *Vitae Patrum*, PL 71:1009–97.
HM	*Historia Monachorum. Cl.* 198. PL 21:387–462. English translation by Norman Russell, *The Lives of the Desert Fathers.* Cistercian Publications, 1982.
HR	Theodoret, *Historia Religiosa*, PG 82:1284–1496. English translation by R. M. Price, *A History of the Monks of Syria.* Cistercian Publications, 1985.
LH	*Palladius: The Lausiac History*, tr. and annotated by Robert Meyer. Ancient Christian Writers, no. 34. Westminster, Md.: Newman, 1965.

3. Ascetical Works

Cass. *Inst.*	John Cassian, *The Institutes of the Coenobia,* tr. by Edgar Gibson, Nicene and Post-Nicene Fathers of the Christian Church, vol. 11. Oxford, 1894; repr. Grand Rapids: Erdmans, 1955.
Cass. *Conf.*	John Cassian, *The Conferences.* Ibid.
Cassiod. *Inst.*	Cassiodorus, *Institutiones. Cl.* 906. PL 70:1105–1150.
Caes. *Serm.*	Caesarius of Arles, *Sermones. Cl.* 1008 (of special importance are *Serm.* 233–37, addressed to monks). Ed. by Germain Morin. Corpus Christianorum, 103–104. Turnhout: Brepols, 1953.
Faustus of Riez	*Sermones ad monachos. Cl.* 966. (*Serm.* 35–44, PL 50:833–59. We indicate within parentheses the no. of the sermon in the collection of pseudo-Eusebius). For *Serm.* 34 (eulogy of Maximus of

	Riez), see Schott, *Bibliotheca Maxima Patrum* (Lyons, 1677) vol. 6, pp. 654– 656.
Greg Nys.	*Gregorii Nysseni Opera*, vol. 8, *pars* 1.
De Inst. Christ.	*De Instituto Christiano*, ed. by Werner Jaeger. Leiden, 1952.
Lib. Ors.	*Liber Orsiesii* in *Pachomiana Latina*, ed. by Armand Boon, Bibliothèque de la Revue d'Histoire Ecclésiastique, fasc. 7. Louvain: University Press, 1932, pp. 109–47.
	Translation by A. Veilleux, *Pachomian Koinonia,* III. Cistercian Publications, 1982.

We cite the *Dialogues* of St Gregory the Great (*Cl.* 1713) according to the edition of Umberto Moricca (Rome: Instituto Storico Italiano, 1924), and his *Letters* (*Cl.* 1714) according to PL 77. The *Dialogues* have been translated from a different Latin edition by Henry J. Coleridge. London, Burns and Oates, 1874.

4. Reference Works

AS	*Acta Sanctorum* (Bollandists).
AS OSB	*Acta Sanctorum Ordinis S. Benedicti*, ed. by L. d'Achery and J. Mabillon, 9 vols. Paris, 1668–1701.
CC	*Corpus Christianorum.* Turnhout: Brepols.
CSCO	*Corpus Scriptorum Christianorum Orientalium.* Louvain-Washington: Durbecq.
CSEL	*Corpus Scriptorum Ecclesiasticorum Latinorum.* Vienna: Hoelder-Pichler-Tempsky.
DACL	*Dictionnaire d'Archéologie chrétienne et de Liturgie.* Paris: Letouzey et Ané.
DHGE	*Dictionnaire d'Histoire et de Géographie ecclésiastiques.* Paris: Letouzey et Ané.
Dict. Spir.	*Dictionnaire de Spiritualité.* Paris: Beauchesne.
PG	Migne, *Patrologia, series graeca.*
PL	Migne, *Patrologia, series latina.*
PO	Graffin-Nau, *Patrologia Orientalis.*

RAM	*Revue d'Ascétique et de Mystique*, Toulouse.
Rev. Bén.	*Revue Bénédictine,* Maredsous.
REL	*Revue des Études Latines,* Paris.
RHE	*Revue d'Histoire ecclésiastique,* Louvain.
RLM	*Revue liturgique et monastique,* Maredsous.
RMAL	*Revue du Moyen-âge latin*, Paris.
RTAM	*Recherches de Théologie ancienne et médiévale,* Louvain.

SELECT BIBLIOGRAPHY

We indicate here some of the works frequently cited in this work, references to which were habitually given in abridged form.

S. Benedicti Anianensis. *Codex Regularum*, ed. by L. Holstenius and M. Brockie. Augsburg, 1759 (Migne, PL 103:393–702).

S. Benedicti Anianensis. *Concordia Regularum*, ed. by H. Ménard. Paris, 1638 (Migne, PL 103:713–1380).

Butler, Cuthbert. *Benedictine Monachism*. London: Longmans, 1919.

________. *Sancti Benedicti Regula Monasteriorum*, third edition. Freiburg-im-Breisgau, Herder, 1935.

Corbett, Philip B. *The Latin of the* REGULA MAGISTRI. *A Guide to the Establishment of the Text.* Louvain University Press, 1958.

Corpus Juris civilis, ed. by C.H. Freiesleben. Mainz, 1789.

Delatte, Paul. *Commentary on the Rule of St. Benedict*. Latrobe: Abbey Press, 1950.

Hallinger, Kassius. "Papst Gregor der Grosse und der Hl. Benedikt," *Commentationes in Regulam S. Benedicti, cura B. Steidle* (*Studia Anselmiana* 42). Rome, 1957; pp. 231–320.

Hausherr, Irénée. *Direction Spirituelle en Orient autrefois* (*Orientalia Christiana Analecta* 144). Rome: Pontifical Institute of Oriental Studies, 1955.

Herwegen, Ildephonsus. *Sinn und Geist der Benediktinerregel.* Einsiedeln/Köln: Benziger, 1944.

Labbeus-Cossartius. *Sacrosancta Concilia*, 18 volumes. Paris, 1671–72.

Linderbauer, Benno. *S. Benedicti Regula Monachorum, herausgegeben und philologisch erklärt.* Metten: Verlag des Benediktinerstiftes, 1922.

Mansi, J.D. *Sacrorum Conciliorum nova et amplissima collectio*, 31 volumes. Florence, 1759–98.

Meester, Placide de. *De Monachico Statu iuxta Disciplinam Byzantinam.* Vatican City: Polyglot Press, 1942.

Il Monachesimo nell' alto Medioevo e la Formazione della Civiltà occidentale. Spoleto: Centro italiano di studi sull' alto medioevo, 1957.

Penco, Gregorio. *S. Benedicti Regula*. See DIVISIONS AND SIGLA OF THE TEXTS, "RB."

Rousseau, Olivier. *Monachisme et vie religieuse d'après l'ancienne tradition de l'Eglise* (*Collection Irénikon*, 7). Chevetogne, 1957.

Steidle, Basil. *The Rule of St Benedict: A Commentary*. See ABBREVIATIONS, p. 485: "RB."

Vanderhoven, Hubert; Masai, François. *La Règle du Maître, édition diplomatique des manuscrits latins 12205 and 12634 de Paris*, avec la collaboration de Philip B. Corbett (*Les Publications de Scriptorum*). Brussels-Paris: Éditions "Érasme," 1953.

Vogüé, Adalbert de, "*Le Monastère, Église du Christ*" in *Studia Anselmiana* 42 (Rome, 1957), pp. 25–46.

SCRIPTURAL INDEX

INDEX OF NAMES

LITERARY AND DOCTRINAL INDEX

CISTERCIAN PUBLICATIONS INC.

Kalamazoo, Michigan

TITLES LISTING

THE CISTERCIAN FATHERS SERIES

THE WORKS OF BERNARD OF CLAIRVAUX

Treatises I: Apologia to Abbot William, On Precept and Dispensation . . . . CF 1

On the Song of Songs I–IV . . . . CF 4,7,31,40

The Life and Death of Saint Malachy the Irishman . . . . CF 10

Treatises II: The Steps of Humility, On Loving God . . . . CF 13

Magnificat: Homilies in Praise of the Blessed Virgin Mary [with Amadeus of Lausanne] . . . . CF 18

Treatises III: On Grace and Free Choice, In Praise of the New Knighthood . . . . CF 19

Sermons on Conversion: A Sermon to Clerics, Lenten Sermons on Psalm 91 . . . . CF 25

Five Books on Consideration: Advice to a Pope . . . . CF 37

THE WORKS OF WILLIAM OF SAINT THIERRY

On Contemplating God, Prayer, and Meditations . . . . CF 3

Exposition on the Song of Songs . . . . CF 6

The Enigma of Faith . . . . CF 9

The Golden Epistle . . . . CF 12

The Mirror of Faith . . . . CF 15

Exposition on the Epistle to the Romans . . . . CF 27

The Nature and Dignity of Love . . . . CF 30

THE WORKS OF AELRED OF RIEVAULX

Treatises I: On Jesus at the Age of Twelve, Rule for a Recluse, The Pastoral Prayer . . . . CF 2

Spiritual Friendship . . . . CF 5

The Mirror of Charity . . . . CF 17

Dialogue on the Soul . . . . CF 22

THE WORKS OF GILBERT OF HOYLAND

Sermons on the Song of Songs I–III . . CF 14,20,26

Treatises, Sermons, and Epistles . . . . CF 34

THE WORKS OF JOHN OF FORD

Sermons on the Final Verses of the Song of Songs I–VII . . . . . . CF 29,39,43,44,45,46,47

Texts and Studies in the Monastic Tradition

OTHER EARLY CISTERCIAN WRITERS

The Letters of Adam of Perseigne, I . . . . CF 21

Alan of Lille: The Art of Preaching . . . . CF 23

Idung of Prüfening. Cistercians and Cluniacs: The Case for Citeaux . . . . CF 33

Guerric of Igny. Liturgical Sermons I–II . . . . CF 8,32

Three Treatises on Man: A Cistercian Anthropology . . . . CF 24

Isaac of Stella. Sermons on the Christian Year, I . . . . CF 11

Stephen of Lexington. Letters from Ireland, 1228–9 . . . . CF 28

Stephen of Sawley, Treatises . . . . CF 36

Baldwin of Ford. Spiritual Tractates . . . . CF 38,41

Serlo of Wilton & Serlo of Savigny . . . . CF 48

** Temporarily out of print*

† Forthcoming

THE CISTERCIAN STUDIES SERIES

* *Temporarily out of print*

† *Forthcoming*

Nicolas Cotheret's Annals of Cîteaux (Louis J. Lekai) .... CS 57

The Occupation of Celtic Sites in Ireland by the Canons Regular of St Augustine and the Cistercians (G. Carville) .... CS 56

The Finances of the Cistercian Order in the Fourteenth Century (Peter King) .... CS 85

Rancé and the Trappest Legacy (A. J. Krailsheimer) .... CS 86

Fountains Abbey and Its Benefactors, 1132–1300 (Joan Wardrop) .... CS 91

Medieval Religious Women

Distant Echoes: MRW, I (L.T. Shank and J.A. Nichols, edd.) .... CS 71

Peace Weavers. MRW II (L.T. Shank and J.A. Nichols, edd.) .... CS 72

Studies in Medieval Cistercian History sub-series

Studies I .... CS 13

Studies II .... CS 24

Cistercian Ideals and Reality (Studies III) .... CS 60

Simplicity and Ordinariness (Studies IV) .... CS 61

The Chimera of His Age: Studies on St Bernard (Studies V) .... CS 63

Cistercians in the Late Middle Ages (Studies VI) .... CS 64

Noble Piety and Reformed Monasticism (Studies VII) .... CS 65

Benedictus: Studies in Honor of St Benedict of Nursia (Studies VIII) .... CS 67

Heaven on Earth (Studies IX) .... CS 68

Goad and Nail (Studies X) .... CS 84

Erudition in God's Service (Studies XI) .... CS 98

Studies in Cistercian Art and Architecture

Studies in Cistercian Art and Architecture, I (Meredith Lillich, ed.) .... CS 66

Studies in Cistercian Art and Architecture, II (Meredith Lillich, ed.) .... CS 69

Studies in Cistercian Art and Architecture, III (Meredith Lillich, ed.) .... CS 89

THOMAS MERTON

The Climate of Monastic Prayer .... CS 1

Thomas Merton on St Bernard .... CS 9

Thomas Merton's Shared Contemplation: A Protestant Perspective (Daniel J. Adams) .... CS 62

Solitude in the Writings of Thomas Merton (Richard Anthony Cashen) .... CS 40

The Message of Thomas Merton (Brother Patrick Hart, ed.) .... CS 42

Thomas Merton Monk (revised edition/ Brother Patrick Hart, ed.) .... CS 52

The Legacy of Thomas Merton (Brother Patrick Hart, ed.) .... CS 92

Thomas Merton and Asia: His Quest for Utopia (Alexander Lipski) .... CS 74

Towards an Integrated Humanity (M.B. Pennington, ed.) .... CS 103

Thomas Merton: Monk & Artist (Victor Kramer) .... CS 102

THE CISTERCIAN LITURGICAL DOCUMENTS SERIES

The Cistercian Hymnal: Introduction and Commentary .... CLS 1

The Cistercian Hymnal: Text and Melodies .... CLS 2

The Old French Ordinary and Breviary of the Abbey of the Paraclete: Introduction and Commentary .... CLS 3

The Old French Ordinary of the Abbey of the Paraclete: Text .... CLS 4

The Paraclete Breviary: Text .... CLS 5–7

The Hymn Collection of the Abbey of the Paraclete: Introduction and Commentary .... CLS 8

The Hymn Collection of the Abbey of the Paraclete: Text .... CLS 9

The Molesme Summer-Session Breviary .... CLS 10–14

STUDIA PATRISTICA

Papers of the Oxford Patristics Conference 1983 (Elizabeth A. Livingstone, ed.)

1. Historica-Gnostica-Biblica
2. Critica-Classica-Ascetica-Liturgica
3. The Second Century-Clement and Origen-The Cappodocian Fathers †
4. Augustine-Post Nicene Latin Fathers-Oriental Texts-*Nachleben* of the Fathers †

FAIRACRES PRESS, OXFORD

The Wisdom of the Desert Fathers

The World of the Desert Fathers

The Letters of St Antony the Great

The Letters of Ammonas, Successor of St Antony

A Study of Wisdom. Three Tracts by the author of *The Cloud of Unknowing*

The Power of the Name. The Jesus Prayer in Orthodox Spirituality (Kallistos Ware)

Contemporary Monasticism

The Influence of St Bernard

Theology and Spirituality (Andrew Louth)

Prayer and Holiness (Dumitru Staniloae)

Saint Gregory Nazianzen: Selected Poems

** Temporarily out of print*

† Forthcoming

Eight Chapters on Perfection and Angel's Song (Walter Hilton)

Creative Suffering (Iulia de Beausobre)

Bringing Forth Christ. Five Feasts of the Child Jesus (St Bonaventure)

Gentleness in St John of the Cross

Distributed in North America only for Fairacres Press.

DISTRIBUTED BOOKS

St Benedict: Man with An Idea (Melbourne Studies)

The Spirit of Simplicity

Benedict's Disciples (David Hugh Farmer)

The Emperor's Monk: A Contemporary Life of Benedict of Aniane

A Guide to Cistercian Scholarship (2nd ed.)

North American customers may order through booksellers or directly from the publisher:

Cistercian Publications
WMU Station
Kalamazoo, Michigan 49008
(616) 383-4985

Cistercian Publications are available in Britain, Europe and the Commonwealth through A. R. Mowbray & Co Ltd St Thomas House Oxford OX1 1SJ.
For a sterling price list, please consult Mowbray's General Catalogue.

A complete catalogue of texts-in-translation and studies on early, medieval, and modern Christian monasticism is available at no cost from Cistercian Publications.

Cistercian monks and nuns have been living lives of prayer & praise, meditation & manual labor since the twelfth century. They are part of an unbroken tradition which extends back to the fourth century and which continues today in the Catholic church, the Orthodox churches, the Anglican communion, and, most recently, in the Protestant churches.

Share their way of life and their search for God by reading Cistercian Publications.